BLOOD AND FAITH

Religion and Politics
Michael Barkun, *Series Editor*

BLOOD & FAITH

Christianity in American White Nationalism

Damon T. Berry

Syracuse University Press

Copyright © 2017 by Syracuse University Press
Syracuse, New York 13244-5290

All Rights Reserved

First Edition 2017
17 18 19 20 21 22   6 5 4 3 2 1

For a listing of books published and distributed by Syracuse University Press, visit www.SyracuseUniversityPress.syr.edu.

ISBN: 978-0-8156-3544-4 (hardcover)
      978-0-8156-3532-1 (paperback)
      978-0-8156-5410-0 (e-book)

Library of Congress Cataloging-in-Publication Data
Names: Berry, Damon T., author.
Title: Blood and faith : Christianity in American white nationalism / Damon T. Berry.
Description: First edition. | Syracuse, New York : Syracuse University Press, [2017] |
    Series: Religion and politics | Includes bibliographical references and index.
Identifiers: LCCN 2017018400 (print) | LCCN 2017031913 (ebook) | ISBN
    9780815654100 (e-book) | ISBN 9780815635444 (hardcover : alk. paper) |
    ISBN 9780815635321 (pbk. : alk. paper) | ISBN 9780815654100 (ebook)
Subjects: LCSH: Christianity and politics—United States. | White nationalism—
    United States.
Classification: LCC BR516 (ebook) | LCC BR516 .B397 2017 (print) |
    DDC 277.3/082—dc23
LC record available at https://lccn.loc.gov/2017018400

Manufactured in the United States of America

NOV **16** 2017

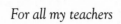

For all my teachers

Contents

Acknowledgments

Any book has a long list of people without whom it would not have been written. This one is no exception. I have space to name only a few individuals, but let me say that a number of teachers, colleagues, friends, and confidants from Ohio State's Department of Comparative Studies helped greatly with the first draft. Many fellows at St. Lawrence University, including the supportive library staff, colleagues in other departments, and my friends in the Department of Religious Studies, Kathleen Self and Mark MacWilliams in particular, have helped me in several ways, personally and professionally. I will always be grateful. And, of course, I owe a great debt to my supportive network of friends and overseas acquaintances, who have provided much needed words of encouragement and support.

I specifically thank Michael Barkun, whose work inspired this project from the beginning and who was kind enough to invite me to submit the initial manuscript for publication. I also thank my gracious long-time teacher Hugh B. Urban, who taught me so very much and guided me through my graduate studies years. In much the same way, I am very grateful for the patient instruction from others, especially David Horn and Merrill Kaplan. Their advice was essential in shaping this book and my thinking in so many ways.

Ruby Tapia, too, was of great assistance very early on in helping me work through much of the foundational thinking that shaped this project even before a single word was written. I also thank Michael McVicar for his input and suggestions as well as for his friendship. I am sincerely grateful to Kay Clopton, Andrew Culp, Josh Kurz, Elizabeth Marsch, Rachelle Peck, Gabriel Piser, Jasmine Stork, Vidar Thorsteinsson, Lee Wiles, and so many others, teachers and fellow students alike, for their fellowship and kindness. And I owe special thanks to Barry Mehler, who did so much to compel me to revise and rewrite key sections of this work from a very early stage. He has been a true friend in his caring criticism and constant belief in the project's value.

I also thank the supportive team of professionals at Syracuse University Press, especially my copy editor, Annie Barva, all of whom were so patient and helpful. There was a bit of a learning curve on my part. Any remaining errors are my own. Everyone with whom I dealt was always direct and responsive to questions and concerns. I hope I have honored their efforts in what is given here.

Finally, I offer my sincerest gratitude to my family, especially to my devoted partner, who has always believed in me. She, too, has struggled and sacrificed as I pursued this project.

BLOOD AND FAITH

Introduction

Racial Protectionism and White Religion

For specific historical reasons, the name "Religious Right" in America has referred exclusively to a politically and socially conservative Christianity that emerged into public view during the presidential race in 1980. This movement, of course, signified a particular wedding of socially conservative evangelical Christianity with conservative politics that continues to shape the Republican Party to this day. But as significant as this meeting point was and continues to be, relationships between Christianity and right-wing politics were by that time hardly new in US history. Certain forms of Christianity have long shared space with the political and nationalist Right in the United States.

The history of white racist religion in the United States has for some time also followed the contours of a conservative and nativist political ideology informed by a certain understanding of Protestant Christianity. For example, the Ku Klux Klan in the 1920s sought to preserve Anglo-Protestant demographic superiority and political supremacy in America in the face of what it saw as a worrisome influx of immigrants from outside western Europe.[1] Later, as Michael Barkun demonstrates in *Religion and the Racist Right*, a particular form of racist Christianity known as "Christian Identity" continued to be popular in some of the most important and dangerous white racist organizations in US history well through the 1990s.[2] That said, racialized Christian mythologies are not the only religious ideologies that have influenced white racist activists in America. In fact, they are no longer the dominant ones.

In her article "The Role of Religion in the Collective Identity of the White Racialist Movement," Betty Dobratz convincingly argues that Christian Identity is not the only racist theology to arise in the United States.[3] She notes that other religions, such as Odinism, a racialized Norse-inspired Paganism, and Creativity, a racialist new religious movement founded in the 1970s, in fact over time supplanted the formerly dominant Christian mythological tropes for an increasing number of American white nationalists. Various authors, including Matthias Gardell, Nicholas Goodrick-Clarke, and George Michael have since 2001 done monograph studies of Odinism, various racialist esoteric movements, and Creativity, respectively, exploring these influential racial-religious movements.[4] In these studies, to be sure, some aspects of the recent developments in religious preference among white nationalists are discussed. However, no one has yet done a study dedicated to describing and understanding why these changes have taken place. That is what I propose to do here.

This book is in some ways related to Barkun's landmark study of racist Christianity in that it continues to examine the relationships between the American racist Right and Christianity. But in this case, rather than exploring further the origins and ideology of Christian Identity, I seek to offer an explanation for why most influential white nationalists in America have regarded Christianity, even white nationalist forms of it such as Christian Identity, as a problem.

The full answer to this question is complicated. In the coming chapters, I discuss many reasons why, some of which differ from one author or activist to another, but a few preliminary points can be made. In the first instance, many American white nationalists have rejected Christianity as an alien and consequently dangerous ideology, often describing it as an inherently "Jewish" religion that weakens one's commitment to the survival of the white race. In the second, some white nationalists argue that an aggressive rejection of Christianity risks alienating Christian Identity–oriented white nationalists, which may hinder the broader white racial unity that is regarded as of vital importance in the effort to preserve the white race. And finally, Christianity is a problem for contemporary white nationalists who have to navigate entrenched hostility toward it while trying to access the conservative movement mainstream, which is still overwhelmingly Christian. As with the former position, the concerns here are not only broader racial unity but also what the legacy of anti-Christianity in white nationalism may mean for efforts at establishing political agreement with white American conservatives on issues such as immigration and opposition to multiculturalism—a strategy that some American white nationalists have developed to preserve the white race in America from an imagined future white genocide.

White nationalist activism in America is far from monolithic, but obsession with white racial survival defines and unites white nationalists more than any other issue. I call this ideological orientation *racial protectionism*. It forms the basis for white nationalists' worldviews and constructs an animating ethic that shapes and informs their thoughts and actions. My argument is that whether Christianity is rejected outright or simply viewed as an obstacle for larger appeal of white identity politics, it is a problem in American white nationalism because it strains the primary obligation and driving moral principle to protect the white race.

Each of the subjects in this study, though they often differ from one another in significant ways, share a common belief that the white race is imperiled and that it is the duty of every white man and woman to do what they must to protect it from biological extinction. This protectionism takes various forms, even the use of violence, but more often it takes shape in combating perceived cultural and ideological contamination. These efforts at ideological purity mirror the fetishizing of so-called biological racial purity and give rise to an orientation in which the one is imagined as linked to the other. Ideological and biological purity then becomes the foci of self-surveillance in the effort to protect the imagined white racial community from destructive and weakening pollution, whether in the form of interracial sexuality or in the form of religious or political ideologies that contradict or undermine one's commitment to white racial survival.

In American white nationalism, scrutiny and purification of one's ideology is central to racial protectionism. To conduct oneself in this way proves to the community and to oneself that one is truly pure and dedicated in one's character and thought to white racial survival. It also proves that one has a truly "white" attitude. Such commitment is indeed regarded as the measure of one's morality. Furthermore, acting upon this obligation binds the individual white nationalist to the white race's fate, providing each individual with an identity imbued with meaning in a mission to overcome imagined racial enemies and thus ensuring the futurity of the white race.

Racial protectionism therefore should be understood as a motive for activity. One can, for example, see it as motivating violence, as was certainly the case recently with the murders perpetrated by Dylann Roof at Emanuel African Methodist Episcopal Church in Charleston, South Carolina. It also motivates many forms of activism, including awareness campaigns such as the website White Genocide Project, the formation of blogs and chat rooms, and print and digital publishing. More to the point of this study, however, racial protectionism motivates constant surveillance of ideology, religious and otherwise, for the purpose of purifying the white nationalist body of thought. Rendering one's racial ideology pure, it is believed, immunizes the racial body to weaknesses that would otherwise lead to social and biological miscegenation and thereby to the destruction of the white race. In this way, racial protectionism positions Christianity in particular as a problem for American white nationalism.

Appreciating the tense relationship between racial protectionism and Christianity in American white nationalism helps us understand why many white nationalists have rejected Christianity as an alien and imperiling influence. Furthermore, it helps us to appreciate the role of religion as a significant element in the formation of white nationalist identity, as Dobratz and others have noticed. Moreover, the relationship between racial protectionism and Christianity reveals that religion is itself a significant site of contest and strategy for American white nationalists, even for those who profess to be atheists. For all of these reasons, the study of racist religiosity is important.

Nevertheless, we may ask why we should care what white nationalists think about Christianity. Why should that which seems to be a subgroup within the racist fringe concern us? My first response is that though this book is about white racist subcultures in America and their relationships with Christianity, it is not simply an investigation of the racist fringe. It is best understood as a case study of responses to racialized demographic anxieties that are far from exclusive to extremists in America. In any case, racism is far from marginal in the American experience. It is indeed a comforting thought to imagine that racist ideation is an aberration in US history, but it is not an honest one. It is likewise comforting to think that we can simply identify the "extremists," isolate and minimize their impact on wider society, and imagine we have nothing further to consider, but this thought is also false. Exclusionary logics supported by racialized religious discourses are in fact troublingly common, pernicious, and very often deadly. News stories about the obscene treatment of minority Rohingya Muslims in Myanmar; the killings of Yazidis, Christians, and Shia Muslims by the Islamic State; and the continual utility of xenophobic politics in western Europe and the United States all demonstrate how important it is to understand discourses of self-protection and social purity that so often motivate states to institutionalize persecution of minorities and private actors to commit heinous acts of violence. I propose that through the study of such instances of exclusionary and persecutory ideation, as I have done in this book, we may gain insight into the ethnocentric logics that produce ethnocidal responses that are often justified as acts of communal self-defense.

I hasten to add, however, that even if such ideation were to be found only among those who can be regarded as marginal, it should still be a priority of scholarship to examine it in light of the extraordinary devastation that can be wrought by even a small number of individuals or even by one person. One might note the Oklahoma City bombing by Timothy McVeigh in 1995 or the attacks in Norway committed by Anders Breivik, to name just two such examples, to argue for the relevance of studies like this one. As Barkun states in his introduction to *Religion and the Racist Right*, to "close the door on a subject because it is distasteful is to pretend a part of the world does not exist and hence to leave open the possibility of facing unpleasant surprises in the future."[5] I therefore hope to open the door, if only a little, so that we can better understand an often ignored world of racism and religious bigotry that, as we have learned from the recent presidential race, has found a place in the ongoing political battles over immigration and multiculturalism in the United States.

Defining White Nationalism

It is prudent to take a moment here to define white nationalism. Because racist movements are sometimes mistakenly understood to be identical, some measure of description is warranted to contextualize white nationalism as it emerged after World War II, to explain how it is different from earlier forms of white racist activism in America, and to clarify how racial protectionism as an ideological force operates within it.

Michael O'Meara has written one of the most thorough descriptions of white nationalism from within the community in *Toward the White Republic*. O'Meara describes a "terminological change" in the 1990s when various racist activists began to refer to themselves as "white nationalists." According to O'Meara, this change emerged from the realization among some of these racial activists, chief among them a man named Francis Parker Yockey, that after 1945 efforts to "maintain the integrity of America's racial character and prevent alien races from intruding" had failed, which led these activists to rethink the practicality of either saving America or seceding from it.[6] These new white nationalists increasingly regarded allegiance to America as either a side issue or direct competition in securing a future for the white race as a global entity. White nationalism is therefore, as O'Meara writes, best understood as "a variant of historic ethnonationalism," by which he means a nationalism that is defined ultimately in terms of imagined biological and cultural connection among whites across the traditional boundaries of the nation-state.[7] These activists' focus was no longer saving America but saving the whole of the white race, some of whose members happened to live in the United States.

Scholars examining white nationalism from the outside have repeated this observation. In 2003, professor of law Carol Swain published a lengthy study titled *The New White Nationalism in America*. In it, she defines white nationalism as first and foremost a threat to America's liberal ideals but also a response to demographic and political shifts in the latter half of the twentieth century. Swain, like O'Meara, sees *white nationalism* as a term descriptive of a phenomenon that culminated in the 1990s. She also says that white nationalism grew out of "the older white supremacy movement" and fueled "a new and expanded white consciousness movement on the part of those Americans of European ancestry."[8]

Another significant component of Swain's description concerns how white nationalists define themselves by their oppositional stance to what they perceive as racial enemies. With this definition comes, argues Swain, a sense of urgency in dealing with what is regarded as an existential threat to white racial survival that these enemies are allegedly responsible for producing.[9] That is to say, white nationalist ideation is obsessed with self-defense against the imagined existential threats posted by racial integration and biological and cultural pollution.

Taking all of this together, we should define white nationalism as a Pan-European ethnonationalism committed to the survival of the imagined global white racial community. The term *racial protectionism* is then meant to capture at once the Pan-Europeanism in American white nationalism and the dominant ethic of communal self-defense that shapes and defines its ideation. So I agree with O'Meara and Swain on those two points. Where we perhaps disagree slightly is on the timeline of white nationalism's emergence in the United States. I contend that it developed much earlier than the 1990s, at least as far back as the end of World War II.

The 1990s was indeed the moment when this new racialism emerged into public view, in part because of the Oklahoma City bombing and the attention the news media paid to the militia movement, which in their coverage was often tied to organized racism. It is therefore understandable why the perception would exist that white nationalism was a new phenomenon of the 1990s. But in fact the history of American white nationalism goes further back. Jeffery Kaplan and Leonard Weinberg have pointed out that transnational cooperation among white racialist organizations is primarily a post–World War II phenomenon, though they also recognize that minor attempts were made in the 1920s to think on a broader scale about white unity within European supremacist frameworks.[10] One only need reference the speeches of Charles Lindbergh, known for his deep anti-Semitism and his position as a spokesperson for the America First movement in the 1930s, or the writings of Madison Grant in the 1910s and of his protégé Lothrop Stoddard in the early 1920s to see this trend prior

to World War II. In these early years, the preservation of "European culture" and the continuance of white domination of the world in the face of
a "rising tide of color," coupled with the desire to avoid another European
war, can be seen as two influences in the early Pan-European impulse.[11] But
efforts to forge a truly globalized racial nationalist movement really bore
fruit only after the defeat of nation-state fascism and Nazism and later in
racist activism during the 1960s.

This new stateless racial activism was inspired by an American named
Francis Parker Yockey and his efforts to define a specifically Pan-European
movement.[12] Yockey's activism began in 1948 with the European Libera-
tion Front (ELF) and his authorship of a deeply anti-Semitic, European
nationalist manifesto titled *The Proclamation of London*, published in 1949.
But his most important work was *Imperium*. According to Kaplan and
Weinberg, this book, originally published in 1948 under the pseudonym
Ulick Verange, combined the anti-Semitic tropes of *The Protocols of the
Elders of Zion* with a Spenglerian reading of history.[13]

Yockey was deeply influential to American right-wing organizers such
as Willis Carto, who is credited with authoring the introduction to the
edition of *Imperium* released in the American market in 1962, and Else
Christensen, the popularizer of racialist Odinism in the 1970s, whom
I discuss in more detail in chapter 4.[14] Yockey also became an important influence for those who were beginning to articulate a message of
racial nationalism that consciously separated itself from conservativism's
increasing focus on American patriotism at the expense, some believed,
of race. And Yockey's influence on white nationalism persists: American
white nationalists still recognize him as a figure worthy of remembrance,
study, and discussion.

Imperium, which has continued to circulate among the American Far
Right to the present, reinterprets all of Western history through the lens of
race and culture, with the particular end desire being the "imperative integration of Europe" as one race and people. Yockey argues that *Imperium* is
meant to present "all the fundamentals" for a new Pan-European movement and to chart a new Pan-European course after World War II.[15] In
dividing the world between members of "High Cultures" and "culture dis-
torters" or "parasites," he does not stray too far from the anti-Semitic and

racist doctrines that preceded him in both the United States and Europe. In the presentation of this racial and cultural Manicheism, Yockey's aim is to argue for a new political unity in the context of a world divided between communism under the Soviet Union and capitalism under the United States. His ambition is to inspire the creation of a Europe independent of Americanism and Soviet communism and to allow the "Western banner" to rest on its "home soil from Gibraltar to North Cape, and from the rocky promontories of Galway to the Urals."[16] His vision is of an aristocratic, Euro-racial nationalism that does not have the borders of the nation-state but rather looks to what he regards as the much more timeless and fundamental unity of western Europe culturally, geographically, and spiritually. And as we might expect, for Yockey the stakes are survival of the race itself. He writes that "the present situation of the West imposes upon it not only a struggle for power" but also "*a struggle for the continued biological existence of the population of Europe.*"[17]

Yockey's influence on American white nationalists' criticisms of the US government is also substantial. In *Imperium*, America, signified as the "Washington regime," is regarded as a place split between its European origins and ideals, on the one hand, and the machinations of the imagined enemy "distorter," on the other, a thinly veiled but traditional anti-Semitic description of Jews.[18] Yockey even describes America as more of a threat to Europe than Soviet Russia. Whereas he sees the fear of the Russian military power and communism as a possibly unifying force for Europe, he sees America as threatening disorder and cultural distortion that will eventually corrupt Europe and Europeans beyond recovery.[19] This description should be understood as one of the roots of contemporary "Zionist Occupied Government," or ZOG, discourse that has been a mainstay of white nationalism since the 1990s.

Yockey, however, like contemporary white nationalists, distinguishes between the US government and what he considers real Americans. Though he argues that America is ruled by the "spiritually alien," he nevertheless sees it as also made of people whom he describes as "the true America," the perpetuators of the "America of Alexander Hamilton, George Washington, John Adams, of the frontiersmen, the explorer, the men of the Alamo," who, he says, in fact belong to Europe.[20] Yockey imagines, as do American white nationalists after him, that an untainted remnant of true European heritage remains in America, though America itself is hopelessly corrupted by the so-called alien rulers who control it. This narrative of a truly Euro-American remnant that bears within itself the spiritual unity of Europe and that is victimized by a government overrun by racial enemies is a powerful trope in white nationalism to this day and further marks the influence of *Imperium* on the movement.

If we then trace to *Imperium* the Pan-European racial protectionist logic that defines contemporary white nationalism, as I think we should, we can see the roots of white nationalism in the immediate post–World War II context, in which state-centered fascisms had failed and Europe was in the hands of the Allies, pinched between Americanism on one side and Soviet communism on the other. But this brings up a problem in using the term *white nationalism* that must be noted before we go further. If the term *white nationalism* was not really in vogue until the 1990s, how was it used before that time?

Many people discussed in this book did not or have not self-identified as white nationalists, among them William Pierce and Revilo Pendleton Oliver, but they nevertheless play signature roles in the development of white nationalism. Some, in fact, often rejected such a label, though I think for reasons often related to public relations. In this sense, when I use the descriptor *white nationalism*, I am speaking of a style of thinking that to varying degrees has the elements described earlier rather than relying on how someone publicly professes his or her affiliation. I also take into account individual levels of influence within this milieu, which allows me to discuss ideologues whose racism seems quite muted next to that of other figures but who are nevertheless important to the history and development of white nationalism in America. For this reason, the nuances of each person's connection to contemporary white nationalism is part of the specific contextualization in each chapter. In other words, the term *white nationalism* is used in this book, alongside the term *racial nationalism*, as a heuristic to describe a complex dynamic of racial activist thinking in America after World War II that has a similar style and substance but not always the same name.

Approaching Religion in American White Nationalism

To clarify my approach in this book, let me first explain where I am look-ing to trace the attitudes toward Christianity in American white national-ism. In their book *American Swastika*, Pete Simi and Robert Futrell argue that white-power advocates construct collective identity through "free spaces" such as gatherings and private communities but most interest-ingly on the Internet as well.[21] Indeed, the Internet has been an important venue through which white nationalists have shared information with one another and with potential sympathizers since at least the latter half of the 1990s. The sociologist James Aho notes that an "essential component of the hate community is its 'literature.'"[22] As we will see, the most signifi-cant articulators of white nationalist ideology have also relied heavily on pamphlets and books, fiction and nonfiction alike. Because of the stand-ing of both the Internet and print resources to white nationalists, and for the purpose of this intellectual and religious history of the movement, my analysis focuses on these two sites of expression. Proceeding this way allows me not only to follow the argumentation of influential white nationalists but also to see what is commonly available for consumers of this rhetoric.

A few more words about my approach to this topic will help the reader follow my discussions in subsequent chapters. First, I read racist language in white nationalism as a type of mythology. That is to say, I see it as a type of discourse, following Bruce Lincoln's definition, that "is not just a coding device in which important information is conveyed, on the basis of which actors can then construct society" but "a discursive act through which actors evoke the sentiments out of which society is then actively constructed."[23] Race is of course a pernicious and powerful taxonomic device, but it is also an idea that is imbued with such force that it creates and conveys strong sentiments, anxieties, and commitments and is there-fore best understood as a myth, which is, as Lincoln states, "an authorita-tive mode of symbolic discourse."[24]

It is important to keep in mind that white nationalists also deploy the historical power of whiteness, shaping it and adapting it to create new meanings and motives. In such a mythology, a Manichean scheme of racialized struggle, racist discourses are always at least implicitly prescriptions for action. When white nationalists describe the world as the stage for enacting racial survival, individuals are put in the position of having to make a moral choice either to fight for racial survival or to let the race die out for their lack of commitment. White nationalist ideation thereby elevates whiteness itself as a transcendent mode of valuation, a means of identification, and a motivating moral trope.

I take this approach to race as mythology à la Bruce Lincoln together with insights from Benedict Anderson's classic work *Imagined Communities*—namely, that the nation, however signified, is imagined as limited and sovereign and as a community[25]—to enable a description of white nationalism as an imagined racial community that owes its existence to an adaptation of historical racial mythologies that construct the white race as a community that must be defended. This combined approach then gives shape to a methodology for reading the interaction between racialized and religious discourses of belonging and exclusion as social mythologies that inform the construction of moral obligations to one's imagined racial community. This approach is attentive to the fact that racist discourses are socially communicated and formative of contemporary racialized social realities and are therefore not simply reducible to an individual's intellectual or psychological failings. Racism is not simply the individual pathology of a failed social subject. It is the expression of a certain mode of socialization.

In white nationalism, the imagined global white community, established through mythologies of purity and imperilment, is reified in the obligation pressed upon the individual white nationalist to protect the race. At the same time, the obligation to defend the beloved racial community produces the white nationalist subjectivity as it binds the white nationalist to the imagined racialist community. Or, as Henri Bergson puts it, "obligation, which we look upon as a bond between men, first binds us to ourselves."[26] The duty to love and protect the imagined community constructs and sustains the imagined racial community as it constructs and binds the white nationalist individual to the community and his or her own social identity. It is in this sense that white nationalism is sustained as a closed loop of self-concern in the preservation of one's own subjectivity, which is bound to the imagined racial community.

Bergson's argument in *The Two Sources of Morality and Religion* is particularly helpful for understanding racial protectionism in American white nationalism. *The Two Sources* was originally published in French in 1932 and then translated into English in 1935. Bergson wrote it out of concern for the possibility of another world war and in the later part of his career as both a famous and influential philosopher and the president of the League of Nations' International Committee for Intellectual Cooperation, the predecessor of the United Nations Educational, Scientific, and Cultural Organization.[27] Bergson has since fallen into obscurity, though Maurice Merleau-Ponty, Jean-Paul Sartre, and Emmanuel Lévinas all acknowledge his influence, and the French philosopher Gilles Deleuze has been responsible for a revived interest in Bergson's thought through his book *Bergsonism* (1966) and his series with Félix Guattari on capitalism and schizophrenia (*Anti-Oedipus* in 1972 and *Thousand Plateaus* in 1980).[28] Interest in his political and social theory has been on the rise in recent years.

Bergson's political theory, especially its relevance to war, has been taken up by others, in particular Frédéric Worms and Philippe Soulez. Selected contributions from these scholars are now collected in a volume edited by Alexandre Lefebvre and Melanie White titled *Bergson, Politics, and Religion*, which is meant to draw attention to Bergson's long-ignored work. Lefebvre and White describe this edited volume as "dedicated to the political and religious aspects of [Bergson's] thought" in the belief that he is "a philosopher who has had an extraordinary impact on the political" and "an extraordinary philosopher *of* the political." *The Two Sources*, Lefebvre and White further argue, was Bergson's effort to "frame a series of political problems in terms of a treatise on morality and religion" and is therefore useful to understand relationships between religion, morality, society, and violence.[29]

Philippe Soulez agrees with Lefebvre and White's assessment of Bergson's contributions to the philosophy of war, but he goes a step farther in the direction I take here by offering a Bergsonian reading of racism. He writes that Bergson was right "to show that the exclusion of the other, which characterizes the political per se, carries the seed of extermination, precisely when the other is seen as a different and of course inferior species or biological race."[30] Here Soulez is describing the basic function of what Bergson called the "closed society": the segmentation of humanity into a binary of familiar selves and enemy others in a social order concerned primarily about and organized for defense. I suggest that we can describe white nationalism as a closed society and thereby understand how racial protectionism has made Christianity a problem in American white nationalism.

The most succinct description that Bergson gives of the closed society is in the final chapter of *The Two Sources*: "The closed society is that whose members hold together, caring nothing for the rest of humanity, on the alert for attack or defense, bound, in fact, to a perpetual readiness for battle." The definitive attributes of the closed society are its defensive bellicosity and the inculcation of that war stance in its members as it fosters exclusivist self-concern. Bergson goes on to say that the closed society perpetuates itself "through a religion born of the myth-making function," what he calls "static religion," and through the "force" of "moral obligation," which he argues "is the very substance of closed society." That is to say, the closed society forms and deploys moral obligation, molded in myth and conveyed through "religion," to form a society, "however small," that is "prepared for war."[31]

For these reasons, I find it useful to describe white nationalism as a closed society organized around the mythology of whiteness to form an imagined racial community that the white nationalist is obliged to defend in the face of imagined racial enemies. More significantly with respect to my point about racial protectionism, this description allows us to see loving attachment to the imagined racial community as producing racist hatred. In the closed society, war and hatred are produced from the very injunctions to love and protect society from destabilizing, alien agents. In other words, expressions of hatred for the racialized other in American white nationalism are at the same time expressions of love for the imagined white racial community. White nationalists prove their loyalty to and love of the white race in their emphatic hatred of the mythical racial enemy. Every act of racist hate speech is therefore at the same time a statement of one's love for the white race. Every act of racial violence becomes the proof of one's loving devotion to the race.

Chapters

The progression of the book is not strictly chronological. For example, it can be argued that the first white nationalist organization was not founded by Revilo Oliver, who is the subject of chapter 1, but rather by James Madole (1927–79), who formed the National Renaissance Party and is discussed in chapter 5. The reason I do not try to be strictly chronological is that this book is not, strictly speaking, conceived as a chronological history of American white nationalism. It is rather an examination of white nationalism's tense relationship with Christianity. Although Madole and the National Renaissance Party are an important part of that story, I contend that we should first consider closely the critiques developed by figures such as Oliver who have more specifically shaped how white nationalists have broadly understood Christianity, especially in relation to their place in the wider political culture of the Far Right in America.

The first three chapters are biographical in nature, examining Revilo Oliver, William Pierce, and Ben Klassen, men who defined white nationalism in very significant ways and set the tone for the critique of Christianity. The final three chapters take a less biographical turn in examining the contexts—Odinism, racialized esotericism, and the North American New Right—in which American white nationalists wrestled and continue to wrestle with the critiques of Christianity developed by racial nationalists in the decades immediately after World War II.

In chapter 1, I discuss the emergence of contemporary white nationalism in the work and words of a figure who has been forgotten in almost all circles except for white nationalist ones, a cofounder of the John Birch Society, professor of classics, and racial nationalist ideological pioneer, Revilo P. Oliver (1908–94). This chapter describes Oliver's early conservative writings published in the *National Review*, his activities in the John Birch Society, and his evolution from a polemical archconservative into a voracious critic of both the conservative movement and Christianity, arguing in favor of a race-focused activism that was especially critical of Christianity as a dangerous and polluting Jewish ideology. Oliver thus in many ways personifies the transformations in Far Right political and religious thought that became so influential among later white nationalists and that have continued to bedevil the efforts of activists who are trying now to unite mainstream conservatives, the so-called alternative Right, and white nationalists.

In chapters 2 and 3, I discuss William Pierce (1933–2002) and his new religion, which he called "Cosmotheism," as well as Ben Klassen (1918–93) and "Creativity," the religion he initiated in the mid-1970s. Though William Pierce has become more well known, both were key figures in white nationalism as it really took shape in the 1970s. Further, Pierce played a significant role in the hypervisibility of radical right-wing movements in the United States after the Oklahoma City bombing when his writings were implicated as inspiration for this act. Although Creativity adherents have also been involved in acts of violence, on a smaller scale, Klassen's ideology as it was succinctly inscribed in the slogan "RaHoWa—Racial Holy War" has become ubiquitous in white-power circles in America and elsewhere. In both Pierce and Klassen, we have people key to the further development of white nationalist ideology who described new religious movements that would supplant Christianity and all other perceived alien ideologies and would make primary the survival and expansion of the white race over the whole planet.

Chapter 4 leaves the more biographically driven narratives of the first three chapters to examine the emergence and development of Odinism, or racialist Paganism, as one of the most important religious trends in American white nationalism today. What is most challenging about this chapter is correctly delineating what is racist in the ways that we understand white nationalism to be rather than simply ethnicized as a religious option for peoples of northern European decent. Because practitioners of Odinism differentiate themselves along these lines, we must consider that there may in fact be a difference that for outsiders is not apparent. Further, certain developments in white nationalist religiosity reference Odinism in significant ways but nevertheless differentiate themselves in name—for instance, Wotanism. In the white nationalist variants of racialist Paganism, Christianity is seen both as an alien ideology in the sense that Oliver, Klassen, and Pierce articulated it and as something that was forced upon European peoples, who should now seek to recover their supposedly true and inherent religion. Through this rejection of Christianity in favor of Odinism or

Wotanism, it is thought, the peoples of Europe will be able to withstand biological and cultural extinction.

Chapter 5 discusses the even more complicated milieu of occult racialism in America. Here we see not simply a rejection of Christianity but also at times a more nuanced and complex redefining of Christian themes, as in the esoteric Hitlerism of George Lincoln Rockwell (1918–67), founder of the American Nazi Party in the 1960s. In other cases—for example, Savitri Devi (born Maximani Portas, 1905–82), who believed Adolf Hitler to be an avatar of Vishnu—Christianity is regarded as essentially Jewish and therefore as counter to true Aryan spiritual instincts. In this trend of religious thought among white nationalists, we see not only another way in which Christianity was thought of as a problem in relation to esoteric, racialist truths but also explicit transatlantic connections emerging in the 1960s with the effort to revive mythical connections between spirituality, biology, culture, and political activism that would ensure the survival of the white race.

In chapter 6, I discuss the emergence of the North American New Right and how it was adapted from the ideas of the European New Right, specifically members of la Nouvelle Droite, or the French New Right, which emerged in France in 1968. In these movements, white nationalists developed what has been called a metapolitical project of European cultural renewal and biological survival, which has been especially influenced by the university-trained academics Tomislav Sunic, Michael O'Meara, and Greg Johnson. This adaptation of the European New Right for the American white nationalist context is, in Johnson's words, "motivated by consciousness of an existential threat" and is engaged in saving "European peoples" from "a cultural and economic system that has set our race on the path to cultural decadence and demographic decline."[32] But here the rejection of Christianity found elsewhere is complicated by some New Rightists' assertion of a certain form of traditionalist European Christianity as adequate for the masses and of a racialist Paganism for the elite, others' suggestion that Christianity can be racially reformed, and still others' argument that the rejection of Christianity is politically inexpedient. These New Rightists suggest religious toleration for the sake of unity in the pursuit of the larger political goal of white racial survival. Among the racialist New Right, the problem of Christianity in American white nationalism is approached not simply by rejection but also by complex compromises shaped by political pragmatism and a broader appeal to the American conservative mainstream, which signals a further change in white nationalist religiosity beyond even what Dobratz noticed in 2001—a trend that reflects once again the centrality of racial protectionist logic among American white nationalists.

In the conclusion, I revisit the implications of the problem of Christianity in American white nationalism, in particular the importance of racial protectionism in understanding it. Of special concern here is understanding the larger story of Oliver, Pierce, Klassen, and others' early disillusionment with both conservative politics and Christianity and what we may be observing now in white nationalist intellectuals' efforts to form alliances with the mainstream American Right once again, particularly by aligning itself with anti-immigrant sentiment and opposition to multiculturalism. Here, I argue, we can see that understanding the internal logic, religious and otherwise, of the racist Right may be important for understanding how so-called extremists are finding voice among the mainstream of the increasingly antimulticulturalism and anti-immigration Right in America. Such a conclusion reinforces the warning that to ignore "extremists" is not only foolish but also neglectful of the fact that extremism easily becomes the norm if we are not attentive to truly democratic ideals in moments of social stress and anxiety.

Finally, I have added a postelection epilogue in which I briefly explore the relationships between what has been called the "Alt-Right" and white nationalism as well as some of the implications for the United States and indeed for the populist New Rightists elsewhere after the election of Donald Trump and his appointment of Steve Bannon as senior policy adviser. My aim here is to offer some much needed terminological clarification and perhaps some suggestions for what we may need to consider as we enter an era that many of Trump's supporters and detractors alike have called "Trump's America."

I

Revilo Oliver and the Emerging Racialist Critique of Christianity

Revilo Pendleton Oliver, though he has been sometimes overlooked or even forgotten, is one of the most important figures in the development of American white nationalism. He of course was not the first person to express racial nationalist sentiment in America, and he founded no organization to compare with the National Renaissance Party, which first came to prominence in the 1950s, or the American Nazi Party, which was likewise active before Oliver exerted his influence in the racial activist milieu. Nevertheless, he played a significant role in defining white nationalist ideas concerning conservative politics and Christianity.

Oliver's writings on these topics still circulate today through the Internet and print publishing, and many American white nationalists consider him to be one of their most influential intellectuals. But Oliver is also important for us to consider first because he in many ways personified the transformation of the old racist Right during the height of the Cold War into a new racial activist Right after World War II. In the 1950s and early 1960s, Oliver was a staunch proponent of American conservatism and an advocate for Christianity's place as the basis of Western civilization. He was an early contributor to William F. Buckley's magazine *National Review*, a cofounder of the John Birch Society (JBS), and a member of "the Council," the leadership organization within the JBS. But by 1969 he was becoming a vocal critic of both conservative politics and its attachment to "Judeo-Christianity." In subsequent decades, Oliver became increasingly harsh in his criticisms of conservatism and Christianity as equally detrimental to the cause of white racial survival. Indeed, Oliver's critique of American conservative politics and his critique of Christianity reflected one another in both their increasing intensity and their conspiratorial anti-Semitism and zealous racism.

Oliver's later attacks on conservatism and Christianity were fundamentally anchored in his firm conviction that neither could secure the survival of the white race, which he had taken to be the first obligation of every sane white person. He eventually came to argue that conservatism and Christianity were actively contributing to the weakening of the very instincts necessary for racial survival and were in fact themselves part of a larger Jewish conspiracy to destroy the white race. In his estimation, both led to a liberalizing, integrationist attitude toward other races and, especially in Christianity's case, taught universal brotherhood rather than the exclusive focus on the survival of the white race. For these reasons, he finally abandoned any defense of either conservatism or Christianity and argued strenuously that other whites should do so as well.

Oliver's focus on racial protectionism clearly compelled him to turn against conservatism and eventually to reject Christianity, even in its racist forms. It is also significant that his opinions concerning conservatism and Christianity prefigured popular sentiment among other early white nationalists and have shaped how they see themselves and organize their activism. And as we will see in chapter 6, these persistent and commonly shared attitudes have presented significant challenges for those white nationalists today who seek to bridge white nationalism and mainstream politics. We should then regard Oliver and his evolving critiques of Christianity and conservatism as the best starting point for our discussion of the problem of Christianity in American white nationalism.

Oliver's Education

No thorough biography of Oliver is available to us, but some details of his life can be gleaned from various print and Internet resources, especially white nationalist sources. Revilo Pendleton Oliver was born in 1908 in Corpus Christi, Texas.[1] He developed an interest in India's mythology early in his college education, beginning with readings of Max Müller's handbooks. He later took his interests to the University of Illinois at Urbana-Champaign to pursue graduate studies and eventually published a translation of the ancient Indian drama *Mrcchakatikā*, or *The Little Clay Cart*, in 1938. He then received his PhD in 1940 under the guidance of the eminent American classicist William Abbott Oldfather.[2] Later in life he also served, as did George Lincoln Rockwell, in the US armed forces for a time, which for many of Oliver's admirers is still as much a point of pride as his academic career. After receiving his PhD, Oliver was granted a professorship in the Classics Department at the University of Illinois at Urbana-Champaign, where he stayed until his retirement in 1977.

It is hard to overstate Oliver's erudition. He was conversant in several topics, especially philology and history. Much of this learnedness, of course, was brought to the service of his fondness for conspiracy theorizing and racism. His academic prowess was more often directed toward antiliberal and racist polemics, though he did publish on academic subjects. He stayed long in the academy, but his true passion was right-wing activism, especially in his writing and speaking engagements to groups such as the JBS, the Citizens' Councils of America, the Daughters of the American Revolution, and later the National Youth Alliance (NYA).

Oliver became officially affiliated with *National Review* as a contributor in 1955, and he continued to write reviews of books for the magazine well into the late 1950s. Buckley and he eventually had a falling-out that compelled them to part company. The main cause for this dissociation seems to have been Oliver's many public anti-Semitic statements.[3] We must also consider that about the time that Oliver stopped contributing to *National Review*, Buckley was already attempting to purge members of JBS and other undesirables from the magazine's staff and even from conservatism as a whole. Buckley and his colleagues at *National Review* and then on the television program *Firing Line* were trying to form a new conservative movement that could not allow itself to be perceived as a refuge for "extremists" and racists. Nonetheless, at least for a time, Oliver published his ideas in what became the flagship magazine of the conservative movement.

Such antagonism was not always the case. Before Buckley and Oliver discontinued their professional relationship, Oliver met Robert Welch through their mutual association with Buckley. Not long after their first meeting, Welch, with some measure of help from Oliver, founded the JBS, in their view, to fight communism and preserve America's Christian spiritual heritage.

The JBS was the result of a particular meeting of politicized Christianity and devout anticommunism. It was named after an American Baptist missionary killed by Communist Chinese in 1945 and included such members as a young Tim LaHaye of *Left Behind* fame. The JBS combined anticommunism and ultraconservatism with a particular political and fundamentalist understanding of Christianity. As Barbra Stone noted in the mid-1970s, "Religious fundamentalism has been a corollary of the John Birch Society from the beginning."[4] Indeed, in *The Blue Book of the John Birch Society* Welch described the Cold War as a "world-wide battle . . . between freedom and slavery, between light and darkness, between the spirit of Christianity and the spirit of the anti-Christ for the souls and bodies of men."[5] Throughout *The Blue Book*, there are references to alleged Communist subversion and spiritual decline in America that the JBS was meant to reverse. It would then seem that, if even for a brief time, Oliver believed this mission had value.

In addition to being a founding member of the JBS and engaged in a position of leadership there, Oliver also contributed consistently to *American Opinion*, the JBS's publication, as an editor and a contributor, writing a column called "A Review of Reviews." And if his anti-Communist bona fides were not established by this connection, Oliver also testified before the President's Commission on the Assassination of President Kennedy (Warren Commission), during which he discussed an article he wrote in *American Opinion* arguing that the Kennedy assassination was a Communist plot.[6]

These associations of course did not last. Oliver seems to have been, at least from what can be gathered from his later writings on the topic, disgusted with the direction of *National Review*. He abandoned Buckley's company willingly and acrimoniously.

So, too, was Welch struggling with some JBS members who he thought were propagating "ideological wedges," people he called "the neutralizers."[7] In his little book *The Neutralizers*, Welch stated that chief among these subversive agents were anti-Semites, whom he regarded as a seditious element within the JBS who were there to purposely derail the society's program or were perhaps led astray by the teachings of British Israelism. He even went so far to state that the Communists had planted anti-Semitism in America to distract anti-Communists and to "weaken" the organization's hold on its membership with accusations that the JBS was "not realistic" on the so-called Jewish issue.[8] And though Oliver is not mentioned by name in this book, this is in fact exactly what he would later accuse the JBS of in his writings. It was known, of course, as Seymour Martin Lipset and Earl Raab note, that Oliver was "the most aggressive Anti-Semite [sic] active in the Society."[9] It is entirely possible that Welch was thinking of him in particular, though Oliver was far from alone in his views on this issue.

It must also be noted that the institutional attitudes of the JBS and *National Review* reflected broader changes in American conservatism, especially concerning religion. During the 1950s, conservatives such as Will Herberg, a Jewish American theologian and intellectual, religion editor at *National Review*, and author of an important book on American religious sociology, *Protestant, Catholic, Jew* (1955), deployed the concept of America as a Judeo-Christian civilization to demonstrate its opposition to godless Russian and Chinese communism. Such an open embrace of Christian and American identity as defined by a certain affinity with Judaism and Christianity as well as the institutional rejection of anti-Semitism were surely all too much for the virulently anti-Semitic Oliver to withstand. He came to see the JBS as a Jewish organization that used anticommunism as a tactic of distraction to prevent white people from focusing on their racial identity and obligations.

In reflecting on his time in the conservative movement, Oliver described his self-removal from the JBS and from conservativism more broadly in terms of utter disillusionment and disdain. He said of American conservatives that "there was no significant intellectual difference between the American bourgeoisie and the cattle one sees . . . on their way to the abattoir."[10] He finally came to regard this break as a positive move that freed him to "write with utter frankness on the dire plight of our race [the white race] and [the] civilization [it] created."[11] Finally, in 1965, after giving a speech in which he assailed Jews alongside Bolsheviks and the Illuminati, he resigned from the JBS.[12] With this resignation, his advocacy of even extreme conservatism came to an end.

Even as Oliver left the anti-Communist camp, his conspiratorial anti-Semitism and increased focus on white racial survival compelled him to start his activism anew in the late 1960s. He began to contribute to the *American Mercury*, which had been founded by H. L. Mencken in 1924 but had changed hands in the 1950s and 1960s to become a mouthpiece for openly anti-Semitic and racist views. Russel Maguire acquired it in 1952 and then sold it to Gerald Winrod in 1961, who then sold it to Willis Carto in 1966. Here, Oliver could voice not only his racism, homophobia, and anti-Semitism but also his displeasure with the conservatives whom he had recently abandoned. He also regularly, perhaps more than any other single person, contributed to *Liberty Bell*, a magazine produced by longtime racist activist and Holocaust denier George Dietz. Oliver continued to contribute to *Liberty Bell* until his death and was eulogized twice in its pages in 1995.

Oliver's connections with *Liberty Bell* and Liberty Bell Publications were significant. The magazine often advertised his collection of essays *America's Decline: The Education of a Conservative* (1981), which included even some of his early essays from his days with *National Review* and the JBS but also significantly some pieces that described his disaffection with conservatism. In 1995, shortly after Oliver's death, Liberty Bell Publications also published selections from his contributions to *Liberty Bell* in a collection titled *Against the Grain: The Writings of Professor Revilo Pendleton Oliver*.[13]

Oliver's political direction after leaving the JBS seems to have been deeply informed both by Yockey's Pan-European vision and Oliver's own efforts to find new associations with an emerging racial nationalist movement in America. The latter assertion is I think easily proven with his work in *Liberty Bell* and *American Mercury*. But perhaps the best view of Oliver's changing political thought and Yockeyian influence during this time comes from a talk he adapted from his article "After Fifty Years," published in *American Mercury* in 1969. The talk was produced and filmed in that same year for the NYA, the predecessor of William Pierce's infamous group National Alliance.[14]

The article opens with a sharp critique of anti-Communist and conservative political efforts to date. Oliver's argument is that conservative organizations, although seemingly sincere in their efforts to "awaken the

American people" and defend the Constitution and Christianity, had failed. He argues further that such efforts have finally reached "the end of the road" concerning their ability to rouse white America. Concerning Christianity, he says that rather than providing a foundation for the preservation of Western civilization, it encourages "pulpit-pinks and pulpit-punks [who] deny the divinity of Christ, spout poisonous rant about 'social justice,' and . . . incite rape and murder."[15] From Oliver's point of view here, Christianity had become either a detrimental socialist ideology hijacked by liberals or the irrelevant faith of a minority. His view of the US Constitution fairs little better. He argues that it was "*no longer possible to restore the Constitution by Constitutional Means*" and that conservatives were naively unaware that that the Constitution had been already successfully "undermined by aliens."[16]

In both the filmed address and the article, Oliver condemns American conservatives and anti-Communists as distracted, lost, and deluded, not simply corrupt. "What is left?" he asks rhetorically in the face of his long list of the conservatives' failures. He answers, "Only the biological fact of race, the yet discernible vestiges of our culture, and the yet fresh memories of what we were not long ago." And further, offering a formula that is echoed in later forms of white nationalism, Oliver opines that those things are "all that we have left from which to create, if we can, a new nation to replace what we lost."[17]

In this talk and in the original article, Oliver introduces Francis Parker Yockey's opus *Imperium* as the principal means of instruction for the youth organization and as a book that "does not tell them [white youth] about the economic advantages of 'free enterprise'" or "dilate on the blessings of freedom to buy a mortgage in the suburbs, run faster in the rat-race, and raise children to be taught that paradise is a place where hominoids with full bellies live in perpetual rut." He describes *Imperium*, in contrast, as a guidebook that "speaks to them [white youth] of honor, loyalty, race, and Western man's will to conquer or die." He states that this guidebook for the NYA, unlike the "lady-like conservatives who insist that we must be careful to love everybody," warns that the "treason of the slimy Ganelon can be defeated only if the Men of the West are still willing to die in the pass at Roncesvalles."[18]

Closing with this reference to the eighth-century French epic *Song of Roland*, Oliver clearly means to contrast Yockey's Pan-European racial nationalism to what Oliver regards as the soft, ineffectual, and blind conservative movement, which insists, in his view, on the liberal inclusion of all peoples rather than focusing exclusively on the survival of the white race and Western civilization over and against perceived racial and cultural outsider-enemies.

We can see clearly that by 1969, the year Oliver gave this talk, he had no love left for his former conservative associates. Such disdain is confirmed in his remarks in a later essay titled "America after the Holy War" in which he attacks *National Review* as a "basically 'Liberal' periodical . . . under the cover of devotion to Catholicism, subject to strict Jewish censorship," that simply purveyed a "kosher 'conservatism.'"[19] Both modern forms of Christianity and Buckley's conservatism are, according to Oliver, complicit in the destruction of so-called Western values in America and are therefore endangering the future survival of the white race. After 1970, Oliver continued to link criticism of American conservatism to the Christianity that he came to despise as racially integrative, neglectful of white racial survival, and bereft of an adequate racial-warrior ethic.

After his filmed address to the NYA, Oliver quickly found affiliations and outlets for his racialist politics in America and abroad. In his talk before the NYA in 1969, Oliver praises Louis T. Byers, then leader of the NYA, and his organization as the first major youth organization of its kind, and though he shies away from making any definite statements about the group's future, he describes it as possibly the "turning point for which we have so long hoped for."[20] His later associations included friendship with William Pierce, who was soon to take the leadership of the NYA from Byers and transform the organization into National Alliance in the 1970s. Oliver also corresponded with Alain de Benoist, a founder of Groupement de recherche et d'études pour la civilisation européenne (Group for the Study and Research of European Civilization), which later became the core organization of the French New Right and the predecessor and catalyst for the European New Right and then the North American New Right.[21]

Correspondence between Oliver and Benoist reveals not only a general amity but a mutual interest in the respective right-wing scenes in America and France. As early as June 1970, Benoist began to write Oliver to discuss the NYA as well as issues of *Attack!*, a periodical edited by William Pierce, and to congratulate Oliver for his "fine work" in making known Francis Parker Yockey's book *Imperium*. In one letter, Benoist also apprised Oliver of the coming publication of his own periodical, *Nouvelle École*, and other projects, such as the translation of W. C. George's pro-segregationist pamphlet *The Biology of the Race Problem* into French (commissioned in 1962 by the governor of Alabama, John M. Patterson).[22]

In a letter from Oliver to Benoist dated April 6, 1971, we learn that in spite of all of Oliver's optimism for the NYA, the organization had failed amid leadership and money problems and that in the wake of its demise a "successor organization . . . headed by Dr. William Pierce" was being started.[23] This is not just an early indication of the emergence of National Alliance but also a clue to Oliver's ongoing interest in Pierce. Pierce's biographer, Robert S. Griffin, draws associations between Pierce and Oliver more closely than even Oliver himself implied. He reports that Pierce met Oliver through Louis T. Byers in 1970 or 1971 and that Oliver and Pierce continued to correspond thereafter. Griffin also reports that Pierce was initially inspired to write fiction by Oliver's suggestion that it would help recruitment for National Alliance. Furthermore, Pierce claimed to have received from Oliver a photocopy of the book *The John Franklin Letters* (1959), described as a template for Pierce's work *The Turner Diaries* (1978), which has been connected to the bombing of the federal building in Oklahoma in 1995.[24] Pierce told Griffin that he went so far as to "buy into Oliver's idea,"[25] which suggests that Oliver was the main catalyst for Pierce's fictional works.

Oliver's activism had clearly shifted since his days with the JBS and *National Review*, and at the center of his new activism was the survival of the white race. In his collection of essays *America's Decline: The Education of a Conservative*, Oliver describes more completely his story of disengagement with the American conservative movement, specifically in the essays titled "The Great Deceit" and "Aftermath." In brief, his narrative is that the JBS was revealed to him to be fraudulent and controlled by Jews, and he calls it "the B'nai Birch." Like Pierce and Ben Klassen, as we will see later, Oliver saw the JBS and the conservatism it promoted as a distraction for "otherwise well-meaning American Aryans" and nothing more than a "Jewish auxiliary."[26]

In "Aftermath," Oliver merges his critique of the JBS with a more general critique of American conservatism, arguing, as he does in "After Fifty Years," that those who wanted to recover or restore America to an earlier time were possessed of "dangerously antiquarian delusions." Such men, in Oliver's estimation, neglected the issue of racial survival. He concludes "Aftermath" by stating in uncompromising terms that "American Conservatism is finished, and its remaining adherents are, . . . merely ghosts wandering, mazed, in the daylight."[27] It is clear that by the 1980s Oliver believed that race, specifically the preservation of the white race, was the only real issue confronting white Americans and that this issue needed renewed attention. The white race was in need of saving, a task that, in Oliver's view, was something well beyond what conservatism could ever accomplish.

We should then understand that Oliver's critique of what he described as "quaint" patriotism and American conservatism was essentially pragmatic in relation to the survival of the white race. He was clearly provoked to attack National Review and the JBS because of the abject presence of persons whom he perceived to be dangerous racial enemies. But we should appreciate that he was more troubled by the perceived impotence and inadequacy of conservative ideology and praxis, of which, for him, the presence of Jews was a sign and symptom. As this rationalistic pragmatism shaped his critic of conservatism, it also shaped his assessment of Christianity. In a review of William Gayley Simpson's book Which Way Western Man (1978) in Liberty Bell in 1980, Oliver went so far as to describe Christianity as nothing more than a collection "Jewish superstitions" that have "paralyzed" the "vital instincts" and "rationality" of the white race.[28]

According to Oliver, Christianity, like conservative politics, inhibits the expression of necessary attributes that would ensure the future survival of the white race. But he did not always feel this way. Like his critique of conservative politics, Oliver's perspective on Christianity changed from his days with National Review, when he saw it as fundamental to the Western tradition. It is to this transformation in his thought that I now turn.

A Westernized Religion Perverted

As discussed briefly already, Oliver's departure from the conservative scene is timed with significant developments in the movement, in particular those related to attitudes toward Jews and especially Christianity in the context of the Cold War. It is important to note that not long before Oliver left *National Review*, Will Herberg, the publication's religion editor, wrote about America's spiritual heritage in his classic study of religion *Protestant, Catholic, Jew: An Essay in American Religious Sociology*, published in the mid-1950s. Herberg's thesis is that Protestantism, Catholicism, and Judaism are in America the "three great branches" of one "American religion" and are now "three culturally diverse representations of the same 'spiritual values.'" Referencing President Dwight D. Eisenhower's appeal to the recognition of God as a fundamentally American disposition, Herberg notes that what we may call Judeo-Christianity had become the "religious creed of Americanism" and the civic religion of the American people.[29] In brief, Herberg, agreeing with Eisenhower, Billy Graham, and the conservative movement almost as a whole, claims that Americanism is now synonymous with Judeo-Christianity.

The notion that America is a country founded upon and defined by Judeo-Christian values gained popularity at the time Herberg was writing his book, in part because of the incredible revival of Christianity in the post–World War II years, spearheaded by Billy Graham's crusades and a general sense that only devotion to liberty and to God could save the free world from communism. According to Mark Silk in "Notes on the Judeo-Christian Tradition in America," prior to the twentieth century the term *Judeo-Christian* served as a referent only to "designate connections between Judaism and Christianity in antiquity" but in the twentieth century had come to refer to a shared "western religious outlook" in the context of Cold War America.[30] Appeals to the Judeo-Christian tradition became a means to define American democracy in opposition to Nazism, especially after the revelations of Hitler's camps, and to Soviet atheism, both of which came to be described together under the newly established rubric of totalitarianism.[31] In 1952, this relationship between Judeo-Christianity and democracy was popularized by President-elect Eisenhower, who deployed it before the Four Freedoms Foundation when he argued that "our form of government . . . has no sense unless it is founded on a deeply felt religious faith" and that for the American people this faith was of course "the Judeo-Christian concept."[32] In this way, Judeo-Christianity came to be regarded, especially among Republicans, including Eisenhower's vice president, Richard Nixon, as the only appropriate foundation for American democracy and defense against communism. As Silk remarks, "Having proved itself against the Nazis, the Judeo-Christian tradition now did duty among the watchfires of the Cold War."[33]

The point here is, of course, that the signifier *Judeo-Christian*, which involved a dense set of relations between religiosity, on the one hand, and the mission and identity of Cold War America, on the other, came to hold a particular importance among anti-Communist conservatives after World War II. At the same time, blatant anti-Semitism, though persistent in American culture, was slowly becoming one of the cardinal sins of politics because it was associated with Nazi totalitarianism and the terrible revelations of the concentration camps liberated only a few years earlier. Beginning in the early 1950s, the dualism of democracy and totalitarianism was balanced on the notion that America is a godly nation dependent on the teachings of Moses as much as on the ideas of Thomas Jefferson. No doubt, Oliver, committed to anti-Semitism and the exclusive preservation of the white race, was not pleased by this direction of rhetoric that mainstream conservatives were increasingly demanding in relation to Christianity. Just as he could simply no longer see a place for himself in the political mainstream of the conservative movement, where he felt Judeo-Christianity defined one's mores, political commitments, and attitudes toward Jewishness, he could no longer speak well of American Christianity itself.

In some ways, then, Oliver's eventual critique of Christianity is simple to understand. At a certain point, he even refused to accept racist forms of Christianity. In a letter to Benoist dated May 14, 1975, Oliver lamented the nearly total resistance to addressing the "*Hauptproblem* of our time"—that is, the "preservation of our race"—by most Americans and especially by Christians, even racist Identity Christians.[34] He went on to offer a counterexample in *The Dispossessed Majority* (1966) by Wilmot Robertson, in which Robertson argues that his book is meant to "supply members of this discomforted and threatened group," white Americans, "with a systematic diagnosis of the diseases and debilities that have laid them low and some suggestions for their recovery."[35] For Oliver, Robinson succeeded most where Christianity and conservative politics failed in that he offered a rational solution to the problem of racial preservation that was not reliant upon polluted and polluting Christian mythologies.

So we can see that by 1975 Oliver had a dim view indeed of Christianity, even in its overtly anti-Semitic and racist forms. But this was not the position at which he had started. It may be that he was an atheist for most of his adult life, but his writings did not always reflect that position. Earlier in his career as a public intellectual, Oliver had thought of Christianity as an authentically Western expression that should be preserved for the sake of the fate of Western civilization. This viewpoint is easily demonstrated in an article he published in *National Review* on March 15, 1958, "Superstitious Materialism."[36]

This essay is mainly a review of Methodist bishop G. Bromley Oxnam's career and his recently released book and of Zoltan Sztankay's book *Christianity, Democracy, and Technology* (1957). It is basically a right-wing polemic against the socialism that Oliver saw as latent in "liberal" Christianity, especially, in his view, as expressed by these two authors. But far from decrying Christianity in general, Oliver defends a certain understanding of traditionalist orthodoxy. He defines the Christianity of Bishop Oxnam and Sztankay as differing from communism "only by an impudent claim to divine sanction" and criticizes their "schemes of social reform" as a distortion of what he understands as authentically historical Christianity. Oliver here defines real Christianity as "a religion of spirit and hence exclusively concerned with moral choices that individuals freely make in their own minds."[37] Historical Christianity is, in his view, not a progressive social reform movement but a personal belief that may transform personal morals. For Oliver, then, the sin of the authors under review is their perversion of traditional Christianity. Making this point more strongly, Oliver closes his commentary by arguing that authentic Christianity is the opposite of "universal love" and that such visions of world peace and a global community that he finds so prevalent in the liberal Christianity of Sztankay and Oxnam are "the hallucinations that precede disaster."[38]

Oliver's fundamental problem was not with Christianity per se but with what he regarded as liberal distortions of truly historical Christianity that he considered probable fronts for Communist goals of social reform. Such a position made Oliver rather unremarkable for his time. But what is important in this article is that he defends a form of Christianity. Given the date and place of publication, *National Review* in 1958, we can see this article as a starting point to understanding how his position on this topic changed as he began to leave the conservative movement. I will, however, draw attention to two particular themes that emerge here and remain linked in his thought thereafter: an appeal to reason and the logic of protectionism. In this review, he finds it historically ludicrous and logically specious to assume that liberal Christianity is truly Christianity. Moreover, he thinks that adopting such an illogical and historically uniformed position is dangerous because such a position is simply Communist subversion in religious garb. His affective attachment to a form of rationality and protectionism take his opinion of religion in a different direction later.

Oliver's shift in attitude toward Christianity can perhaps be most clearly observed in his essay "Christianity and the Survival of the West," originally written in 1969, the same year he recorded his address to the NYA. He begins this essay by arguing that the Western world is in peril and that if it is to be saved, it will be done "by observing reality objectively and by reasoning from it dispassionately." The point of this essay is to assay the "actual strength Christian tradition" at that time.[39] Already, as in Oliver's review of Oxnam's and Sztankay's books, we can see that he positions reason at the center of his analysis as protectionist logic dominates his approach. Nevertheless, he does not yet attack all Christianities. He argues rather early in the text that "Christianity is a religion of the West, and for all practical purposes, *only* of the West." He argues further that what began in sacred books, such as the Bible, which deals with the "activities of Israelites and Jews," had become imbued with elements that he regards as peculiar to Indo-European peoples.[40] Historical Christianity is in fact here properly understood to be European Christianity Aryanized, reflecting the disposition of Europeans.

There are already some obvious similarities between "Superstitious Materialism" from 1958 and "Christianity and the Survival of the West" from 1969, but, unlike in the earlier piece, in the later article Oliver racializes his take on historical Christianity and does not simply draw a distinction between liberal and traditional perspectives. Relying much on the Aryan myth, he constructs a narrative in which Western or true Christianity was specifically adapted by Aryans for Aryans and as such is unfit for other races. The Christianity he lionizes here is neither a "Semitic cult" nor a universal religion but a tradition that had come to embody "the moral instincts" of the white race.[41] Plainly stated, real Christianity is of, by, and for so-called Indo-Europeans because of its long habitation in Europe.

At this stage in the development of Oliver's thought, Christianity is still imagined as the exclusive heritage of the West and of Western peoples as well as the glue of Western civilization itself. This is of course why in "Christianity and the Survival of the West" he regards the loss of the Christian faith as the loss of the "West's bond of union" a "disaster" that resulted in a catastrophic "spiritual vacuum," which he traces to the eighteenth century. He argues that the intellectuals of that time undermined traditional Western Christianity and propagated preposterous superstitions such as Rousseau's "fantasies" of democracy. For Oliver, this revolution in European thought replaced Christianity's "faith in the unseen" with "faith in the visibly and demonstrably false." The unreason Oliver saw in the liberal philosophers of democracy, in particular what he saw as their argument for universal equality, had become in his view a "grotesque caricature of religion" that by 1969 had come to dominate the United States and Europe as the religion of democracy and equality.[42]

Again, this view was not for Oliver yet a great departure from the opinion he held in 1958. He can therefore be read thus far as a defender of a certain historically western European Christianity and at the same time as an animated critic of liberalism in Christianity. In 1969, Oliver still hoped that a traditionally oriented, Pan-European-minded Christian minority in the United States would realize that the West had protected itself "at Châlons, and at Tours, and at Vienna . . . not by book, bell, and candle, but by grace of the shining sword in a mailed fist directed by a dauntless heart."[43] That is to say, he hoped that Christianity could be used to cultivate a defensively bellicose and racially aware Christianity to preserve the West. But his view of Christianity in 1969 was nevertheless mostly a dim one. Save those few traditional Christians, he argued, Christianity is simply the carrier of the mental detritus called "liberalism" and had thereby become an agent of decay in Western civilization rather than an agent of its preservative.

Oliver's remaining optimism about the chances for Christianity to again act as a unifying force for European peoples, already diminished in 1969, was soon completely discarded. In the postscript to "Christianity and the Survival of the West," written in 1978, not ten years after the original article was published, he argues that in spite of the few Christians who still held to racialist ideals, the Christian Church was finished. He further decries how popular it had become among clergy to replace the term *Christian* with *Judeo-Christian*, causing what he describes as a regression away from the Christianity of the West to a "primitive 'Christianity' of the Nazarenes and Ebonites [sic]."[44] In other words, the use of the term *Judeo-Christianity*, which was so significant in Cold War America, signaled to Oliver a reversion to the Jewish roots of Christianity at the expense of what he assumed to be the historical, European Christianity developed by and for Aryans. Those claiming salvation under the guidance of "Billy Graham and the many other big time salvation hucksters" were now for Oliver nothing other than the very evidence of decline as people were called away from rationality to Jewish myths and "a particularly insidious and irrational form of occultism."[45]

This acrimony for the modern American Christianity typified by Billy Graham was mingled with Oliver's harsh treatment of conservative and anti-Communist organizations that in his view had abandoned race as the only really crucial issue and had focused simply on secondary issues.[46] Though he still clung in this postscript to a notion of a "historical Christianity" that was a benefit to the West at a certain time, he had by 1978 written off all modern Christianity as simply hucksterism that allied white people to Jews and their irrational mythologies. In his writings after 1969, he further emphasized his attachment to what he described as rationality and the *Hauptmoral* of racial protectionism, which then become hammer and chisel in his efforts to chip away at racial nationalists' attachment to any form of Christianity.

From a Western Faith to an Alien Influence

Oliver's critique of what he thought of as the dominant modern liberal Christianity, demonstrated in the essays and reviews discussed earlier, soon metastasized into a full critique of all forms of Christianity as alien to the so-called racial instincts of Western man. For Oliver, the noble traits of the Aryan, such as imagination and hard rationality, make the white race peculiar in its sensibilities and therefore not served well by alien religions or ideologies. Even in "Christianity and the Survival of the West," where we see a sympathy for a form of militaristic, mediaeval European Christianity, Oliver claims that the thought processes peculiar to the Indo-European, such as the "innate need to know and master the physical world," compel him to mandate logical consistency and that this assumed rationality conflicts with the "alien elements" "latent" in Christianity's scriptures and teachings.[47]

After this point, though, Oliver's description of Christianity began to take an even more negative direction. He began to argue that Christianity, though perhaps transformed in a sense into a Western tradition, did a measure of damage to the Western racial psyche. And as he eventually concluded regarding conservative thought, he came to see Christianity in any form as a dangerous, alienating, and alien ideology. In 1979, just one year after he wrote the postscript to "Christianity and the Survival of the West," he penned "The Enemies of Our Enemies," a three-part review and response to Francis Parker Yockey's work *The Enemy of Europe*, published first as an essay in the journal *Liberty Bell* in 1981 and then as a book by Liberty Bell Publications that same year.[48]

In "The Enemy of Our Enemies," Oliver's critique of Christianity sharpens significantly as he describes the Christianization of Europe as nothing less than "the imposition of a Magian religion on a Faustian people" and argues that Europe was from this time on "infected by a Levantine religion."[49] This language, of course, comes from Oliver's reading of both Yockey and Oswald Spengler, from whom he gets the notions of the "Faustian" and the "Magian." But in these essays Oliver goes further than even Spengler and Yockey in this regard. In particular, he marvels that neither

Spengler nor Yockey says much about this "prime example" of a "startling pseudomorphosis," an imposition of "Magian" Christianity on the "Faustian" Europeans.[50] The basic point for Oliver is that Christianity, far from simply supplying the West with its historical identity or culture as it was molded into an expression of the Aryan mind, had been from the beginning the most significant factor inhibiting the might of the West and the full development of Western man's racial protectionist instincts.

Such statements already mark a significant break from Oliver's position in 1958 and to a degree also from his position in 1969. Though it must be said that some of his anti-Communist rhetoric remained as he argued that the acceptance of Christian conversion, especially notions of the incrementalist takeover of a geographic area and liberal notions of helping the poor, had prepared the West for Bolshevism.[51] Nevertheless, his position had hardened against anti-Communist conservatism from his earlier days. And as the break with conservatism afforded him the opportunity to find new associations and inspiration among fellow anti-Semites and racial nationalists, it was followed by an increased animosity toward Christianity.

In his review of *The Enemy of Europe*, Oliver particularly favors Lawrence R. Brown's neo-Spenglerian text *The Might of the West* (1963). According to Oliver, Brown uniquely and correctly described the deleterious infection of the European consciousness resulting from the infusion of Jewish thought via Christianity. Quoting directly from Brown's text, Oliver affirms with Brown that because of the imposition of Christianity on the West, Europe had become "a society whose inward convictions have been at hopeless variance with the outward professions the events of history have forced it to make." Oliver further uses Brown's conclusions to bolster his own that Christianity is at odds with the Aryan's rational instincts. This "spiritual tension," as Oliver calls it, has, as he quotes from Brown again, "destroyed the peace of mind of every able man in the West for a thousand years."[52]

In a sense, Oliver revisits his own thesis from 1969 and states that Christianity in the West differed significantly from the early Christianities in Palestine and Asia Minor, but he nevertheless concludes that the Bible and its mythology were at odds with Europeans' racial soul as expressed in the literature of the medieval West. The Bible was indeed not a benefit for Europeans. It was, he argues, "an incubus of which Western Christianity could not rid itself" and had produce irreparable harm to Europeans' "racial psyche." "Even at its best . . . Christianity [had] powerfully and, indeed, immeasurably distorted [Western] culture."[53] Here, even historical Christianity in the West was nothing but an infection that inhibited the full flowering of the West's potential and the full racial awareness of Europeans.

By the time Oliver wrote "The Enemy of Our Enemies," it was apparent that the anti-Semitism that drove his rejection of American conservatism was also shaping his rejection of Christianity. This anti-Semitic acrimony toward Christianity is apparent also in his essay "The Jews Love Christianity," first published in the August 1980 edition of *Liberty Bell* under Oliver's oft-used pseudonym Ralph Perier. As Perier, Oliver claims that key to developing racial consciousness is the recognition that "Christianity was a Jewish invention," designed to destroy "civilized" peoples' racial instincts, peoples "on whom the Jews were preying in antiquity and have preyed ever since." Here, borrowing from Nietzsche, he describes Christianity as a "mental virus." But Oliver goes further still in describing the Church Fathers as a "knavish lot" who were "probably Semites or descendants of one of the other Oriental peoples that swarmed into the mongrelized Roman Empire and displaced or replaced the Romans."[54]

Anti-Semitism in Christianity, in Oliver's view, did not and cannot now inoculate the white race from Christianity's Jewishness and nonrational mysticism. Oliver does, however, confess sympathy for the present manifestation of Christian anti-Semitism, calling such believers the "best of Christians" because they can identify Jews as the "eternal enemies" of the white race. But he also compares these Christians to the Marcionites, an ancient sect of Christians who rejected anything Jewish, including the Old Testament scriptures, who, he argues, "believed that the Jews were 'the synagogue of Satan'" but who were nevertheless not rescued from what he calls a hopelessly flawed belief system that distorted their worldview. So it is, he argues, with contemporary Christian Identity believers. Oliver plainly states that the doctrine taught by Christian Identity is "historically preposterous" and, worse still, "demoralizing." Christianity, even anti-Semitic Christianity, is pernicious in its Jewish origins, has distorted the racial identity of Europeans, and has allowed Jews to masquerade as a different religion rather than to reveal themselves as an alien race.[55]

Oliver's position had hardened about this time, between 1978 and 1981, and under his pseudonym he proposed an uncompromising position that Christianity was a Jewish plot devised to destroy Europeans' racial identity and will to resist the Jew. Even anti-Semitism among Christianism was not enough to redeem it from its Jewish origins and its usefulness to Jews for their own ends. He concludes that Christianity had "dominated and distorted the mind of [the white] race for fifteen centuries—and continues to do so," especially in the United States.[56]

It is important to note that Oliver wrote "The Jews Love Christianity" under a pseudonym. One wonders if he felt that such an assault on Christianity would alienate those who might be his allies in all respects apart from his perspective on Christianity, or maybe he was concerned that he would face such criticism from other racialists that his ideas would fracture alliances among racial activists. It is possible the reason was a mix of these concerns. Whatever Oliver's concerns may have been, "The Jews Love Christianity" did in fact elicit a critical response from another contributor to *Liberty Bell*, "Major" Donald V. Clerkin.

In the August issue from the same year, Clerkin wrote an essay titled "A White Christian Defends His Faith." His thesis was similar to Oliver's in "Christianity and the Survival of the West," that Christianity, though "Magian–Semitic at its birth," in the end "took on a Gothic physiognomy."[57] For Clerkin, Western and racialist Christianity was still the best hope for the preservation of Western culture and the preservation of the white race. More to the point for him, it was God's true path for his chosen people, the Aryans.

Oliver quickly replied to this criticism, once again under his nom de plume, in an essay titled "Religion and Race" in the November issue of *Liberty Bell*. Here he argues that "the question is a practical one" and that any discussion must have as its central point that which will best serve the white race.[58] Again, the issue of efficacy in relation to white racial survival emerges strongly in his response. Oliver reiterates his point that even racialist Christianity is alien and mystical rather than rational and fully focused on the white race's innate potential. He remains unconvinced by Clerkin's counterargument and rebuts that whites now shudder at the word *Aryan* and are often convinced to act out of Christian charity for non-whites around the world, all because, he claims, the "cancer of Christianity" "has at last eaten into their brains."[59] Christianity has warped whites' minds, Oliver affirms without equivocation, so the only logical course of action is to reject it completely.

A short time after his reply to Clerkin, Oliver began to be even more outspoken and brazen in his attack on conservatism and Christianity, though he did not immediately get rid of his nom de plume. In September 1980, in *Liberty Bell* once again under the byline "By an Observer in Hollywood" he published another article critical of Christianity, "The Old Actor and the Jews," this time focusing on the new Religious Right movement. The purpose here was to critique Ronald Reagan, whom Oliver called, as he did Buckley, a "kosher conservative," and to establish further parallels between them.[60]

Oliver was by this time already well clear of any admiration for conservatism in general, but it is worthy of notice that what seemed to bother him the most were Reagan's associations in Hollywood and his pro-Israel stance. Such things were all that Oliver needed to condemn Reagan as an agent of Jewish interests. Reagan, though quickly becoming the hero of Christian conservatives in the newly formed Religious Right, was for Oliver just another example of the failure of the increasingly pro-Israel, anti-Communist conservative movement to prioritize the survival of the white race. Reagan's relationship with conservative Evangelicals proved to Oliver once and for all the ineptitude of both Christianity and conservatism.

Oliver continued to assail conservatism and Christianity alike, especially in the pages of *Liberty Bell*. But it was in the posthumously published unfinished work *The Origins of Christianity* that he tried to develop more completely his critical history of Christianity as a means of discrediting it in the eyes of fellow racialist activists. This work represents in many ways Oliver's final word on the subject of Christianity and its relationship to white racial survival. In this manuscript, Oliver further plays upon his attachment to rationality and the accompanying rejection of anything that approaches mysticism, arguing instead for "an objective and dispassionate" assessment of the problem facing European peoples in the practice of Christianity.[61]

Oliver's treatment of Christianity in *The Origins of Christianity* does not offer much more than what he writes in "Why the Jews Love Christianity," apart from more historical data in the effort to try to support his conclusions about Christianity's detrimental impact on the "Aryan." There are, however, two points in *The Origins of Christianity* that are only implied elsewhere in Oliver's work, each of which relates directly to how Oliver imagined religion in general and Christianity in particular.

In chapter 5, Oliver argues that the "spiritual mongrelization" that was the result of alien religious ideologies encountering the unique and superior Aryan peoples "largely preceded and certainly facilitated the biological mongrelization."[62] In this particular passage, Oliver is not directly discussing Christianity but rather Georges Dumézil's hypothesis about Indo-European religion and the eugenicist Hans Friedrich Karl Günther's racial theories. He does so to draw a particular conclusion about the effects of ideological mixing. He argues that biological racial destruction through biological "miscegenation" has its roots in the initial influence of alien ideologies. For him, such histories as that of Rome and India offer for him insight into the "puzzling episodes" in the history of the white race that precipitated destruction through ideological and then finally biological miscegenation.[63] His clear point is that Christianity, an alien religious ideology, was the initiating force behind interracial sexual permissiveness that ultimately spelled and spells the end of Aryan dominance in any particular area. Ideological miscegenation always results, so the formula goes, in racial suicide through sexual miscegenation.

Oliver goes further in his book to describe religion as a whole and principally Christianity as a "corrosive acid" that has dissolved "all the natural bonds of society, kinship, family, social status, race, and even government, and replaces them with the fractious and unnatural bond of unanimity and superstition." He argues that Christianity in particular compels its adherents to "replace race with a church" and has thereby become a "deadly racial poison" that has brought the white race "to the point of death." And because all such vestiges of religious mysticism, especially Christianity, are so dangerous to the future of the white race, they must be abandoned if the race is to survive. Any such trappings are simply incompatible with civilization.[64]

Oliver had by the early to mid-1980s reached the conclusion of his journey from conservative defender of Western Christian orthodoxy to uncompromising critic of Christianity, indeed of all religion, even in their racist and anti-Semitic forms. With an author as prolific as Oliver, it is not possible to comment on every piece in his oeuvre, but the selections discussed so far indicate a trajectory that parallels his developing critique of conservatism and Christianity. What we can conclude, finally, is that Oliver hated both conservativism and Christianity in his later years because they equally represented to him an ideological poison that was alien to the best instincts of the white race to defend its existence. It is clear, therefore, that racial protectionism was the driving force behind his rejection of Christianity. It is also clear that he was not alone in having these views. Oliver stands even now as one of the most important early voices in American white nationalism on that topic.

Oliver's Legacy

Revilo Oliver's place in American conservatism in the 1950s and 1960s, however neglected or hidden, is established with credentials possessed by few other individuals in the white nationalist milieu after him. His associations with the Right ran deep and broad, from Buckley and Welch to Benoist, Byers, Carto, and Pierce. But the greatest indication of how important Oliver is for white nationalism are the testimonies of his admirers and recent interest in publishing his works by the likes of the anti-Semitic Historical Review Press and former National Alliance member Kevin Alfred Strom.

Further testament to Oliver's place in the construction of contemporary white nationalism comes from the introduction to the collection *America's Decline*, written by Sam G. Dickenson, then director of the Council of Conservative Citizens, an extension of the anti-integrationist White Citizens Councils, and contributor to the racialist periodical *Occidental Quarterly*. In that introduction, Dickenson describes Oliver's place in the racial nationalist movement as "philosopher, leader, and participant" and notes Oliver's description of nationhood as "an historical, cultural and racial community."[65] That is to say, Dickenson esteems Oliver as one of the foremost intellectuals of racial nationalism in America and as a fellow in the cadre of those describing and shaping what Carol Swain calls the "new white nationalism in America."[66]

Oliver has also been lionized by publishing organizations and on websites that are sympathetic to the white nationalist cause and that still make available his work in print and online. Among the most significant publishers are Counter-Currents Publishing and Historical Review Press, both of which facilitate the distribution of works from neofascist and racialist authors, Holocaust denial literature, and so-called radical traditionalist texts. It is of course also significant that Counter-Currents publishes the journal *North American New Right*. In chapter 6, I discuss the North American New Right as a movement in much more detail, but here it is important to note that this most recent manifestation of racial nationalism in America—one that in many ways revisits Oliver's earlier thinking about Christianity as a Western religion—has served as a medium for some of Oliver's essays and books. So important is Oliver to this newest movement within American white nationalism that in 2011 the Counter-Currents editor, Greg Johnson, described him as a man of extraordinary erudition and "an avowed racial nationalist."[67]

Oliver's work has been archived and cataloged for easy Internet access by Kevin Alfred Strom, a onetime leader in National Alliance who defines himself on this website as "a friend of the eminent American classicist and writer Revilo P. Oliver."[68] Strom also wrote the preface to *The Origins of Christianity* in 2001. Significantly, Strom lauds Oliver as one who rightly judged that "one of the weaknesses of our nation and civilization was its religion" and describes *Origins* as Oliver's "most important work."[69]

By the time Oliver took his own life in 1994, the Pan-European racial nationalism that he was so significant in articulating from the late 1960s through the 1980s had been established as a complex movement encompassing an array of groups, organizations, and individual ideologues. By this time, too, Oliver's criticisms of Christianity and conservative politics had become popular sentiment in the emerging white nationalist milieu. Like him, later racial nationalists saw conservatives as weak, ineffectual, and hopelessly distracted from the real problem of white racial survival.

Many also came to see Christianity as a source of pollution to the racial psyche and therefore a threat to the future of the white race. But where Oliver came to see rationalistic atheism as the only means to counter the infection of "Jewish Christianity," others still held that religious alternatives to Christianity were best. In the next chapter, I discuss one of these alternatives, William Pierce's Cosmotheism, and the particular critique of Christianity that emerged from it.

2

William Pierce and the Cosmotheist Critique of Christianity

I n the previous chapter, we saw that Revilo Oliver had become one of the staunchest racial nationalist critics of Christianity and American conservatism, which he essentially felt were ideological hindrances to the survival of the white race and therefore had to be rejected totally. Oliver's one-time interlocutor, William Pierce, shared the core of Oliver's convictions in that regard, though he seemed not to have had to undergo such a dramatic transformation as Oliver. As founder of National Alliance and the author of the infamous *Turner Diaries* (1978), he continues to be a dominating presence in American white nationalism today. According to the Southern Poverty Law Center, he was "America's most important neo-Nazi for some three decades until his death in 2002."[1] But even across the Atlantic, racialist organizations such as the French group Jeune Nation (Young Nation) have posted material approvingly discussing Pierce's work and have even reproduced some of his writings on their websites.[2] Furthermore, Pierce's relationships with the Nationaldemokratische Partei Deutschlands (German National Democratic Party) and other European racial nationalist organizations are well known.[3] Pierce, like Oliver, has been memorialized on the Counter-Currents website created by Greg Johnson, who describes him in admiring terms as an activist who gave up his academic career to "work full time on white racial preservation."[4] And numerous websites make Pierce's writings and speeches available for posterity.

In short, there is really no way to overstate Pierce's importance to contemporary white nationalism. As a consequence, his thoughts on

Christianity should be taken as authoritative for those in the movement. Although Pierce and Oliver held exactly the same opinion about the John Birch Society, of which Pierce was also a one-time member, and of conservatism more generally, they differed on matters of religion. Oliver thought any form of religious "hocus pocus" was nothing more than a distraction from a logical approach to racial survival, whereas Pierce ventured in a more mystical direction. Though he is known as the founder and leader of National Alliance as a political organization, what is less appreciated is that at the heart of this project was the creation of a new religion that Pierce called "Cosmotheism."

Through Cosmotheism, Pierce articulated a specific program of racial survival and a religious alternative to Christianity. He presented Cosmotheism as a transcendent ideology that would support a sustained program for white racial survival. Its principles were therefore not marginal to National Alliance and the other activist work that Pierce undertook but rather deeply informed his understanding of what racialist activism should be about and what should drive it. His claims to a supposedly timeless, metaphysical, and racialized truth in Cosmotheism ultimately shaped and authorized his racial politics and his whole worldview, through which he critiqued Christianity.

In this chapter, I outline in brief William Pierce's activism with the American Nazi Party, his brief membership in the NYA, and finally his founding of National Alliance after the NYA's collapse in the 1970s. This outline, as in the discussion of Revilo Oliver, is intended to contextualize Pierce's views on religion and to situate his rejection of Christianity within a broader understanding of his religious and political thought, which I explore later through examinations of his writings and talks, especially as they are preserved for white nationalists today online and in print.

I argue that Pierce's rejection of Christianity emerged from the racial embodiment of Cosmotheist principles that rests on the assertion of a transcendent metaphysical evolutionary racial struggle and spiritual progress that ultimately defines all life in terms of hierarchy. For Pierce, the struggle between races is not simply a biological fact played out in a Malthusian contest among competing organisms, as Oliver saw it, but also a transcendental metaprinciple that must be properly interpreted and acted upon.

Furthermore, I argue that such an approach to understanding Pierce's activism helps us appreciate the importance of his religious thought to his political ideology and situates National Alliance as an organization that was meant to give form and political expression to Pierce's metaphysical racialism. As Pierce saw it, racial protectionism is an obligation derived from metaphysical principles upon which the cosmos is predicated and ultimately resulting, if properly followed, in the elevation of the superior man, the white man, to deity.

Cosmotheism is thus properly understood as the metaphysics of white racial advancement to eventual godhood. Christianity from the perspective of Cosmotheism is an impediment to that progress and therefore a danger to the white race and its possible glorious and divine future. To protect that destiny and even the white race itself, Christianity must be rejected.

An Activist Life

A comparatively large amount of scholarly attention has been paid to Pierce and National Alliance as compared to Oliver. This is not so surprising given the publicity that surrounded Pierce. Since the revelation of the ties that Pierce's magnum opus *The Turner Diaries* had to the bombing of the federal building in Oklahoma in 1995 and the association drawn between him and the activities of the terrorist organization the Order, also known as the Brüders Schweigen (Silent Brothers), founded by Robert Matthews, an admirer of Pierce, numerous articles have been dedicated to him, and even more references have been made to him in journalistic and scholarly books. He was even featured in a documentary titled *Dr. No?* produced for West Virginia Public Broadcasting, WNPB-TV, in 1990.[5] I do not repeat here all of the biographical information spread across these many sources. The point is simply to offer some context for Pierce's thought on religion, his development of Cosmotheism, and finally his critique of Christianity through his new religion.

William Luther Pierce III was born on September 11, 1933, in Atlanta, Georgia.[6] His family moved around after his father's death in 1942, and the young Pierce graduated from Allen Military School in Texas in 1951 and later attended Rice University in Houston.[7] He went on to complete his

PhD at the University of Colorado and took an assistant professor position at Oregon State University, where he taught physics from 1962 to 1965. With his expertise in physics, he later worked for Pratt Whitney as an engineer.[8] Pierce was, it is easy to see, relatively successful in his field, and his academic and professional experience obviously later impressed Greg Johnson of the North American New Right. But at each turn in Pierce's academic and professional life, his energies were directed in some form toward racialist and political activism.

While Pierce was at Oregon State, he joined the JBS, as he explained to his biographer Robert Griffin, because he felt that it was an anti-Communist organization, which was reason enough for him at the time to warrant joining.[9] But much like Oliver, he soon left the JBS because he came to feel it was not aggressively dealing with the race problem.[10] Pierce expressed disappointment to Griffin because the JBS was opposed to the civil rights movement, "but they weren't willing to deal with it on a racial basis."[11]

Pierce's main objection to the JBS was basically the same as Oliver's—that the JBS was misdirecting attention from race to the canard of anticommunism. Both Pierce and Oliver in this sense represent an early expression of a common attitude among the emerging white nationalist movement in America regarding politics: conservatives, even those on the far right, had abandoned race as the central focus of political activity. Whereas Oliver never became deeply involved with any organization after he left the JBS, Pierce seemed to be drawn to organized activities, especially those that presented themselves as the vanguard of white racial survival.

In the 1960s, Pierce became associated with the American Nazi Party (ANP) under the leadership of "Commander" George Lincoln Rockwell and then became the editor of the party's periodical, *National Socialist World*.[12] Pierce found in Rockwell a fellow traveler in the opinion that the central issues around which to form organized activism were the preservation of the white race in America and the education of white Americans on the alleged scheming and machinations of world Jewry and the so-called Zionist conspiracy. During his time with the ANP, Pierce came to be one of Rockwell's closest associates.[13] Unlike the JBS, Rockwell's party linked conspiratorial anti-Semitism and the imperilment of the white race in an attempt to awaken white Americans to what party members thought presented an existential threat to all of America. There is no doubt that Rockwell and Pierce shared a focused racialist activism. They also shared a distaste for passivity. Rockwell wrote in his autobiography, *This Time the World*, "We recognize a great proportion of Jews have been, and are the leaders of this criminal Bolshevik mutiny and conspiracy against the race of humanity and will not shrink from the task of utterly destroying such poisonous human bacteria."[14]

Pierce and Rockwell shared a penchant for conspiratorial anti-Semitism, a Manichean and militaristic view of the world as the scene of racial conflict, and a myopic focus on white racial survival as the only goal worth fighting for. But these similarities notwithstanding, the relationship between them was not always amicable, and their association was definitively terminated with Rockwell's assassination by a disgruntled member of the ANP at an Arlington, Virginia, strip mall on August 25, 1967.[15]

This event punctuated a longer trend of disharmony in the ANP; things were tending toward a break in the organization even before Rockwell's assassination. The night before the murder, according to Rockwell biographer Fredrick Simonelli, Pierce and another high-ranking member named Matt Koehl had an "acrimonious showdown" with Rockwell that was so vocal and venomous that there was speculation, though unsubstantiated and ultimately unconfirmed, that Pierce and Koehl had something to do with the assassination.[16] Twenty-nine-year-old John Palter was eventually convicted of the murder in a Virginia commonwealth court.[17] After the shooting and following a brief affiliation with Koehl's National Socialist White People's Party, Pierce found his way to the NYA and then founded National Alliance in the wake of the NYA's collapse.

This brief discussion of Pierce's early affiliations demonstrates his place in the emerging white nationalist movement in the 1960s as well as his long-lasting commitment to the racial nationalist cause. I could go a bit further, though, by highlighting that Pierce's major efforts on behalf of the ANP centered on publication and writing. This was his major function early on in his activism, and he never strayed too far from writing even after he became the leader of his own organization. In the pages of

National Socialist World, he was able to insert much of his own perspective through editorial prerogative.

Pierce's personal and academic interest in so-called race science was connected to what he imagined to be the ANP's proper political mission.[18] But his interest in racial esotericism also became a feature in *National Socialist World*. Significantly, Pierce sought to publish a condensed version of the mystical racialist book *The Lighting and the Sun* by Savitri Devi in *National Socialist World*.[19] I discuss Devi's writings more in chapter 5 but can note here that this book was an important work by one of the most important articulators of occult National Socialism in the postwar period, and it is noteworthy that Pierce took the initiative to expose American racialists to it. Nicholas Goodrick-Clarke summarizes Devi's writings as "an elaborated and extraordinary synthesis of Hindu religion and Nordic racial ideology," wherein she identifies Adolf Hitler as an "avatar of Vishnu" and an Aryan savior. He further describes Devi as a "leading light of the international neo-Nazi underground" who had become influential for both Rockwell and Pierce.[20]

Pierce had indeed become deeply interested in Devi's ideas, sought to popularize them among the ANP's readership, and wanted further to have her ideas influence the ANP. His own religious thought and the construction of Cosmotheism were influenced by those ideas. *National Socialist World* reproduced her work and described her as possessing "mysterious and unfailing wisdom" that was the "basis of a practical regeneration policy of worldwide scope."[21] Her combination of metaphysical insight and practical application was indeed what Pierce had been looking for. He claimed not only to have made editorial decisions regarding reproductions of Devi's work but to have hatched the idea on his own and proposed it to Rockwell.[22]

The distribution of Devi's work under Pierce's charge, according to Goodrick-Clarke, "represented [Devi's] literary debut in international neo-Nazi circles" and brought to a broader readership her ideas about "National Socialism as a religion of nature, the Hindu cycle of the ages, and Hitler's world significance as an avatar."[23] That is to say, we can credit Pierce's early editorial efforts regarding Devi's work with opening up a new way of thinking about racialism for him personally and with playing a role in introducing Devi's ideas to the early American white nationalist milieu.

After his involvement with the ANP came to an end, Pierce became an adviser for the NYA and a close associate of another disgruntled racialist defector from the JBS, Louis T. Byers, who was also the founder of the Francis Parker Yockey Society.[24] The NYA was launched in 1968 as a specific response to leftist campus activities and perceived Communist agitation and as an organization specifically for the youth of the racialist Right.[25] It grew out of Youth for Wallace, an organization headed by Willis Carto, whom biographer George Michael describes as "the central figure in the post–World War II American far right."[26]

During this period, Pierce borrowed two thousand dollars from Byers to start the periodical *Attack!.*[27] It was the official publication of the NYA and therefore not exclusively the expression of Pierce's opinions. However, *Attack!* later became the outlet for the first serials of what eventually became *The Turner Diaries* and was the foundation for Pierce's own publication for National Alliance, *National Vanguard.*[28] But as important as publishing and writing were to Pierce and his mode of activism, he always thought that embodying his ideas in an organization was important. Much of his writing reflects such an ambition.

Pierce was finally able to realize his ambition to found an organization in the wake of the NYA's demise. As we saw in the letters from Oliver to Alain de Benoist, the NYA was troubled early in its existence. The disruptions and infighting within it led to serious dysfunction and eventual collapse. Pierce was able to steer the remnants into a new group under his control and to begin anew as its leader. According to Leonard Zeskind in his history of white nationalism, *Blood and Politics*, this result was no accident. Pierce actively sought to put himself in a position of leadership.[29] By the time the dust had settled from the skirmishes, William Pierce was firmly established as the leader of the faltering NYA, which he eventually renamed and redesigned as National Alliance.[30]

In 1974, Pierce confirmed the demise of the NYA and announced the beginning of National Alliance, modeling its entire structure on his own ideas adapted from previous experience among the American Far Right.[31] This meant taking his criticisms of other movements and forming an organization that he felt would not have the same vulnerabilities as they had. Moreover, his organization had a spiritual message that certainly did not reflect the conservative Christianity of the Birchers or even the racist message of Christian Identity. Pierce intended his organization to be supported by a cohesive metaphysics of race that likely drew inspiration from Devi's work. Perhaps he hoped this metaphysics would be more coherent and scientific. More to the point, he clearly hoped that it would provide the basis for a vanguard of racial activism that would secure the future survival and advancement of the white race.

Giving Form to a Cause

In the mid-1970s, clearly affected by his previous experiences in failed right-wing organizations, Pierce argued for the need for "a new revolutionary force, with the spiritual basis that conservatism lacks, and advancing with even more boldness and determination than the forces of the Left."[32] The goals of the newly formed National Alliance were broader than those of its predecessor organization. Whereas the NYA was, as the name suggests, a youth organization focused primarily on college campus recruitment and activism, National Alliance's scope was truly global and was meant to reach anyone of European descent anywhere he or she might live.[33] Pierce, given his experience, was most of all concerned with signifying how different his organization would be from those that had come before it or indeed from any other right-wing group,[34] a distinction he spelled out near the inauguration of National Alliance.

In a talk given in 1976 titled "Our Cause," Pierce differentiated his new organization from others on the right by contrasting its ambitions to the "mental pigeon holes" that were so important to the JBS and other anti-Communist groups. He argued that National Alliance "is neither a conservative or right-wing group," but something new. National Alliance, he expected, would be far more effective for the purposes of racial survival than the conservatives who touted individualism over collective racial survival and ignored what Pierce and Oliver imagined to be a Jewish conspiracy against the white race. His organization would address the real issues. Nor would the US Constitution be its guide, argued Pierce, though it had "served a certain purpose well for a time."[35] Conservatives and other right-wing activists were, according to Pierce, living in the shadow of a fallen idol to imagine that the old American forms of government or

Christianity, for that matter, could save the white race. These statements are strikingly close to what Oliver said about conservatives and indeed were to be pretty closely mimicked by white nationalists exposed to both men's writings and speeches.

Pierce wanted nothing less than to foster a revolution of values centered on race, and that is what he created National Alliance to do. He regularly described National Alliance as a vanguard organization: the gathering point for the best people the white race had to offer, who would lead the way to a new white racial awakening. In his talk in 1976, he spoke of National Alliance as the beginning of "a mighty army whose task is . . . to conquer an entire world."[36] As he stated elsewhere, National Alliance was also to provide guidance for the "survival and progress" of all European peoples everywhere.[37]

The scope of National Alliance was truly transnational, but Pierce later compared what he was doing with European nationalist movements. He intimated to Griffin that National Alliance was in a sense analogous to the British National Party or the National Democratic Party in Germany in that it focused on racial nationalism as a political platform and shunned populism, libertarianism, and other political platforms.[38] National Alliance was racial nationalist in orientation and placed the survival of the white race as its top priority.

National Alliance's main activity, according to Pierce, was educational, focusing on countering what he regarded as the Jewish-controlled news and entertainment media, political parties, public schools and universities, labor and trade unions, and, as far he was concerned, nearly all mainstream Christian churches.[39] Pierce wasted no time in starting this campaign by promoting his organization through print and later other means. He immediately took to publishing and in 1975 began the serialization of what eventually became The Turner Diaries.[40] In that same year, he began to hold weekly Sunday night meetings for Alliance members, during which he would show films and give talks.[41] He subsequently began to publish National Vanguard, which took the place of Attack! in 1978.[42] In 1987, Pierce further advanced his publishing activities when he formed Vanguard Books, through which he published and distributed materials such as Devi's works and William Gayley Simpson's Spenglerian reflection

Which Way Western Man (1978).[43] In 1991, Pierce took another step in marketing National Alliance and his ideas when he started the radio show *American Dissident Voices* and broadcast weekly messages on a number of topics from a white nationalist point of view.[44]

A short time after National Alliance began broadcasting this radio program, it made an appearance on the web with natvan.com, where one could find prerecorded and sometimes live programs, news reports, and links to sellers of racist and Holocaust denial literature.[45] By this time, Pierce had left almost no avenue unexplored to get the word out about National Alliance and its project—including what was in the late 1980s and early 1990s a new medium for the public, the World Wide Web. But as he was making inroads in print, radio, and the Internet, he sought one more avenue to educate the white youth.

National Alliance set its focus on purchasing a music label called Resistance Records to further its outreach agenda. Resistance Records first emerged out of the skinhead music scene in the early 1990s, but in 1997 the company's properties and assets were sold off. After the label passed through the hands of Willis Carto and then Todd Blodgett, a former Republican official and Reagan White House staffer, William Pierce purchased it.[46] He later described the music promoted through Resistance Records as a counter to both the alien influences of mainstream music and what he regarded as the nihilism of Black Metal and Death Metal. The music of Resistance Records would in his estimation play an "important role" in the "quest for roots, community, and meaning."[47] As with National Alliance's website, which was at one time available in fifteen European languages, Pierce wanted to reach an international audience for the music produced by Resistance Records. According to a *Time* article published in 2001, Resistance Records acquired a Swedish label, Nordland Records, in 1999 and was able to establish markets in Greece, France, Italy, Poland, and even Serbia, bringing in revenue of $1.5 million annually.[48] Pierce was by this time the major voice in popularizing the Pan-European white nationalism that we know today.

These various activities and acquisitions of media emerged from the self-imposed imperative to recruit quality people who Pierce imagined would lead the resistance to preserve the white race. Although there can be no doubt that all such efforts were important for what Pierce wanted to do politically, the principles that guided his vision were grounded in racialized metaphysics. Behind the publishing, writing, and organizing lay his racialized philosophy. Griffin states that Pierce's motivation for creating Cosmotheism was in fact to provide "the spiritual basis" for the direction he wanted National Alliance to take and that he always felt should be at the heart of any racialist organization.[49] For Pierce, the survival of the white race depended not just on rational action, as Oliver believed, but also on the apprehension and application of the fundamental concepts in the new religion that he created.

Engendering a Cosmotheist Consciousness

Pierce articulated his first in-depth description of Cosmotheism in his pamphlet *The Path*, published in 1977. In that same year, he also elucidated its meaning in a talk titled "Cosmotheism—Wave of the Future." He later produced the second and third pamphlets in what became known as *The Cosmotheism Trilogy: On Living Things*, published in 1979, and *On Society*, published in 1984.[50] These are indeed the main sources for understanding Cosmotheism, but we should also recognize, as Pierce's successor Kevin Alfred Strom has remarked, that a "Cosmotheist thread" runs through all of Pierce's writings, including *The Turner Diaries* and even his less-familiar novel *Hunter*.[51] Therefore, to unpack the content of Cosmotheism, we ought to consider, as much as possible in this chapter, the breadth of Pierce's work, fiction and nonfiction alike.

Pierce first described Cosmotheism publicly in 1977, but his focus on spirituality, to use a term that approximates his own, was not new. Since the 1960s, even during his brief involvement with the National Socialist White People's Party, he wrote about the importance of a spiritual basis of National Socialism.[52] And he claimed that from the very moment he formed National Alliance, it was his primary mission to help the white race make "spiritual advances."[53] As early as 1976, two years after the founding of National Alliance, Pierce mentioned the core of Cosmotheism, though he had not named it yet, in stating that the white race was imbued with an "upward surge," a "divine spark," which he understood to be situated within an spiritual-evolutionary model that formed the "spiritual basis" for political activity.[54] That is to say, Pierce was interested in the metaphysics of racial embodiment ultimately articulated in Cosmotheism even before he finally described Cosmotheism in 1977.

Furthermore, we should understand that Pierce's subsequent efforts at organizing were guided by Cosmotheism. He admitted this in a *National Vanguard* article titled "A Program for Our Survival" in 1984, where he describes a three-part plan for appealing to people on a "spiritual level." In organizing what he called "community building," Pierce claimed that he ultimately wanted to establish a "reservoir" of activists from which would emerge the racially and spiritually aware men and women who would be prepared to "act when the time comes."[55] But, again, to begin to understand what he wanted to achieve, we should begin with his first attempt to explain Cosmotheism.

In *The Path*, Pierce articulates his vision of the transcendent truth that defines our material existence and that ultimately must be served for an individual life to have its fullest meaning. Cosmotheism as described in this pamphlet is fundamentally pantheistic. As Pierce explains, the "tangible universe is the material manifestation of the Creator." The diversity of life, including the various races of human beings, is an expression of the "Creator's" being, will, and purpose. But though Pierce's model is pantheistic, there is still dualism within it. He writes in the very next passage that "the Creator has a spiritual manifestation" in addition to its material one, and this is what Pierce calls the "Urge."[56]

The "Urge" in Cosmotheism is, as Pierce describes it, the binding force in the universe that harmonizes the material and spiritual dimensions for one singular purpose—the Creator's "Self-Completion."[57] This sort of metaphysical notion of self-realization by the "Creator" is the very engine of history, which speaks to a Hegelian influence and is ultimately the transcendental justification and framework for Pierce's racialist logic. All of life is understood as rightly organized in nature according to the Creator's will, and thus "races" are understood as natural manifestations of the Creator's will. In this context, man best serves the Creator's purpose through a union of "awakened consciousness" and "true reason" that Pierce calls the "Divine Consciousness." The ultimate purpose of the white man is therefore to realize this truth and to enact it in his life in order to realize the "Urge," which will advance man, who is above the "sub-man," to the "higher man," who then must advance toward "Godhood."[58] That is to say, racial hierarchy is the manifestation of the larger metaphysical drama in which the Creator comes to realize itself in one's individual choice to realize and enact its evolution in one's very body and consciousness.

Pierce's goal in articulating Cosmotheism was to instill within the reader a disposition toward his or her own racial embodiment. In *The Path*, he finally asks the adherent of Cosmotheism to cultivate a life in service to what he calls "Cosmic Truth" and to "cast off alien ways." Doing so will allow the adherent to engage with the Creator's purpose and eventually become that superior man and, one day, that deity. But consistent with the racial protectionist logic to which Pierce was beholden, this destiny is not ensured. If one does not fully commit to enacting the Creator's will, the whole of creation's purpose is placed at hazard. Ensuring the survival and advancement of the white race depends on those "Awakened" people, the "crossers of the threshold," the "pointers of the way, of the Path of Life," disciplining themselves for the sake of all life.[59]

As noted earlier, in the same year Pierce released *The Path*, 1977, he delivered an address titled "Cosmotheism—Wave of the Future," in which he elucidated the principles described in the text.[60] He summarized the content of Cosmotheism and how his doctrine related to race and politics. First, Pierce explained, he understood Cosmotheism as communitarian in nature. He stated in the beginning of this talk that *The Path* exists as a guide for the racial community and as a recruitment tool. He also explained that Cosmotheists are not people who are concerned primarily with politics, culture, or economics, but with accomplishing their task as the "bearers of the Creator's purpose." He continually affirmed the primacy of spiritual belief over politics and subordinated politics to race, which was for him the first principle in Cosmotheism from which other principles ought to be derived. He told the audience that this emphasis distinguished his attitude from others in the racial activist milieu: he and his organization did not "put the cart before the horse." Pierce claimed here that only Cosmotheists in National Alliance were working "for ultimate things, for eternal things, for infinite things."

Pierce's statements about his organization demonstrate a general elit-ism inherent in his thought, but it also emphasizes the often overlooked primacy of Cosmotheism in his approach to racist activism, which he felt would and should in time become universal. Pierce nevertheless lamented in "Cosmotheism—Wave of the Future" that *The Path*, in spite of its central importance in describing the basic truths of Cosmotheist teachings, was too esoteric for most people to understand it properly. This was indeed a source of tension between Pierce and his contemporary racialist organizer, Ben Klassen, whom I discuss in chapter 3. Because of the esoteric nature of Cosmotheism, Pierce also worried about the danger of misinterpretation of this doctrine, particularly that his hierarchical pantheism could be mis-read as egalitarian. In keeping with his racialist pantheism—of a certain kind, of course—Pierce affirmed that all people are part of a metaphysical and material whole, that each particular being plays a role in the Creator's purpose, and that all things share in a divine nature. But he emphasized that Cosmotheism still stratifies the races and even stratifies the individu-als within a race according to what he imagined as the Creator's design. He therefore argued in "Cosmotheism—Wave of the Future" that whites "are brothers to the blacks, but in the same sense we are brothers to the rattle-snakes, the sea urchins, to crabgrass, and even to every stone and clump of dirt." For Pierce, racial differences and various individual and communal aptitudes are a necessary part of the singular reality of the Creator in a dynamic and developing material and spiritual reality.

Pierce went on in the talk to argue that Cosmotheism was not, like other religions, passed down via tradition. Rather, he imagined it to be an impulse that moves within the consciousness of European man. In this way, the cosmic racial order is embodied in the white individual, whether that individual knows and acknowledges it or not. Pierce claimed that one can find incomplete expressions of Cosmotheist truth in the writings of pre-Christian thinkers in Europe and among some outstanding intellectu-als in the Middle Ages, in spite of what he regarded as the fundamental contradictions between Cosmotheism and the teachings of the Christian Church that suppressed it. He recognized Cosmotheist principles in par-ticular in the works of later philosophers such as Johann Gottlieb Fichte and G. F. W. Hegel as well as in nineteenth-century romanticism. These philosophical innovations and the scientific discoveries of the twentieth century signaled for Pierce a return of Cosmotheist principles in the face of the diminishment of Christianity in public life, demonstrating that a Cosmotheist thread indeed ran through the spiritual and intellectual history of the white race.

The allegedly unique giftedness of the white race, according to Pierce, is demonstrated in this philosophy, the prominence of the sciences in the West, and the aesthetics of romanticist art and music. The latter, in particular, he thought, typified the Cosmotheist notion of beauty and feeling as well as the supposedly unique emotive capacity of European peoples. Of course, this belief is not at all far from what Oliver proposed in his writings. But rather than seeing this feeling as a detriment in a cold modern world of Malthusian rationality, as Oliver did, Pierce saw it as a sign of the innate spiritual superiority of the white race that could be tapped into for racial advancement and survival. For Pierce, the mix of the rationality of Western science and romantic aesthetics, rooted in a racialized and pantheistic metaphysics, should live harmoniously in the "race-soul," a word he used often, of the European people. Cosmotheism was in Pierce's estimation the fullest expression of that harmony and the most comprehensive program for white racial advancement.

In the talk Pierce gave in 1977 as well as in his pamphlets and other works, Cosmotheist truth is constructed as timeless, if sometimes dormant in the face of suppression. Now that the oppressive Christian dogmas that had long stifled Cosmotheist truth were waning, Pierce thought, this truth could emerge in full flower. Cosmotheism, he proclaimed, "is an idea whose time has come."[61]

Such a description of Western religious and intellectual history strongly juxtaposed Cosmotheism with Christianity, which Pierce regarded as inhibitive, detrimental, and alien to white racial consciousness. He viewed Western religious history as a struggle between the "static view" under Christianity, as he called it, and the dynamic view he considered both the inherent disposition of white racial consciousness and the basis of Cosmotheism. The domination of Christianity over the intellectual life of Europe, Pierce argued in clear agreement with Lawrence R. Brown and a later Revilo Oliver, was a detriment from the start and could be nothing else. Its presence in the West did not lead to enlightenment, nor was Christianity Westernized, as Oliver once believed. Rather, it held the creative, intellectual, spiritual capacities of Western man captive to a corrupting and destructive alien ideology.

In "Cosmotheism—Wave of the Future," Pierce illustrated the way in which the institutional church suppressed Cosmotheist ideas with a brief discussion of the mystic Meister Eckhart. He argued that because the Christian Church opposed Cosmotheism, people such as Eckhart were the object of persecution. In Pierce's narrative, the church's opposition to Eckhart and the charges of heresy leveled against him did not come from his denial of the virgin birth or of the divinity of Christ but from his "deepest philosophical writings" that expounded what Pierce identified as Cosmotheist principles. That is to say, in Pierce's narrative, when the church recognized the thread of Cosmotheism in Eckhart's work, Eckhart was attacked in keeping with this alien institution's basic function—to keep whites unaware of their true potential and destiny.

Pierce certainly thought of the diminishment of Christianity as an opportunity for Cosmotheism. But this moment also presented for him a certain danger. In the wake of the decline of the Christian Church, another enemy had taken its place—liberalism. Liberalism was for him simply a "disease of the soul." He argued in his talk that it uses not reason but "peer pressure"—a clear reference to what became known as "political correctness," as he specifies later in other writings—to obstruct the full awakening of whites to the truth. He did not specify a lineage of liberalism from Christianity, as Oliver did, but it is clear that he saw both liberalism and Christianity as opposed to and inhibitive of Cosmotheism and consequently equally dangerous to the white race.

Immediately after this delineation of the historical enemies of Cosmotheism in his talk, Pierce gave a comparative analysis of how Cosmotheism differs from other religions. He distinguished it from what he called the "purely subjective religions of the East" and from "the pure rationalism" of science that is uninformed by Cosmotheism. In contrast to the "Maharaji [sic]" and other "Yogas [sic]," the Cosmotheist cannot "get away with babbling whatever nonsense enters [his] head." And unlike in the

rational sciences, "observations of the universe" do not dominate the Cosmotheist's perception. Knowledge for the Cosmotheist "comes from the
soul." Because of this, argued Pierce, "everyone who shares the same race-
soul, the same genes," will naturally gravitate toward a similar truth. This
is why he claimed that though Cosmotheism has been and in some ways is
still repressed, it runs the length of the white man's evolution. Cosmotheism is that perfect union of all the elements of the white race, the "blending of the universal consciousness" with the white "race-soul"—immanent
within the race's genes—and with rationality.

Cosmotheism is thus described as intrinsic and powerful, residing in
the genes and expressed in the race consciousness of Western man if he
is unencumbered. But, for Pierce, though Cosmotheism is innate and
powerful, it is nevertheless imperiled by the presence of Christianity and
liberalism, both of which are thought to inhibit its full and meaningful
expression. And alongside these two enemies, there is a third enemy, "the
Jew," who, Pierce believed, is ultimately behind the other two. Pierce
was everywhere concerned about Jews, whom he imagined to have set
out to deliberately subvert the Cosmotheist message for centuries. He
regarded Jews as having a race-soul contrary to that of the white race—
one that is not simply different from that of whites but also inimical to
Cosmotheist truth.

The danger Pierce saw as coming from this imagined alien agent is
one of infiltration in that Jews have played a singular and significant role
in the intellectual life of the West. He argued in "Cosmotheism—Wave
of the Future" that though some Jews perceived some Cosmotheist truths,
they had corrupted this truth and provided a perverse interpretation of
it. A prime example that Pierce used to support this narrative is Baruch
Spinoza, whom he described as "one of the foremost founders of pantheism
in the Seventeenth Century." Pierce emphasized that because Spinoza was
a Jew, he developed a pantheism contrary to that of authentic Cosmotheism and gave it a distinctly Jewish inflection. For Pierce, this inflection was
only natural, though he found it repugnant because Spinoza was, after all,
not white but Jewish. Racial antagonism was for Pierce a significant part of
the cosmic drama of Cosmotheism, innate to the genetic makeup of Jews
and whites alike. The two groups' imagined racial souls were and could

only be in competition for ultimate survival, even when Jews and whites agreed on other points of philosophy.

Pierce ended his talk with instructions on how to avoid such dangers by cleaving unto the teachings of Cosmotheism and enacting them in one's life and political activity. For him, the concretization of the principles of Cosmotheism is carried out not only in pamphleteering and speaking out but also and perhaps more importantly for him at this point in making an effort to "embody" Cosmotheist ethics and racial and social policy in a "living, growing community of consciousness and blood." To ensure the fullest expression of Cosmotheism and to thwart the plans of the Jews and other imagined racial enemies, Cosmotheism must find expression in racially conscious individuals who will cooperate within a community guided by its principles.

In the second pamphlet in the *Cosmotheism Trilogy, On Living Things*, Pierce emphasizes again the evolutionary metaphysical hierarchy of being by drawing a clear distinction not only between races but also within them. He also emphasizes that there is unity but not equality among the people, even among people of the same race. Only the most aware and insightful regarding Cosmotheism are fit to participate in the vanguard that will bring about the full realization of the divine mission. But in the last pamphlet in trilogy, *On Society*, Pierce specifically reflects on the social and political role of Cosmotheism.

In this last installment, the embodiment principle specifically discussed as Pierce's focus begins to shift to the organization he calls the "Cosmotheist Community." Pierce identifies four qualities needed for an individual to enact the Creator's will in the world: the "Divine Spark," "the strength of his true reason," the "strength of his true character," and the "constitution of his body," which allows him to "act in accord with the urgings of his race-soul."[62] Pierce imagines the person thus guided as someone who will eventually direct the advancement of his race, someone who will fully realize the fullness of Cosmotheism "in full consciousness of his identity as the substance of the Creator and the agent of the Creator's Purpose."[63] Such individuals will ultimately be gathered together, guided by Cosmotheist principles, and organized in a community that will serve as the vanguard of the white revolution and as the example for the coming white society.

But without the full embodiment of the principles of Cosmotheism in the life and activity of those aware of its principles, nothing is certain except devolution and despair. And without the communion of these like-minded individuals engaged in common purpose, individual awareness is of no benefit to the race as a whole. The community, in Pierce's scheme, guides the individual and sets the foundation for a future age in which the race advances toward deity.[64] We should therefore conclude that the Cosmotheist Community and National Alliance were Pierce's attempt to enact that personal and organizational embodiment.

Such a conclusion should then affect the way we read Pierce's fictional work, especially when we find the Cosmotheist thread that runs through it. In *The Turner Diaries* (1978), *Hunter* (1989), and the comic book produced by National Alliance, *The Saga of White Will* (1993), not only do the characters describe the Cosmotheist principles that Pierce defines in his religious and political writings, but the narrative demonstrates how the characters come to realize the importance of becoming part of an organization. We should in fact understand organization itself as a Cosmotheist principle, especially in light of the third pamphlet, *On Society*. We then should read Pierce's fiction as further elucidation of Cosmotheism and consequently the criticisms of Christianity therein as further descriptions of his attitude toward it.

As we have discussed in the first chapter, Pierce's first efforts at fiction were likely the result of his being given a copy of the novel *The John Franklin Letters*, published in 1959.[65] This novel, like the later *Turner Diaries*, is structured as a collection of diary notes from the hero of the story, John Franklin, as a group of patriot Americans, a remnant, struggle against repressive antipatriot forces who seek to subjugate America and subsume it under a Communist world government. But whereas John Franklin's letters discuss a patriot group's efforts to fight a one-world, United Nations–led government seeking to impose socialism through martial law, *The Turner Diaries* tells the story of Earl Turner and a group of racial patriots who fight the repressive forces led by Jews and "Negros" who want to disarm whites to more easily subjugate them in a forced multiculturalist dystopia.

The Turner Diaries, originally published in its completed form by Pierce under the nom de plume Andrew MacDonald in 1978, is widely considered one of the most racially violent books ever written. The novel not only celebrates the murder of racial enemies and race traitors in a revolution that begins with the attack on a federal building but also, through Earl Turner's diary entries, is presented as the found historical narrative of the construction of an all-white racial utopia that would emerge after the events described in the diary and indeed because of such acts of gratuitous viciousness and the genocide of racial minorities in America. Because of its racialism and conspiratorial narrative about lone white patriots fighting a corrupt "system," *The Turner Diaries* has become especially popular among white nationalists and some in the survivalist milieu.[66]

There is certainly much to be discussed when talking about this particular novel, but my interest here is specific. In *The Turner Diaries*, though there is no reference to Pierce's religion by name, one can easily see Cosmotheist principles spoken through the novel's protagonist. For example, when talking about the recruits for the guerilla warfare unit the "Order," the main character in the novel, Earl Turner, remarks that although the new recruits come from "basically sound human stock left in this country," most were still corrupted by "the instilling of an alien ideology and an alien set of values in a people disoriented by an unnatural and spiritually unhealthy lifestyle."[67] That is to say, the same degeneration of the white race-soul and consciousness discussed in the *Cosmotheism Trilogy* and in "Cosmotheism—Wave of the Future" plagues the characters in the novel.

Such a description of white decrepitude may indeed be regarded as an attack on liberalism, and certainly liberalism is implicated, but I think the main target is Christianity. This seems to be the case especially if we read that passage alongside an earlier one in which Earl Turner describes the "Jewish takeover of the Christian churches" and the nearly complete corruption of Christian ministries, which at that point in the novel are wholly in the service of Jewish interests.[68] Furthermore, at the close of Turner's "diaries" we get the starkest contrast between Pierce's imagined *Übermensch* and conservative Christians:

> Knowing full what was demanded in character and commitment of each
> man who stood before me, my chest swelled with pride. These were no

soft bellied conservative, business men assembled for some Masonic mumbo-jumbo; no loudmouthed, beery red-necks letting off a little ritualized steam about "goddam niggers": no pious, frightened churchgoers whining for the guidance or protection of some anthropomorphic deity. These were real men, White men, men who were now one with me in spirit and consciousness as well as in blood. . . . They are the vanguard of the coming New Era.[69]

This passage should be read as a literary expression of the Cosmotheist ideal of white manhood as opposed to, among other things, the timidity taught in Christianity. Here the metaphysical embodiment principle is expressed in the fantasy of white racial revolution in the face of the destruction of the white race. On the previous page in the novel, Turner proclaims his joy to play such a vital role in "determining the ultimate destiny of mankind."[70] If we read this proclamation with an understanding of Cosmotheism as Pierce articulated it a year before the book was published, it is clear that Turner references the very Cosmotheist awareness that Pierce claimed is manifest in all racially aware white people. The character of Earl Turner is in this sense a fictional embodiment of the principles of Cosmotheism, just as the novel is a narrative embodiment. Turner's indictment of Christianity is unambiguous. Christianity is simply a timid doctrine that emasculates white men and keeps them from realizing the truth behind and the need for white revolution.

In Pierce's second novel, *Hunter*, published in 1989 and again written under Pierce's pen name, the basic teachings of Cosmotheism permeate the book, though it remains unnamed here, too. The novel is based on the infamous activities of Joseph Paul Franklin, who was eventually put to death in 2013 after years on death row for the vicious crimes he committed through the 1970s and into the early 1980s, which included the murder of an interracial couple and several African American men as well as the attempted murders of Larry Flynt, whom he targeted because of interracial sex scenes published in *Hustler* magazine, and National Urban League president Vernon Jordan.

In *Hunter*, the main character, Oscar Yeager, whose last name is the German word for "hunter," proceeds very much like Franklin in attacking and killing racial minorities, interracial couples, race traitors, and anyone whom he regards as responsible for the degeneration of the white race. Cosmotheist principles emerge throughout the book in his reflections and interactions with other characters. For example, early in the book Yeager's disposition toward other races is described as having been formed during his experiences with black soldiers and the Vietnamese people whom he knew while serving in Vietnam. He did not "hate" them as such but came to realize that they were "races apart" and that what he describes as "innate differences" between the races are "products of race-souls totally alien to his own."[71] Yeager's own racial identity is bolstered by this revelation of the alleged truth of the racial order of things. He realizes that his race is in fact endangered by racial integration, which he believes is promoted by Christian churches and liberal politicians as well as by the ubiquitous Jewish conspirators. And like Earl Turner, Oscar Yeager seeks to take on the "System," which he blames for the corruption of the white race. He wants to do so through violence, initially targeted shootings of alleged racial enemies in a lone-wolf fashion.

The novel is not simply about violence but rather about using violence to bring about change that will begin with awakening the racial consciousness of other white people. In that sense, *Hunter* is a deeply Cosmotheist novel, like *The Turner Diaries*, that is fundamentally about confronting racial enemies by awakened racial activists enacting revolution to secure the future of the white race. As in Pierce's first novel, in *Hunter* the Christian Church is established as a serious obstacle for that mission's success. Moreover, discussions of religion in the novel reveal the Cosmotheist impetus behind Pierce's writing, in particular regarding Christianity. In discussion with other racialists on the topic of the Bible and the Jews, Yeager remarks on religion in general in a way that echoes Pierce's own theory of religion: "Well, races generally create their religions in their own images . . . a religion which is truly native—which came from the soul of a people instead of being imposed by a conqueror . . . a study of the religion would at least give some insights into the character of the people."[72] This passage points to the Cosmotheist conviction that the Bible is properly understood as an expression of the Jewish race-soul and Cosmotheism as the proper expression of the white race-soul.

As in *The Turner Diaries*, so too in *Hunter* the Christian churches are presented as part of the "System" of racial degeneration that the protagonist means to stem. While musing on the disgust he feels toward liberal attitudes regarding what he calls "mud-colored mongrels," Yeager recalls a moment a few years earlier when white clergymen stood side by side with politicians, businesspeople, and black activists outside the South African embassy as insults and abuse were heaped upon a blond woman who was passing by.[73] He later describes churches as "easily the most vociferous boosters of race-mixing" and accuses them of having joined forces with "race-mixing groups, the homosexuals," and other such groups that he believes actively seek to weaken white racial consciousness and to subvert the chances that the white race will survive into the future—the primary sin, according to Cosmotheism.[74]

Christian churches must be overcome if the white race is to survive. In Yeager's discussion with another racialist named Harry, we see the precise description of Christianity as an imposed alien religious sensibility that Harry, echoing Lawrence R. Brown and Revilo Oliver, feels has distorted the European peoples' racial mindset. Harry asserts that Christianity is simply "a religion of equality, weakness, of regression and decay, of surrender and submission, of oblivion." As his monologue continues, he states, "If our race survives the next century it will only be because we have gotten the monkey of Christianity off our backs and have found our way back to a genuinely Western spirituality again."[75]

Like the hero's actions in *The Turner Diaries*, Yeager's individual actions as a revolutionary white warrior are buttressed by organizational activity that is meant to awaken delusional whites to their peril. Yeager is originally interested in joining forces with other racialists through his contact with an organization called "the National League," which at the end of the novel is the force that will eventually, with Yeager's individual "hunting" activities, carry on an organized campaign against the enemies of the white race.[76] Here once again the lone white hero joins forces with a vanguard organization of like-minded racial warriors to awaken and liberate the white race and thereby secure its future. As I have argued, this process, too, should be read as an expression of Cosmotheism. In this way,

Pierce's art imitated his life's ambition for himself, for his new religion, and for National Alliance.

The organizational aspect of Cosmotheism is also clearly present in the comic book *The Saga of White Will*, published in 1993 as issue number 1 in Pierce's venture New World Order Comix. In the comic, a strapping white high school student named Will battles out-of-control "blacks" and a permissive school administration that has been overtaken by political correctness, a particular target in this narrative. In the name of racial tolerance, the Jewish-controlled school administration disenfranchises white students, who are the victims of bullying and threats by the black students. Will, like Turner and Yeager, confronts the institution, or the "System," by exposing so-called discrimination against white students, which is framed as reverse racism. He also commits acts of violence against a student of color who, it is charged, sexually molested a white female student. Will calls the offender "a beast" as he literally knocks his teeth out. He then continues to pummel the offender's associates, who object to the "honky pig" punching their "soul brother."[77]

So far the same pattern demonstrated in Pierce's other fiction is clear in *The Saga of White Will*—the taking on of an antiwhite establishment and the violent retaliation against perceived injustices. But the Cosmotheist thread is most apparent when Will is later inspired by his own outrage to confront the System. With the guidance of an older man from National Alliance who instructs Will and his friend on the new world order conspiracy to indoctrinate white students in political correctness, Will stands before the collected student body to explain to them the truth he learned from the older National Alliance member.[78] The student body is gathered to hear a message of tolerance and multiculturalism by the student president, an African American named Roosevelt Washington, but Will, overcome with frustration, snatches the microphone from Washington and proclaims that America was exclusively made by and for white people and that whites share a fundamental, even mystical affinity because of what lies "very deep in our nature," which goes "back tens of thousands of years in our EUROPEAN ANCESTRY."[79] Cosmotheism is clearly what Will is explaining to the students, even if he does not name it as such.

Racial strife in the school intensifies to the point of a race war, much as it does in Pierce's other fictional works, though on a much smaller scale. Finally, the comic ends like *Hunter*, with Will and his revolutionary student Vanguard, supported by the elder from National Alliance, preparing to continue the struggle.[80] So, like Pierce's other fiction, *The Saga of White Will* should be read not only as an expression of National Alliance's political aspirations but also as an expression of the fundamental points of Cosmotheism. But it should be noticed that this particular piece of fiction had a clear function when it was published. On the inside of the cover page, Will invites the "kids" who were meant to read the comic to join him in getting "the word out" so they, too, can help "blow the lid off of this rotten system."[81] And at the end of the comic, the older National Alliance character, O'Brian, invites the "kids" once more to join National Alliance in its struggle once they turn eighteen and to write for more information about the "most politically incorrect organization that ever was." And as if there were any ambiguity as to what National Alliance is about, on that same page we read, "If the White race is to survive we must unite our people on the basis of common blood, organize them within a progressive social order, and inspire them with a common set of ideals."[82] Once again, Cosmotheism is expressed, though not named, as the fundamental realization that will save the white race from extinction.

Christianity and Christian churches are not mentioned specifically in *The Saga of White Will*, as they are in *The Turner Diaries* and *Hunter*, but the Cosmotheist thread is still easy to identify. In the comic, there is a veiled reference to universal love as a danger to the future of the white race. Pierce elsewhere blames Christianity for teaching universal love to whites and thus corrupting their racial protectionist instincts. But more significant are the other common elements needed to organize exceptional white activists—those who do violence consistently to racial enemies and race traitors—into an organization guided by Cosmotheism. In Pierce's fiction, the heroes recognize the need to embody their convictions and express them in direct and often violent action and finally to have their activities organized in a vanguard group that embodies the principles of Cosmotheism for the future survival of the white race, which is consistently presented as the highest moral value.

These fictional works speak to National Alliance's larger project. Grounded in the principles of Cosmotheism, with a deep criticism of Christianity and a commitment to organized resistance, National Alliance was to be the base for the group that would create a communal space, even if only virtual, for white activists to learn, share ideas, and prepare for and perhaps enact the coming white revolt.[83] Pierce imagined the Cosmotheist Community within the political organization National Alliance as an organized religious order that functions as the elite within the cadre of the larger political organization and would become the "concrete embodiment" of the ideas formulated in the meetings at which he spoke and described in the pamphlets he wrote as well as a place of spiritual support for the political and educational activities of National Alliance.[84] As Brad Whitsel has rightly noted, the beliefs of the Cosmotheist Community and National Alliance are composed around a "single, great truth" that provides "the community with a spiritual understanding of its mission."[85] We should then understand Cosmotheism not only as an expression of Pierce's particular racialism but also at the same time as an expression of an organized ideological criticism of Christianity that was intrinsic to his activities, literary and other.

The Cosmotheist Critique of Christianity Summarized

The Cosmotheist critique of Christianity is easy to comprehend at this point. In his numerous writings, fiction and nonfiction alike, we can clearly see that Pierce viewed Christianity as inauthentic to the white race-soul and therefore inhibitive of a full spiritual awakening that will inspire white men to fight for the preservation and advancement of their race. In this sense, Pierce's critique is not dissimilar to Oliver's eventual position. Christianity is too soft, too complicit in "race mixing," and too influenced by Jews and their interests to save the white race. Pierce therefore attempted to awaken white people's racial instincts through literature and political tracts and to organize the vanguard of a white revolutionary force, as described in his novels and comic book, into a new and explicitly non-Christian "Community of Divine Consciousness" to serve the Creator's purpose.[86] For Pierce, then, the rejection of Christianity was inextricably tied to his new religion. But where he most directly discusses this rejection is his article "On Christianity," published in 1982.

In that article, published first in *National Vanguard* and later disseminated across the Internet, where it can be found still today, Pierce replies to complaints directed at him by those who had detected an anti-Christian perspective in his writings.[87] He identifies two positions in the criticism that he and National Alliance had received in this regard: "I am a Christian. Why are you attacking my religion?" and "I am not a Christian, but many White people are[,] . . . [so] to attack Christianity is divisive." These positions are reminiscent of "Major" Clerkin's response to Oliver's criticism of Christianity. Furthermore, the second objection, as shown in chapter 6, will keep coming up for white nationalists of all religious persuasions. The issue of pragmatics with regard to racial survival is something that appears time and again in white nationalists' rejection of Christianity, as is the retort from others that this rejection is divisive and possibly detrimental to united white opposition to racial enemies. But in "On Christianity" Pierce reminds his critics that though he had avoided this contentious issue to date, he and National Alliance have an "obligation to deal forthrightly with *all* issues of vital concern to the welfare and progress of [the] race."

Pierce responds in a way that does not specifically reference Cosmotheism by name but still insists on "feelings" that emerge from "deep within the White race-soul [and that] existed long before the advent of the Christian church" as well as on the importance of following the direction of those feelings rather than imposed alien ideologies. He remarks that National Alliance is not a principally "a religious organization . . . in the usual sense of the word," but he quickly follows with a veiled reference to Cosmotheism in stating that the organization nevertheless has a "strong spiritual element" in its message. Pierce then asserts his personal sense of responsibility to address Christianity, especially in the face of the Moral Majority's and other right-wing Christian groups' growing strength and active political participation as well as their outspoken support for Israel.

As Oliver eventually came to believe, Pierce also argues in "On Christianity" that all significant Christian denominations had situated themselves as enemies of the white race: they had "openly aligned themselves" with racial enemies and "vigorously" supported racial mixing and Zionism.

This is of course exactly what his characters in *The Turner Diaries* and *Hunter* say. For Pierce, as he argues in the article, such positions are destined to intensify and become more important in the struggle to preserve the white race in the years ahead, especially as "the churches become more and more involved in social and political issues." Just as his fictional characters come to realize, he sees the Christian churches not only as anti-revolutionary but also as a significant source of opposition to the goals of National Alliance and the principles of Cosmotheism.

Pierce is clear that Christianity, with its Jewish mythology and racially alien teachings, especially the trope of universal brotherhood and the use of it to teach race mixing and sympathy with Zionism, is totally at odds with National Alliance's ultimate goal, proper racial consciousness, and is therefore necessarily opposed to white racial survival. Pierce finally asserts in the article that the white race "must look to [its] racial roots," rid itself of the Jewish religious influences, and endeavor to establish itself under new, authentically white principles.

In these statements, we can clearly see that although Cosmotheism is not mentioned by name in this article, Pierce is critiquing Christianity on the spiritual grounds established in Cosmotheism. That is to say, Pierce is critical of Christianity primarily because it is at odds with Cosmotheist principles and therefore with the desire to promote white racial advancement and survival.

A New Consciousness, a New Order, a New People

Since Pierce's death in 2002, National Alliance has faded from its former glory and respected position in the white nationalist community. Mark Potok of the Southern Poverty Law Center reported in July 2012 that the National Alliance, once a "radical-right powerhouse," had been transformed into "a tiny band of small-time propagandists, criminal thugs and attention-seeking losers."[88] But largely through the efforts of Pierce's admirers, especially Kevin Alfred Strom, his writings and speeches are still easily found on the Internet, and his books are still available for purchase through Amazon and other booksellers.

Pierce is still considered one of the most important voices in the white nationalist movement and one of the signal interpreters of its meaning, though he often denied that there was such a movement. The doctrines of Cosmotheism also still circulate on the Solar General website, self-described as the "most censored" site in the world. Adherence to Cosmotheism by name is still quite uncommon, but, the central principles that Pierce propagated through National Alliance and his writings remain common—namely, that the highest principle is racial survival and that this principle is not only a material reality but also a spiritual or metaphysical one. Like Pierce, contemporary white nationalists look for or wish to inspire a revival of racial instincts that will lift the white race to a supreme and indomitable position on the planet and therefore ensure its survival. Furthermore, Pierce's sphere of influence has always been broader than the United States. As Martin Durham notes in his article "The Upward Path: Palingenesis, Political Religion, and the National Alliance," Pierce never sought an exclusively American racial consciousness but one "spanning whole continents," touching all European peoples wherever they might be.[89]

Pierce imagined that his Cosmotheist principles would someday direct the racial vanguard to accomplish this goal in time and that these ideals would form a new racial state guided by Cosmotheism into the racially pure future imagined in *The Turner Diaries*.[90] However fantastic these claims and aspirations may appear to those of us outside the white nationalist movement, they nevertheless offer significant insight into the ideology and personality of one of the most significant figures in white nationalism. They also demonstrate the role of religion, in particular Christianity, in the construction of the white nationalist movement in America after World War II. So far we have seen Revilo Oliver and William Pierce offer both the intellectual foundations for a new form of racist activism and the vigorous criticisms of Christianity that were inherent to their broader agendas. We must conclude, therefore, that the new white nationalism in America had from its beginning a strong antipathy toward Christianity, even in its racialist forms.

In the next chapter, I turn to a contemporary of both Oliver and Pierce who likewise came from the John Birch Society and who had connections with conservative politics before he turned his back on it to pursue racial nationalism: Ben Klassen, the founder of the World Church of the Creator.

In much the same way as Pierce, Ben Klassen devised an alternative religion, what he called "Creativity," that was to provide the spiritual and ideological basis for the expansion and advancement of the white race. He signified this religious ideology in the slogan "RaHoWa—Racial Holy War," which has since become a rallying cry for many white nationalists today. And like Oliver and Pierce, he offered both a foundation for the emerging white nationalism in America and a harsh criticism of Christianity as an alien and imperiling ideology that threatened the survival of the white race.

3

Anti-Christianity in Ben Klassen's "Racial Holy War"

When one discusses racism on the far right, one risks diverting attention from its centrality to the American experience. Discourses concerning racist extremists tend to marginalize or obscure everyday racism and institutionalized forms of discrimination that still exist. Moreover, we should remember that the "extremists" did not invent racism, even if they have often expressed it in shocking and anachronistic ways. As we have seen already with Revilo Oliver and William Pierce, white nationalists often lament the abandonment of older, establishment racist ideals, an abandonment for which they blame liberals, Buckley conservatives, and in some cases Christianity. It is therefore incorrect to imagine that American white nationalists formed from whole cloth the racism they advocate. In fact, they have formed their logic of racial protectionism from what was once common, openly accepted, and even established popular and scientific discourses in America.

The ideas that defined American white nationalism in the years after World War II were not born in the subterranean currents of the extreme right in the middle and late twentieth century but in the mainstream colonialist logic that began to take shape five hundred years earlier. Such was, of course, the assessment of Nazism by Hannah Arendt and Aimé Césaire—that the murderous logic of the camps was forged in the crucible of European imperialism.[1] Racialist logic was also common even among some of those who fought Nazi aggression. Winston Churchill, for example, said before the Palestine Royal Commission in 1937, "I do not admit . . . that a great wrong has been done to the Red Indians of America, or the black

74

people of Australia. I do not admit that a wrong has been done to those people by the fact that a stronger race, a higher race . . . has come in and taken its place."[2] As Europeans colonized the Americas and elsewhere, to quote Charles Long, "the notion of race became the theatre of the entire European myth of conquest."[3] This myth of racial superiority and of right through might for the white man to rule over the earth, a myth born in colonialism, served as the basis for later mutations of racialist logic such as white nationalism.

Racism, to use shorthand for a complex and shifting network of institutionalized ideas and practices, became a significant guiding principle of social organization that was often validated by religious institutions. In the United States, race not only was written into the codes that regulated slavery but also justified ethnic cleansing of First Nations Peoples throughout North America. It was woven into the dreams of Manifest Destiny during the Mexican-American War and in the occupation of former Spanish territories after the Spanish-American War. It was also established in de facto and de jure modes of racial segregation and deeply informed immigration laws through 1965. One's racial signification in America influenced nearly everything from where one might live to one's opportunities for education, one's voting rights, and where and with whom one might worship.

In the eugenics movement, which was enormously influential in the United States during the 1920s and 1930s, the so-called science of heredity as the basis of social organization was used to uphold antimiscegenation laws and was directly applied to immigration policy, particularly in 1924 with the passage of the Immigration Restriction Act, also known as the Johnson–Reed Act. The motive, of course, was to control perceived contamination and devolution of Anglo-American racial stock. This kind of defensive language was often used in the enforcement of policies shaped by eugenics. For example, in the opening address of the Second International Congress of Eugenics in 1921, the famous paleontologist and curator of the American Museum of Natural History Henry Fairfield Osborn said, "The right of the state to safeguard the character and integrity of the race or races on which its future depends is, to my mind, as incontestable as the right of the state to safeguard the health and morals of its peoples."[4]

Protection of Anglo-American stock and political power was also clearly the motive for the immigration quotas set in the Johnson–Reed Act. President Calvin Coolidge, who signed the infamous immigration restrictions into law in 1924, stated plainly after the act's passage that "America must be kept American,"[5] by which he meant of course that its racial status must be preserved as predominantly northern European. Such policies did not simply mean the exclusion of racial others, though that was indeed much of the motive with respect to immigration. It also meant the numerical diminishment of so-called dysgenic individuals who were considered racially "white" but nevertheless genetically inferior or undesirable.

Sterilization of those institutionalized for "feeble-mindedness" or "imbecility," actual diagnostic labels at the time, was common. For many leading social and scientific thinkers in America in this era, having hereditarily deficient persons give up or, rather more accurately, have taken from them the ability to reproduce was a small sacrifice to ask of them for the betterment of society as a whole. As Supreme Court justice Oliver Wendell Holmes infamously wrote for the majority in *Buck v. Bell* (274 US 200 [1925]), the decision that upheld that institutions could sterilize "feeble-minded" persons, "It is better for all the world, if instead of waiting to execute degenerate offspring for crime or to let them starve for their imbecility, society can prevent those who are manifestly unfit from continuing their kind. . . . Three generations of imbeciles are enough."[6]

Policies enacted through a deep sense of national and racial imperilment and supported by some of the most significant legal and scientific authorities in America were designed to protect the ruling and assumed superior Anglo-American racial stock from infiltration by outsider racial aliens and from degeneration from within by marginalizing or exterminating the "unfit" or by not permitting them to breed.[7] It can be said that the logic of racial protectionism, now of course much more broadly imagined in the context of American white nationalism, had its roots in the mainstream racist, colonialist, and eugenic thought that matured in the late nineteenth and early twentieth century.

There are numerous examples of racist attitudes and institutionalized practices throughout US history, but the point should be clear from just this brief discussion that we must understand racism and racial protectionist ideation in one form or another as a significant element in that history. But we must also recognize that racism is never a static notion. As David Theo Goldberg says, race is "one of the central conceptual inventions of modernity," although, as he rightly recognizes, "the significance of race transforms theoretically and materially as modernity is renewed, refined, and redefined."[8]

Through innumerable encounters, institutionalizations of knowledge, and resistances, various mutations of the idea of race and racism emerged and transformed over the five hundred years of European colonialism. Part of that story is the development of what came to be called "white nationalism" in America. For ideologues such as Oliver, Pierce, and their contemporary Ben Klassen, recovering and recoding old-time racism was not simply a political strategy to draw disaffected white southern Democrats into the new base of the Republican Party, as it had been in Nixon's Southern Strategy. Their projects were attempts to fix what they regarded as conservatives' failure to keep central the ideals of race that had previously guided immigration policies, upheld segregation, and maintained white control of central private and public institutions. What critical race theorists have correctly identified as institutionalized forms of racism in current political policies and praxis early white nationalists looked at as only half-measures.

In their attacks on conservatism and Christianity, Klassen, Pierce, and Oliver began to offer a redefinition of race-based activism for their newly imagined racial community. But they did not completely agree on all matters, particularly when it came to religion. Though they all despised Christianity and conservatives, they differed on what political or religious activity would best serve their mutually sought goal of white racial survival.

In this chapter, I discuss Ben Klassen, the religion he called "Creativity," and especially how he articulated a critique of Christianity through the ideas this religion codified in its creed, "Racial Holy War." Klassen thought that a racial religion formed for the purpose of ensuring the future of the white race was the only way to avoid its extinction. He shunned politics to pursue the development of that religion, but, like Oliver, he had no patience for mysticism or unrealistic claims, as he understood them. As Martin Durham remarks in *White Rage*, at the core of Creativity was "a fiery rejection" of the "spooks in the sky" narrative.[9] Nevertheless, he believed strongly that there was psychological power in evoking religion that was unique.[10] Klassen wanted to harness that power in Creativity and use it to wage a race war to defend white people everywhere.

In Creativity, Klassen, like Pierce with respect to Cosmotheism, emphasized an evolutionary naturalistic perspective. And this emphasis, too, took on a particularly bellicose tone. In a statement that resonates with Churchill's statement in 1937, Klassen argued that it was "Nature's program" that superior races "colonize into new territory and expand to the limit of your abilities—no holds barred."[11] In Creativity, rather than the ideas of universal brotherhood and love for one's enemies that he found repugnant in Christianity, he elevated what he called "Racial Holy War" to the foremost religious dogma and practice of the properly oriented white activist. This dogma came to dominate every aspect of the church's doctrine and every part of the church member's life if he or she adhered properly to it. Creativity was not simply a list of demands placed on one but a moral appeal for the reformation of one's life and attitude toward one's racial embodiment, one's physical and social environment, and one's inner commitment to the project of racial protectionism.

From Anabaptism to Creativity

As we saw, especially with Revilo Oliver, the first generation of leaders within the new American white nationalism had come from other, sometimes establishment political and activist movements. The same is true of Ben Klassen. He was involved for a time in politics as a member of the John Birch Society and even served briefly in the Florida State legislature. But somewhat differently from Oliver, whose revolt against conservatism was mainly political and antireligious, Klassen moved away from all mainstream politics as such in favor of religion. By the early 1970s, he had come to believe that a truly white religion was the only effective way to begin to fix white people's thinking and to save the race from impending extinction. This belief is easily explained if one understands what religion meant to him from his early life and how that meaning changed until he eventually founded his own racial religion in the early 1970s.

Bernhard "Ben" Klassen was born into a Mennonite family in the village of Rudnerweide in southern Ukraine on February 20, 1918.[12] In his infancy, his family experienced the turmoil of the Bolshevik Revolution. This event was significant to him both in that he later criticized Mennonite theology along with other forms of Christianity and that his Mennonite heritage was personally important.[13] In 1924, his family fled Russia for Mexico, where they stayed only until 1925, when they moved to Canada. Klassen later enrolled in the University of Saskatchewan in 1935, where he developed an acute interest in comparative religion and history. As events in Europe began to catch his attention, Klassen, who was fluent in German, read *Mein Kampf* and was inspired. In his autobiography, he states that the events of 1938 and his reading of *Mein Kampf* had a profound effect on his "Weltanschauung" and his "philosophical outlook on life as a whole."[14]

Through World War II, Klassen remained sympathetic to Germany for what he felt was the cause of national self-determination and anti-communism. Such sympathies were likely inspired to some degree also by his recollection of German troops' protection of his family in Ukraine. But it should be noted that his Germanophilia was much more clearly influenced by what he described as Hitler's compelling ideas. Even as he joined the Canadian Officers Training Corps, Klassen remained sympathetic to Nazi Germany and longed to help establish the "New Order" to which it aspired.[15]

From 1942 to 1943, Klassen studied electrical engineering at the University of Manitoba. After completing his university studies, he got a job at Northern Electric in Montreal. But he was unsatisfied there and wanted to move to the United States. As he tells the story, he left Canada on V-J Day, August 15, 1945, and eventually made his way to California, where he started a real estate firm and did quite well for himself.[16]

Klassen and his wife moved from California to Nevada and back again to California. They also traveled widely and eventually relocated to Florida. During this period, Klassen established a number of businesses and invented products, including an electric can opener he called the "Canolectric."[17] By 1959, he and his family were living in a newly constructed house in Pompano, Beach Florida, where they enjoyed a life of relative leisure.[18]

However, Klassen soon began to reflect on issues that mattered to him and to write a bit, if only for himself as he and his family traveled Europe and other destinations through the early 1960s. In 1962, he recounts, when he saw Governor George Wallace "heroically" stand against integration and later after the Kennedy assassination, he became an active member of the JBS.[19] His political career, however short, began at this time when he was elected to a brief term in the Florida State legislature in 1966, where he represented Broward County, served on the Committee for Banks and Loans, and as a representative sat for a special session on state government organizational efficiency.[20] He was, however, defeated in his bid for the Florida State Senate in 1967—a loss he blamed on Jewish machinations to keep him from further official influence—and thereafter participated in other forms of political activity in the state.[21] He became an active supporter of segregationist governor George Wallace's presidential campaign in 1968, but seeing how the Republican Party treated Wallace, he broke with the party in 1967. He later founded the American Independent Party, mainly on an antitax, state's rights platform.[22] That year he also established a Florida chapter of the Citizens' Councils of America, an anti-integrationist organization, and was a high-profile JBS member until he resigned in 1969.[23]

Like Oliver and Pierce, Klassen abandoned the JBS after becoming suspicious that its anticommunism was a distraction from the issue of race, and he also shared Oliver and Pierce's suspicion that Jews were controlling the organization's agenda.[24] He, like Oliver, was by this time thoroughly disgusted by the politics of the conservative movement, to which he formerly belonged. He began to explore other options. He flirted for a time with Nazi organizations, such as the National Socialist White People's Party and the World Union of National Socialists, which emerged out of the American Nazi Party.[25] But, alas, as Pierce experienced, Klassen found no true place for his ideas in these organizations. He went on to found the Nationalist White Party in 1970 as yet another third party, but this time on a more overtly racist platform.[26] This woud be his last effort at forming a political movement. Hereafter he would focus on religion and its potetial to organize the white race into a sacred community dedicated to its own survival.

Klassen's later political explorations reflected a similar diasallusionment with fledgling racialist movements that Oliver and Pierce also experienced in the 1970s. But Klassen's aspirations shifted dramatically from political activism to exclusively religious activities, unlike what we saw with Oliver and Pierce. He initiated his own religious movement, Creativity, to address the religious shortcomings he saw in other racialist movements—namely, their failure to capture the power of religion in a significant way. In 1971, while the Nationalist White Party was still active, he began to write the sacred dogma that would guide the fight to save the white race, and in 1973 he established the Church of the Creator (CoTC) and a short time later named himself its "pontifex maximus."[27]

Creativity—A History of Violence

The beginnings of the CoTC are recorded in George Michael's history of the organization, *Theology of Hate*, so it is not necessary to cover all the details that Michael covers in his book. I instead remark on some significant moments in the development of the church, especially its later history after Klassen committed suicide in 1993. It is particularly important for my purposes to look at how Klassen described the origin and development of the CoTC as a clear and comprehensive religious program for the survival of the white race. It is also important to understand that he imagined this religion as a direct response to the deficiencies in other religions, especially those he found in Christianity.

In his autobiography, Klassen describes the genesis of the CoTC as coming foremost from the desire to provide the white race with a religion of its own, something that he argues it never had before. He says that he had already determined while studying comparative religions in college that Christianity was just one religion among many and that Christ was just another fanatical religious figure, like Mohammad, who preached nonsense. He had by this time already begun to drift from his Anabaptist upbringing, but in 1971, as he recounts in his autobiography, he reread the Sermon on the Mount in the Gospel of St. Matthew and had an epiphany. He read the words "love your enemies" and "blessed are the meek" with new eyes and concluded that such prescriptions were "the kind of suicidal advice you would give your worst enemies if you wanted them to destroy themselves." Christianity now appeared to him as simply a Jewish plot designed to destroy the white race. And to oppose Jewish Christianity, he decided to formulate a "powerful new dynamic RACIAL RELIGION" for the white race so that it might be rescued from self-destruction through Christianity.[28]

Klassen pondered how best to anchor his new religious thought so that it did not repeat any of the mistakes of even racialist Christianity, especially an attachment to what he regarded as spiritual mumbo jumbo. Finally, he decided that he would found his religion on what he thought of as the *Eternal Laws of Nature*.[29] In contrast to the idea of the universal brotherhood of all people taught by Christianity, he argued that "Nature," a term that he always capitalized, had rooted a biological imperative within each organism to advance its own kind through a struggle between species or races, as the case may be. He maintained that any teaching to the contrary, especially the lessons of the New Testament, were not only illogical but contrary to natural law and would mean the eventual extinction of any race that refused to do its biological duty to defend itself. His doctrine turned everything he saw in Christianity on its head, regarding everything it taught as evil because it could only direct white people away from right thinking and action on behalf of their race.

Klassen anticipated opposition to his new religion from Christians, especially those within the then still active Nationalist White Party. He did in fact receive significant pushback when he discussed his ideas. But he was committed to this new direction and was convinced that his ideas were the only way to prevent the extinction of the white race. He thereafter dedicated himself to developing the creeds and teachings of a new racialist religion regardless of the consequences for his previous commitments.

The first earnest effort at making this vision a reality began with his writing what became the first of the "holy books" of Creativity, *Nature's Eternal Religion*, in 1972. He initially had difficulty with the first printer, he claims, because the owners claimed to be devout Christians who objected to his attacks on their religion. It was not long, though, before he found a willing printer, and the first copies of his book were delivered on February

22, 1973. In that same year, he decided upon the name "Creativity" for his religion and "Church of the Creator" for his organization and received a corporate charter for it as a nonprofit.[30]

His two other major works, *The White Man's Bible* and *Salubrious Living*, followed in 1981 and 1982, respectively. In 1983, Klassen also began producing the CoTC's periodical *Racial Loyalty*, which continued circulation for several years, and numerous articles he wrote for it were eventually reproduced on the Internet and in volumes of collected essays: *RAHOWA! This Planet Is All Ours* (1987), *A Revolution of Values through Religion* (1991), and *On the Brink of Bloody Racial War* (1993).[31] Klassen eventually relocated his family and his organization from Florida to North Carolina in 1985, where he continued to strive to "play a significant role in in the survival, expansion, and advancement of . . . the White Race."[32]

Klassen's refutation of Christianity, at the center of his efforts to develop Creativity in the first place, was controversial among some racialists, to be sure. He discusses this controversy in the later parts of his autobiography, and as we know from Martin Durham's excellent summary of racist activism in America, *White Rage*, white nationalists were not always in agreement and often verbally attacked one another for various reasons.[33] But Klassen's religion and its direct assault on Christianity proved to be extremely attractive to others, especially skinhead youth. Early in the CoTC's history, Klassen made connections with Tom Metzger, the founder and leader of White Aryan Resistance, or WAR. Klassen also enjoyed a relationship with William Pierce, though they were often in disagreement over tactics and recruitment. Pierce, for example, stated that he thought that Klassen's approach was fairly crude and "guarenteed to appeal to mostly rednecks and skinheads and other people at the bottom of the socio-economic ladder."[34] But perhaps it was Klassen's intent to rally a zealous youth rather than to intellectualize the movement.

In spite of their differences, Pierce provided Klassen with real assistance during times of significant financial and legal troubles. In 1991, one of the CoTC's "reverends," George Loeb, was convicted of murdering Harold Mansfield Jr., an African American Gulf War veteran. With the aid of the Southern Poverty Law Center, Mansfield's family filed a civil suit against Klassen and the CoTC and were successful in pursuing restitution.

In particular, the CoTC's North Carolina headquarters had to be sold to pay the settlement. Pierce, however, intervened, bought the property, and later sold it for a profit. The proceeds from the sale of the North Carolina property were later recovered through a court order in 1996, almost three years after Klassen's suicide, and the Mansfield family received the $85,000 earned from Pierce's resale of the property.[35]

The CoTC was popular but suffered from several problems, epsecially in its leadership. Klassen spent his final years before his eventual suicide searching for a successor, but with little success. His first choice was unable to take the position because he was serving a six-year sentence for selling tainted food to Florida public schools. Klassen then settled for a Baltimore pizza delivery man, Charles Alvetar. Klassen was soon disappointed once again and appointed in Alvetar's place a Milwaukee skinhead, Mark Wilson, to the position. Wilson ran the organization until January 1993, when he had to abdicate after he was convicted of wreckless endangerment for placing a bomb on the doorstep of the home of a Baltimore County police officer. Finally, after a series of dissapointments, Richard McCarty, a man well known in racialist circles at the time, was promoted to full leadership of the CoTC.[36]

It was amid this turmoil that in August 1993 Ben Klassen took his own life at the age of seventy-five by swallowing four bottles of sleeping pills.[37] McCarty's was now the lone voice of leadership, which caused a split within the group and a succussion of leaders that ushered the CoTC into yet another series of crises.[38] Under McCarty, the Church of the Creator found itself in more legal trouble. Some members, along with members of a local skinhead group, the Fourth Reich Skins, were arrested in California under suspicion of planning to bomb the largest African American church in Los Angeles and to assassinate the police beating victim Rodney King in 1991.[39] Some days later other members of the CoTC were arrested in Solinas, California, for shoplifting. Later investigations of one of the men arrested, Jeremiah Knesal, revealed several plots to attack Jewish and African American targets, military installations, gay bars, and radio and television stations. Under questioning, Knesal implicated himself in even more serious crimes when he confessed to the firebombing of a National Association for the Advancement of

Colored Peoples office in Tacoma, Washington, on July 20, 1993. Under subsequent legal pressure from the Federal Bureau of Investigation and the Southern Poverty Law Center, McCarty gave in to demands for the liquidaton of the church's assets.[40]

The Church of the Creator had stagnated by the mid-1990s but soon found inspiration for recovery under the leadership of a twenty-four-year-old law student from Illinois, Matthew Hale. Hale had become a member of the CoTC in the early 1990s while attending Bradley University. In his youth, he had experimented with various forms of racial activism, including a brief interest in David Duke's National Association for the Advancement of White People, and he even founded his own group, the American White Supremacist Party. However, after reading a copy of *Racial Loyalty* and borrowing a copy of *Nature's Eternal Religion*, he became fascinated with Klassen's ideas and joined the CoTC. In 1995, Hale dedicated himself completely to the church, rose quickly in its ranks, and later established its new headquarters in Peoria, Illinois. Finally, on July 27, 1996, the elders of the CoTC, known as the Guardians of the Faith Committee, named him pontifex maximus.[41]

As leader, Hale played a vital role in popularizing the church on the newest field of competition—the Internet. But recognition came to the group less from Hale's efforts than as the result of even more instances of violence. In April 1999, the Illinois State Bar Association turned down Hale's application for a license to practice law even though he possessed a law degree. He quickly appealed this decision in July that year but was rejected once again. Within hours of this announcement, twenty-one-year-old CoTC member Benjamin Smith, a personal friend of Hale, began a string of shootings of minorities across Illinois and Indiana, killing two people and wounding several others. When capture seemed inevitable, Smith turned his gun on himself and committed suicide.[42]

The media immediately made the link between Smith and the CoTC, and many asserted that the shooting spree resulted from Smith's rage at Hale's rejection by the bar. In spite of Hale's repeated denials that the State Bar Association's rejections were the cause of the shootings, the assertion rang true. Hale responded that this shooting spree was in fact the result of a young white man frustrated with a world that had worked against him his whole life. According to Hale, Smith was not a criminal but rather a "white warrior" who would be missed.[43]

Other violent acts committed by church members followed. In 2001, another twenty-one-year-old man named Joseph Ferguson killed five people and wounded a California Highway Patrol officer before he killed himself. When Ferguson's residence was searched, CoTC literature as well as other racist materials were found.[44] Though police were reluctant to ascribe racist motives to the killings, neighbors told reporters that Ferguson had stockpiled weapons, kept affiliations with skinheads, and had a collection of white supremacist materials.[45] These violent acts compounded the CoTC's reputation as an extremely violent organization. But this was hardly the end of the chain of events that affected the church into the first decade of the twenty-first century.

In 2000, just a few months before the shootings in California, an Oregon-based nonracist religious organization, the TE-TA-MA Truth Foundation, filed a lawsuit on the grounds of copyright infringement against the CoTC over the name "Church of the Creator," which TE-TA-MA claimed to have copyrighted. Hale argued that his organization had been using the name long before the plaintiffs and should therefore be allowed to use it still. Presiding judge Joan Humphrey Lefkow originally sided with Hale, but in 2002 the Seventh US Circuit Court of Appeals reversed her decision. Judge Lefkow, who acted under the superior court's ruling, then ordered Hale to cease the use of the name immediately. Hale responded by filing a lawsuit against Judge Lefkow, challenging the ruling. The judge's name and address appeared on websites alongside assertions that she was "a probable Jew" and a "nigger loving traitor." The conflict escalated when on January 8, 2003, Hale was arrested for soliciting Judge Lefkow's murder: he asked Tony Evola, an undercover Federal Bureau of Investigation agent who had infiltrated the church, to kill her in exchange for $72,000. In April 2004, Hale was found guilty of soliciting violence and three counts of obstruction of justice. For the original charges, he was sentenced to forty years' imprisonment in 2005.[46]

This was still far from the end of this story, however. On February 28, 2005, Judge Lefkow's husband and mother were found murdered in the basement of their home in what seemed like an execution. It appeared at first, against Hale's protests, that the Church of the Creator was responsible. But the perpetrator turned out to be an unaffiliated person named Bart Allen Ross, who was disgruntled after Judge Lefkow had dismissed his medical malpractice complaint. Mr. Ross, when pulled over for a traffic violation in Wisconsin, shot himself, leaving no reason to suspect that Hale or his followers were responsible.[47]

In spite of Klassen's suicide, the succession of failed leadership, and Hale's imprisonment, websites of World Church of the Creator or the Creativity Movement or simply Creativity, names used after the copyright suit, are still available, and the organization is still visible in the larger white-power subculture. Many white racialists have adopted the acronym RaHoWa, "Racial Holy War," as a logo for those who want to show themselves as the most committed to white survival and is often displayed on T-shirts, bumper stickers, and hats as well as in tattoos. Klassen's description of a racial holy war to the finish, culminating in a planet dominated by the white race, proved to be deeply inspirational. As George Michael notes, the violence associated with Creativity made it a special target of law enforcement and watchdog groups.[48] This violent approach had indeed made the CoTC a byword even among some white nationalists, who thought this sort of tactic was counterproductive to the cause. As discussed in chapter 6, other white nationalists exerted much effort to distance themselves from such activity in favor of more mainstream political access.

Creativity's particular formulation of the ethics of a closed racial society makes clearer the bellicose realities of white nationalism. According to Creativity, the ethic of racial protectionism captured in the slogan RaHoWa colonizes every aspect of the Creator's everyday life. The church demands nothing less from its followers than a total commitment of mind, body, and soul to total holy war to defend the white race. A significant aspect of this war thinking is dealing with Christianity, which Klassen and his followers were convinced had poisoned the collective mind of the white race and taken it from the true path to racial survival. Fundamentally, as stated in a number of different ways in Klassen's books and numerous articles in the journal *Racial Loyalty*, Creativity proposes a war on Christianity and on the racial extinction Christianity is believed to promote, a war to be fought by rigorous culling of undesirable ideas and traits through a process of eugenics, self-surveillance, and ideological combat, with the ultimate goal of eventually removing Jews and other racial enemies from the world.

This commitment to racial warfare penetrated even the very bodily practices of Creativity adherents as Klassen insisted that eating habits, exercise, the rejection of established medical practice and prescription drugs, and especially breeding are part and parcel of the war to preserve the white race. In rooting out all that is dysgenic and debilitating within the imagined personal and social racial body, the race can pass on a pure white world free of crime, disease, and poverty. But at the core of the religion is a strict rejection of Christianity. Ultimately, one has to conclude that the major point of Creativity is to replace Jewish Christianity so that the white race can adequately confront its enemies with what Klassen regarded as an unvarnished, uncorrupted, and uncompromising commitment to white racial survival.

RaHoWa and Christianity

Klassen's statements on Christianity leave no room for misunderstanding his opinion about it. It is already clear from what I have discussed so far that he rejected Christianity because of its Jewishness, even to the point of regarding it as a plot by Jews to convince the white race to commit racial suicide. It is also clear that he rejected what he considered Christianity's "spooks in the sky" narrative in favor of something that he thought was grounded in natural law, defined in terms of racial Darwinian competition and conflict and a segregation of "species." But we should take a moment to think about the role that attacks on Christianity played in the construction of Creativity and ultimately what this role tells us about Christianity in American white nationalism.

In *Nature's Eternal Religion*, the first of the three "holy books" of Creativity, Klassen sets forth to establish the principles upon which he is going to build his church and to define his new racial religion. Those principles are, as he understands them, "the eternal Laws of Nature, logic, common sense, and reality," which he contrasts with "myth and fantasy."[49] This is, of course, how he saw all religions. I discuss in a moment his comparative religions project, wherein he contrasted Mormonism, Hinduism, Islam,

Buddhism, and other major religions with Creativity to demonstate the latter's superiority. He argued that Creativity is the only religion ever to place "Nature's Laws" at the center of its creed, thereby excluding even, as we will see in chapters 4 and 5, racialist Odinism and Identity Christianity. But we should keep in mind that he was concerned mainly with the failings and dangers of Christianity above all else.

The goal of Creativity is also unique, Klassen argues in *Nature's Eternal Religion*. The objective of his new religion is to push toward the "noble objective" of preserving and expanding the white race over and against racial enemies, something that he is convinced only Creativity can accomplish.[50] By so orienting his religion, Klassen had already at the very beginning of Creativity established that racial warfare is not only good but also natural and morally right. That is to say, though he had not yet described his church's program in the terms of racial holy war, which he finally does in the article "Recognize Your Enemies! RAHOWA," published in *Racial Loyalty* in 1986, the fundamental elements of Racial Holy War are there in his first book.

In *Nature's Eternal Religion*, Klassen spends the first chapters describing what he means by the "Laws of Nature." All of this elucidation fundamentally points to segregation of species and to each species' natural striving for its own survival as well as that of its kind, locked in a zero-sum struggle for space and resources. Referencing Madison Grant's work *Passing of the Great Race* (1936), Klassen asserts that personal and communal life is one of constant struggle with other racial groups, or "species," and that such conflict is natural and good.[51] In keeping with his reading of Darwinism as survival of the fittest, he argues that only constant competition can ensure the survival of the best individuals within a given species as well as the survival of the species itself. Anything to the contrary is incipid and illogical and ultimately condemns the race or species to extinction. If the white race does not fight for its survival, it will be condemned by nature itself, according to its laws, and pass away forever.

Of course, Klassen's understanding of species is quite unscientific, but the main point is, if we remember his discussion of the Sermon on the Mount in his autobiography, that he reverses all that he found noxious about Christian teachings by appealing to the most ardent and racist interpretations of social Darwinism to form what he thought of as the antithesis to Christianity—a religion to surpass and replace it in the minds of otherwise intelligent white people. Indeed, Klassen discusses the Sermon on the Mount in some detail in the later chapters of *Nature's Eternal Religion* and concludes that such "irrational ramblings" of a deranged mind can and should be rejected, as they are by the Church of the Creator.[52]

Klassen's first attacks on Christinaity in *Nature's Eternal Religion* are on its Jewish roots. His opinions of Judaism and the Old Testement, as one can guess, are quite harsh. He condemns the Jewish scirptures on every point, calling them lurid and obscene and otherwise revealing of the Jews' desire to subjugate the rest of humanity. The Old Testament God, for Klassen, is simply a tribal god who, according to the writings of Jewish scribes, was invented by them for their own purposes, is nasty and cruel, and approves of the most base kinds of lasciviousness. His examples include King David's sexual appetites and the sexualization that he finds objectionable in the Song of Solomon and especially in the Book of Esther. He finds the latter, among other historical books, to be false but otherwise exposing the Jews' desire to subjugate the peoples of the world and to use their religion to justify that subjugation.[53]

But on this account Klassen reveals another side to his condemnation of biblical Judaism. Though he despises the Jews for their use of religion and their claimed position as God's chosen people to authorize their attacks on the white race, he admires them in a sense and argues that they discovered that religion was a powerful unifying force for them and that such ideolgy put forth in the Old Testement allowed them to construct a program of world conquest. Jews, he argues, discovered that religion could be "an amazingly powerful weapon . . . defensively and offensively."[54] Klassen hates and fears Judaism for the threat that he thinks it presents to the white race, but he manages to use this perceived threat as evidence for white people's need to develop a similar strategy: to use religion to unify the race and propel it to world conquest.

Klassen likewise praises Islam in the chapter titled "Mohammedanism—the Power of a Militant Religion." He is not much kinder to Islam or to the Arabs, who he thinks are close to Jews genetically. He sees them also as an alien race with whom the white race must contend for space and resources and considers their religion as a farce. But he also argues that "Semitic Arabs" were united through their religious zeal to conquer large parts of the world and to challenge even Europe.[55] The white race could learn, he argues, from this history—namely, how religion united the Arabs and compelled them to early military greatness. Again, he argues that the white race should likewise form for itself an equally powerful religion.[56]

Though he is deeply critical of Islam and Judaism as bogus mysticism and ultimately as threats to the white race, he still sees in both examples what he hopes to create—a racial religion that will unite white people everywhere for territorial supremacy that will ensure the future survival of the race. Unlike Christianity, which had "castrated the virile Roman," Judaism and Islam offer a glimpse of the power of religion to advance warfare against racial enemies while uniting the race as a singleminded unit. In Creativity, reflecting exactly what Henri Bergson describes as the core of the closed society, "Loyalty and Love for Its Own Kind" and "Hatred for Alien Races and Their Exclusion from Its Mindset" would be the guiding morality for the foundations of a new white social order.[57] That is to say, Klassen's religion would be a powerful force that would create and sustain mores fitting for the cause of white racial survival.

In this white religion, there is no god, no supernatural, as Klassen understood it. It simply relies on the "Eternal Laws of Nature" that have produced the white race, which he describes as the "greatest miracle."[58] In *Nature's Eternal Religion*, Klassen is clear that the power of a racial religion, guided by reason and the cold laws of nature, is the only way to form and sustain a future for white people everywhere. In the next "holy book," he continues to develop the religion that will be based on these principles.

Klassen describes *The White Man's Bible* as a companion book to *Nature's Eternal Religion*, the focus of which is to describe Creativity as a "four dimensional religion based on the philosophy of **A Sound Mind in a Sound Body in a Sound Society in Sound Environment**." His stated hope is that the church will concentrate on these elements to form a comprehensive program, at the center of which is the "golden rule": "**What is good for the White Race is the highest virtue; what is bad for the White Race is the Ultimate sin.**"[59] As in the previous book, this view is contrasted with that of Christianity in transparent terms. But there is something more in *The White Man's Bible*, especially in the discussion of what Klassen calls "salubrious living," which he discusses also in the third "holy book," which uses this phrase for its title. Specifically, aspects of a person's health and hygiene and a program of eugenics are the focus of *The White Man's Bible*. In such an emphasis, we can see again the application of Klassen's racialist form of Darwinism set against what he calls the "spooks in the sky swindle"—that is, Christianity.[60] But what is significant here is the emphasis on the white body and its relationship to the laws of nature as well as on what maintenance of the racial body means to the imagined white racial community.

In *The White Man's Bible*, Klassen spends chapters 43–57 restating his criticisms of Christianity. In chapter 50, "Why We Indict Christianity so Strongly," he argues again that Christianity is a suicidal hoax perpetrated by Jews against whites, that it is hypocritical and illogical, and that it perpetuates Jewish superiority by teaching that Jews are God's chosen people. But more importantly, Christianity inhibits strong instincts for racial preservation and stands as an impediment to forming a truly white religion.[61] But such a rejection of Jewish Christianity is set within the previous description of Creativity as a four-dimensional religion. That is, Christianity does not and indeed cannot agree with the basic premises upon which Klassen has founded his religion. In a question-and-answer session recorded in the last pages of *The White Man's Bible*, Klassen states that Christianity is the antithesis of science, which he considers the foundation of Creativity. He says that whereas science is "organized common sense" and "seeks the truth" dispassionately, Christianity has "stifled knowledge and progress."[62] Whereas science has advanced the white race, Christianity has inhibited further progress by perpetuating superstition.

Such a contrast has further meaning for Creativity in its program of hygiene described as "salubrious living." The word *salubrious* means simply "health," "agreeable," or "wholesome." What Klassen means when he uses the full term is an "effective, systematic program for the upgrading of the health vigor of our precious White Race."[63] This definition is classified in the book as Creative Credo Number 5, which means that for the purposes of the religion, salubrious living is understood as a mandatory part of the adherent's belief system and religious practice. It includes such practices as eating fresh, organically produced foods; working to produce a cleaner, unpolluted environment; performing strenuous exercise; getting appropriate rest and recreation; getting proper socialization; discontinuing the use of medicines and other drugs; fasting occasionally; and so forth.[64]

Of course, much of this doctrine was developed from the earlier Natural Hygiene movement of the ninteenth and early twentieth centuries, and Klassen credits in particular the works of Herbert M. Shelton for inspiring his ideas here.[65] But Klassen insists that there are strong differences between that movement and his doctrine. First, he says, salubrious living focuses on perpetuating the white race and is not an ideal beholden to "health faddists." Second, perhaps most significantly, he argues that "**CREATORS strongly emphasize Eugenics** as an integral part" of their program.[66]

Each of the points that constitute salubrious living are discussed individually in subsequent chapters in *The White Man's Bible*, but a look at the chapter on eugenics is particularly helpful in making a couple of points about the position of race war in Creativity.

The chapter on eugenics follows a chapter that argues that the white race should protect its gene pool, which is a particular target, Klassen claims, of the Jewish conspiracy to destroy the white race.[67] Protection of the gene pool means for Klassen, of course, the prevention of interracial sexuality but more precisely protection from the deleterious effects of modern living and the tendency for unfit individuals to pollute the gene pool. The CoTC's proposed program of eugenics should then be contextualized within the felt need to prevent the genetic degeneration of the white race and its displacement in a world infested with racial and genetic inferiors.[68]

Eugenics, a word coined in 1883 by Francis Galton, a cousin of Charles Darwin, means simply "of good birth" or "well born." After the turn of the twentieth century, eugenics became quite popular and came to inform policies enacted in the early twentieth century, perhaps most famously in the Immigration Restriction Act of 1924, in Virginia's sterilization act of that same year, and finally in Nazi Germany's Law for the Protection of German Blood and German Honor, enacted in 1935.[69] We should thus be aware that Klassen was not so much inventing a program for race betterment as borrowing, somewhat nostalgically, from earlier mainstream positions on race and breeding.

As Klassen understands eugenics for his religion, it means improvement of the white race by cleansing it of all traces of the "mud races" and by breeding whites to improve the race's intelligence, increase its physical and mental health, and allow it to become "aesthetically finer." Part of Klassen's program, as it was for earlier eugenicists, is also to encourage "the best whites" to have more children while inducing "less-desirable" whites to have fewer children. Again, in *The White Man's Bible* Klassen contrasts his program, described as nothing less than a religious obligation, with Christianity, which, he argues, has encouraged the white race toward "down breeding" in every "creed and tenent . . . that it has espoused for the last 17 centuries."[70]

His prescriptions for the program are straightforward: remove "alien mud races" from among white populations, encourage the "more desirable" specimens of the white race to have large numbers of children, limit the number of children among undesirables, and sterilize the "misfits, idiots, and genetically diseased."[71] Such steps will, he claims, release the full potential of the white race and allow it to prosper. The alternative is a world overrun by blacks and other racial inferiors that will ultimately push whites to extinction.

Klassen's Racial Holy War was not just against Jews, blacks, Asians, and Hispanics but also against even those members of the white race that he deemed genetically deficient. This was also true of eugenics in the early twentieth century, when elite American Anglo-Protestants were concerned about immigrants and "idiots" overrunning America and destroying the genetic health of the race through improper breeding. So again we can see that Klassen was adopting already existing racialist ideals for his religion, but more to the point we can see that Racial Holy War not only creates a Manichean notion of whites versus racial others in a battle for a future white utopia but also cuts through the white race itself, turning the war against everyone who might present a genetic threat to the race. Creativity turns the adherent into a self-surveilling racial warrior whose commitment to white survival will shape how whites view their very embodiment.

Elsewhere in *The White Man's Bible* Klassen emphasizes such things as environmental consciousness, the need to eat organic foods, and the awareness that medicines are part of a misleading and dangerous medical institution. In these passages, he emphasizes the need for better eating and self-care practices, but it is in his next book that we see the extent of his religious instructions to maintain one's white body.

In the third "holy book," *Salubrious Living* (1982), Klassen sets out to expand on the ideas given in *The White Man's Bible* and on "the subject of health in greater detail."[72] The bulk of the text, apart from the introduction and a concluding chapter on eugenics, both by Klassen, was written by the natural hygienist Arnold DeVries, who basically repeats what he wrote in *The Fountain of Youth*, originally published in 1946. Klassen embraced the ideas in that book not only because he considered them "logical," "comprehensive," and "entirely based on the Eternal Laws of Nature" but also because they could provide specific instruction on health management to CoTC members.[73]

DeVries's contribution is indeed comprehensive. It covers such topics as proper nutrition, the benefits of fasting, the origins of disease, proper sleep, and exercise as well as a deep critique of established medicine. Like most people involved in the Natural Hygiene movement, DeVries sees "primitive man," especially aboriginal Australians and Polynesians, as ideal types to contrast with modern Americans and Europeans. The Aborigines' and Polynesians' lack of medical sciences and agriculture had, in his view, kept them safe from the various ailments that Europeans and Americans suffered from. Moreover, he is concerned not just with the European peoples' physical well-being but also, like Klassen, with their aesthetic appearance. "The newer knowledge," DeVries argues concerning his studies, "gives people opportunities for beauty that they have never had before," and such advances permit "the creation of a race whose normal possession is real beauty."[74]

In the chapters written by DeVries, we find detailed and specific advice for the maintainence of the body through the exercise of its various parts, including the feet and the eyes. Such exercises, combined with a form of paleodiet, would in his view enhance one's health and thereby one's beauty, making one a better specimen and prolonging youth. Moreover, DeVries gives specific instructions to women on how to present themselves as fit mates for strong males. He also discusses offspring, but he emphasizes that it is the female's duty to properly feed herself so that her milk will properly nourish the infant. In short, there is no aspect of physical life that is not the object of focus for betterment. Klassen adds in his conclusion that all of these ideas need to be combined with a commitment not to breed genetic deficients and to engage in the process of "culling the herd" in order to "upgrade" the white race.[75]

We have to understand that what is intended in these instructions is nothing short of the colonization of everyday life for the members of the Church of the Creator. From the care of one's teeth and eyes to attentiveness to diet, the cultivation of beauty, choice of mate, and the willingness to strenuously discipline one's morality to the point of euthenizing undesirables, Creativity proposes war on the weaknesses even in one's own body for the benefit of the white race. This is what Klassen means when he describes his religion as a "fourfold religion"—the complete application of the so-called Eternal Laws of Nature in every aspect of life. And these laws teach above all else that one should look to the survival of one's own "kind."[76]

Bellicosity is the central feature of Creativity. It is indeed one of the main points that Klassen emphasizes to distinguish Creativity from Christianity. But nowhere is this emphasis more clear than in an essay Klassen published in 1986, "Recognize Your Enemies! RAHOWA!" In this essay, Klassen defines "Racial Holy War" and blends a white persecution fantasy with a moral call to defend the white race primarily from the ongoing racial war that the Jews had allegedly unleashed upon all the peoples of the world, but primarily on whites. He begins with the statement that the mud races and Jews have "ganged up in a fierce and deadly racial war" to destroy the white race. The main problem for Klassen is not that racial enemies are doing this. In a sense, he regards such activity as simply natural because he believes competing races should use their advantages for the good of their own kind according to their own interests. The main problem, Klassen explains, is that whites have not properly recognized this reality because their minds have been deranged by Christian teachings.[77]

In several pages in this essay, Klassen details the history of this racial war perpetrated by Jews, surprisingly by focusing on contemporary Palestine as an example. He describes the Israeli–Palestinian conflict as a "microcosm" of the "Jewish struggle to enslave the world."[78] In his historical narrative, the Jews, under the auspices of being God's chosen people who have been granted the biblical homeland, tricked Western powers into aiding them in settling Palestine and setting up a nationalistic base for further activity. For him, Zionism is simply a religio-nationalistic doctrine through which Jews justify their claim to world domination while persecuting and destroying any other race that stands in their way. Of particular concern for him is not that the Palestinians are suffering under Israeli policy but that this conflict demonstrates Jewish hostility and Jews' ultimate plans for the United States. He argues that they first destroyed Nazi Germany, which during the war he regarded as the most competent opposition to world Jewry; they then moved on to destroying Palestine and used England to assist it in doing so. Finally, he argues, because all other opposition to Jewish advances has been neutralized, white America is now stuck in a "meat grinder" and "marked for destruction."[79]

This paranoid assessment of world history since the signing of the Balfour Declaration in 1917 and the defeat of the Third Reich in 1945 is meant to bolster his initial claim that though most whites are not aware of it, the Jews are planning an ultimate extinction of the white race through race mixing, sympathy for the Zionist cause, material assistance in their war against Arab states, and ultimately propagation of the delusions of Christianity. His response at the conclusion of "Recognize Your Enemies! RAHOWA!" is that the white race needs "a planned and deliberate program of blueprinted warfare."[80] Once again, as we have already seen in his earlier writings, Klassen demonstrates admiration for Jews and Arabs alike in that he wants whites to adopt what he regards as the Jews' and Arabs' fierce racial defensive posture. Like the Jews, he argues, whites must prioritize racial survival through warfare.[81] In appreciation of the militancy that he finds in Islam, especially in the practice of jihad (as he understood it), he argues that whites must adopt their own religious doctrine of racial self-defense, which he calls "Racial Holy War," or RaHoWa.[82]

For Klassen, RaHoWa is the "total answer" to the war that Jews have allegedly waged against the white race and indeed is the only logical response to it.[83] Key to this program of survival, which he insists is nascent in his previous books, is the recognition that in fact there is a racial war already going on. In "Recognize Your Enemies!" it is most clear how the fantasies of persecution and the resentment aimed at racial enemies inform the CoTC's ethnocidal logic. Klassen's argument is not simply that Jews should be wiped out because they are Jews. Rather, he argues, Jews are actively seeking the destruction of the white race, so RAHOWA is simply a logical and natural defensive response to an existential threat. The paranoid and conspiratorial assessment of world events since the end of World War II shapes a racial protectionist response to perceived danger to the beloved white race that makes ethnocide an expression of supposed healthy instincts. In this way, Creativity is the most succinct distillation of the racial protectionist logic that defines white nationalism. At the core of this response is the rejection of Christianity as a debilitating and suicidal ideology invented by Jews, which the white race must replace with their own ideology to have any chance at survival.[84]

RaHoWa is then best understood as the CoTC's final response to Christianity, especially to the "poison" advice given in the Sermon on the Mount, which Klassen consistently rejected from his first efforts to define his new racial religion.[85] RaHoWa also ecapsulates the general nostalgia for Euro-American hegemony that permeates American white nationalism. In "Recognize Your Enemies!" he laments the days when the white race was the "foremost species" on the planet, territorially and intellectually.[86] But in his earlier writings he also expresses this nostalgia for white American colonialism in references to Manifest Destiny. In *Nature's Eternal Religion*, he dedicates a whole chapter to that destiny. He argues there that "despite the shackles of Christianity," white Americans exercised the "natural" imperative to conquer space, wresting the land from an inferior people. As such, Manifest Destiny should serve, he argues, as another historical lesson that verifies Creativity's approach.[87] In *The White Man's Bible*, too, he argues that Manifest Destiny and the "winning of the West" serve as "prototype[s] for winning the world."[88] All of this in every instance stands in stark contrast to Christianity and is something that only the Church of the Creator can provide.

Racial Holy War was for Klassen and the other CoTC members the most sacred charge and measure of one's commitment to the survival of the white race. Creativity's battle cry "RaHoWa!" signals the clearest expression of the exterminationist logic of racial protectionsim in its nostalgia for genocidal colonialism, its fondness for eugenics, and its ambition to populate the world with only the white race by shrinking the populations of other races across the globe. It also demonstrates the ferocity of anti-Christian sentiment in American white nationalism. In so doing, it further demonstrates the central place of religion for American white nationalists as they consider how to proceed in ensuring a future for the white race. And to return to the central Bergsonian point I want to make, for Klassen the rejection of Christianity in favor of Creativity, which alone can save the white race, is a measure of one's moral commitment to the race. "It's all a matter of persistence," he argues in *Nature's Eternal Religion*, "a matter of conviction, a matter of how much do you care, a matter of dedication."[89]

Creativity and the Closed Society

Oliver, Pierce, and Klassen rejected Christianity on similar grounds—that it is an alien, universalizing, weakening, and imperiling ideology that must be overcome to secure the future survival of the white race. But although each of these men saw racial warfare as inevitable, I have argued that Klassen's ideation and his rejection of Christianity were more consistently bellicose that even Pierce's, specifically in that he articulated his position on racial and religious activism through the doctrine of Racial Holy War.

Oliver had at moments clearly embraced violence as a means to preserve the white race, but the full genocidal implications of his white nationalism were somewhat veiled by his intellectualism, and of course he only later publicly claimed his final more extreme position on Christianity. Pierce never rejected violence, and he was always at his most violent in expressing his white nationalism, especially his antipathy toward Christianity, in his fiction. When confronted on his violence, especially in the documentary *Dr. No?*, Pierce claimed that the calls for violence in *The Turner Diaries* were simply fiction. But Klassen never backed away from statements calling for violence; indeed, his ideas were based on the absolute necessity of violence to save the white race. Klassen's position is clear in his inversion of the Sermon on the Mount, stating that Creativity teaches that "[you should] hate your enemies and love those that are near and dear to you—your family, your friends, your own race."[90] The inherently genocidal logic in white nationalism as a closed society—one that owes its existence to systematic exclusion to form exclusivist identities—is most clearly expressed without reservation in Klassen's religion.

As we have seen in these first three chapters, religion was one of the primary objects of debate and argument for Oliver, Pierce, and especially Klassen, even if they did not agree completely on what religion meant to the white nationalist movement. In focusing on these three significant leaders of American white nationalism, my aim was to define the historical moment in which they operated as that moment when white nationalism became what we understand it to be to this day. In particular, I wanted to demonstrate how the rejection of Christianity was inextricably tied to these men's understanding of what it means to really commit oneself to the preservation and expansion of the white race and the white race alone.

In the following chapters, I shift from this biographical focus to a focus on specific movements in contemporary American white nationalism. This shift is meant to draw our attention from the foundations of American white nationalism to the ways in which anti-Christian rhetoric has existed in significant religious perspectives within the larger movement and to what that means for white nationalist perspectives on religion today, particularly with respect to some white nationalists' efforts to gain more mainstream political appeal.

I begin this shift in the next chapter by focusing on Odinism and other forms of racialized Norse Paganism. Odinism is one of the most popular religious movements in American white nationalism today. But unlike in the white racialist movements discussed so far, there is no one single founder of this Pagan movement or one person at the center of Odinism. I discuss Else Christensen, whom some Odinists refer to as "the folk mother," but she is better recognized as one of several significant figures in this particular milieu.

I cover a trend in the diffuse networks of white nationalism today that centralize what I have called "racial protectionist logic" and the resulting commonly negative attitude toward Christianity. More particularly in the case of Odinism, I discuss how such attitudes shape and inform identity claims that are centered on discourses of religion, specifically the claim that Christianity was forced upon Germanic peoples in an attempt to eradicate resistance to imperialism as well as to extinguish the white race culturally and even biologically.

4

"Authentic" Whiteness and Protectionism in Racialist Odinism

Since racialist Odinism first emerged in the early 1970s, it has become one of the most popular religious alternatives in the white nationalist milieu. The attraction to Norse myth as an articulation of original and untainted Europeanness and to the imagery of berserker Vikings as well as the use of runes as religious objects are ubiquitous in the white nationalist milieu. Such imaginings of a Viking past muted and tamed by Christianity more generally seemed to speak to white racialist activists after the 1960s—people who longed for a sense of authenticity and strength as well as community. In this context, Odinism in particular apparently provided a strong racioreligious identity. As Matthias Gardell remarks in the conclusion of *Gods of the Blood*, racialist Odinists "mobilize history to further strengthen the separateness of the imagined community, tracing the racial or ethnic nation back to Europe and beyond Christianity to the perceived point of cultural origin." Gardell also notes in this regard that "the tide of racist and ethnic paganism in the United States is linked with the processes of globalization and with the mainstream redefinition of the American 'nation' to include as co-nationals all people in its territory irrespective [of] race, ethnicity, or religious preference."[1] That is to say, of all the mythologies that could substantiate white nationalist identity claims since the 1960s, Odinism has been one of the most robust.

The popularity of racialist Odinism should also be understood in the context of the emergence of white nationalism after disillusionment with conservatism and Christian patriotism among the racial Right after the passage civil rights legislation, racial integration, and the liberalization of immigration policy in the United States. These shifts in US law and social practice, as we have seen in the previous chapters, placed racist activists in a situation of uncertainty concerning the future. The pluralization of Americanness in efforts to more fully include Americans of other racial identities raised the issue of identity for white Americans, who sought answers, though not always in racial separatist terms, to complex questions about their own ethnic past.

Michael Omi and Howard Winant remark on the shifts in understandings of ethnic whiteness and the place of these understandings in identity politics after the mid-1960s and into the 1970s, pointing out in *Racial Formation in the United States* that the "revitalized presence" of white supremacist groups after the 1960s was not simply an economically driven response but "also a political response to the liberal state and reflected a crisis of identity" in which the Far Right sought "to develop a new white identity, to reassert the very meaning of *whiteness*, which had been rendered unstable and unclear by the minority challenges of the 1960s."[2] In *Roots Too: White Ethnic Revival in Post–Civil Rights America*, Matthew Frye Jacobson also further discusses this change in attitudes toward ethnic whiteness, addressing the "surge in popular 'ethnic' concerns in the 1960s and after" and its political significance, particularly to notions of "white ethnic revival" that had "eased the conscience of a nation that had just barely begun to reckon with the harshest contours of its history forged in white supremacy."[3]

It was thus at this historical moment that Odinism provided an ideological and identitarian center of mass for white racialists in America who felt otherwise thrown about in a complex and changing ethnic sociological landscape. By providing a sense of an authentic, timelessly essential, and religiously anchored whiteness that was, as the narrative goes, stolen from them by Christianization more than a thousand years ago, Odinism became a response to the challenging questions of the historical and social place of whiteness.

Racialist Odinists contrast the bland, merely political whiteness of the conservative and overwhelmingly Christian American Right to the romantic images of strong, virile Nordics come to set the world ablaze again as they are inspired by their ancestral gods. But as romantic as these notions are, on an even more mundane level for racialist Odinists this is what real whiteness is supposed to look like. For them, Odinist whiteness is unadulterated by millennia of cultural taint by an Eastern religion that has tamed the supposedly natural instincts of communal protection and aggressive expansionism. Such a commitment to the development of the Viking warrior ethic, as they understand it, is significantly bound to racial protectionism.

Such an emphasis is clearly seen in an article published in *The Odinist* in 1974, "Why We Are Odinists," where the author, Bjorn, argues, "We have made a promise—to ourselves and to our kin—that we will . . . fight all things which we . . . find detrimental to the good of our people, and work ceaselessly for the preservation of our cultural and biological heritage."[4] Most significant in such a project is the rejection of any Jewish or Christian influences that would weaken one's attachment and commitment to the gods and the folk. I therefore argue that the rejection of Christianity in racialist Odinism is an expression of a reimagining of white racial identity that takes as its central project the reclamation of an imagined essential, religious, pre-Christian white identity over and against so-called Jewish Christianity.

The Heuristics of Racialist Odinism

To continue my discussion of racialist Odinism, I must define it, especially in relation to nonracialist forms of Neopaganism. This definition is particularly important because the study of Neopaganism is often fraught with particular concerns that responsible scholars should handle with care. Not only have Neopagans often been treated with suspicion and even actively discriminated against in the United States, but the issue of racism in contemporary Paganism is a source of contention within the broader community of Pagans in America. For example, various websites, in particular the Heathens against Hate site (www.heathensagainsthate .blogspot.com), host articles by and conversations among explicitly antiracist Pagans who consistently and aggressively denounce racism, sexism, homophobia, and transphobia in Paganism more broadly and in Odinist organizations particularly.

One of the most concise statements against bigotry among Heathens, an alternative name for those who follow this form of Paganism, comes from the "Declaration 127" site (www.declaration127.com), wherein the authors, in a statement endorsed by a number of Neopagan individuals and groups, specifically denounce Asatru Free Assembly (AFA), an Odinist organization, for its exclusion of "non-white" people and "LGBT Heathens." The statement proclaims that the signatories of the declaration will no longer engage in any way with AFA, that the AFA's "views do not represent our communities," and that the signatories "do not condone hatred or discrimination carried out in the name of [their] religion, and will no longer associate with those who do."[5] Other Heathens have independently taken exception to groups such as the AFA. For example, specifically referencing this declaration, an independent writer in the Heathen community, Stevie Miller, wrote on her blog titled *Grundsau Burrow*, "There is no folkish versus universalist debate. We will not hide your shame any longer. If you are a bigot, you are not a Heathen."[6]

It is clear that we have to make a distinction between different attitudes within Odinism and not simply label all Odinists racists. But, as we can see with the use of terms so far, we have to attend to the different terms used for referencing revivals of the pre-Christian religions of northern Europe, often referred to broadly as "the Northern Tradition."[7] The name "Odinism" refers to reverence of the ancient Norse deity Odin and has been used at times interchangeably with names such as "Heathenry" and "Ásatrú." The name "Ásatrú" means "faith of the Aesir," referring to one of the group's deities in Norse mythology. It is often used in place of "Odinism," especially in places such as Iceland, where practitioners prefer to use the native term. Some use the name "Heathenry," which is a more general reference to revived Germanic Paganism. And, finally, there is Theodism, which is described as the "pre-Christian folk religion" of the "Anglo-Teutonic" peoples.[8] This name is specifically used for that designation and is therefore understood not as a replacement name for Odinism, Heathenry, or Ásatrú. But it is still included as one of many specific paths within the Northern Tradition.

The main point to consider is that when discussing the religions that call for a revival or recovery of ancient Germanic religions, however they are understood, one must note that there is no monolithic Odinism to be considered, whatever name we use. Self-described Pagans are often but not always eclectic in their approach, in any case, and tend to shun central-ized authority. No organizing body regulates, so to speak, the expression or understanding of traditions in Paganism. So for my purposes here I use the terms *racialist Odinism, nonracist* or *universalist Odinism,* and *folkish Odinism,* all of which I discuss at length in a moment. The point is to make distinct racialist Odinism as the object of my analysis.

These heuristic distinctions are complicated and the subject of ongo-ing debate, as I have pointed out already. Fully engaging this complexity would in itself require a separate project. But my distinctions serve the purpose of focusing our attention on the rejection of Christianity among white nationalists who self-describe as belonging to the Northern Tradi-tion or as Odinist. I am not concerned with nonracialist Odinists, nor am I necessarily interested in so-called folkish Odinists either, apart from where they contribute to the development of racialist notions. Furthermore, for the most part I use the name "Odinism" because it is the name most often self-applied by those whom I discuss and is historically and rhetorically significant to that community. This use shifts slightly when I finally dis-cuss Wotanism. Here we have another variation in name, with "Wotan" serving not only as an alternative name for "Odin" but also as an acronym, WOTAN, for "Will of the Aryan Nation."[9]

References to a revival of Odinism go as far back as 1848 in Orestes A. Brownson's "Letter to the Protestants," in which he referred to a "revival" of "odinism" in Norway and Denmark.[10] It is important to note, however, that whether this was a revival of the older tradition or the tradition actu-ally survived is a point of debate. This issue reflects much of the similar debate within Neopaganism in general, whether there is pure revival of the tradition or the tradition is being made anew in a new time and place, especially in relation to the development of Wicca by Gerald Gardner.[11] Since this early recorded mention of Odinism by Brownson, as Margot Adler notes in *Drawing Down the Moon,* Odinism, by whatever name we call it, is often viewed by other Pagans as being "more conservative in its values and ideas . . . , stressing concepts like family, courage, and war-rior virtues."[12] But even this general truism does not hold in the modern debates within Heathenry, so once again we have to return to more precise definitions of the terms and names in use here.

The first division to discuss is those described sometimes as ascribing to "nonracialist" or "universalist" Odinism. These Heathens do not regard Odinism to be a racially specific or otherwise ethnically restricted tradition but rather see it as a path available to anyone who wishes to engage with it no matter one's assumed ethnic or racial background. It is in fact not unusual to find Pagans in America working together with Ásatrú and other traditions, including Native American traditions and other forms of Neopagan practice. For many Pagans, one's chooses one's gods or goddesses in ways that are often highly complex and deeply personal, not simply according to one's assumed racial background.

This division, of course, stands in contrast to the division of "folkish" and "racist" Odinists, who place a high value on finding one's ancestral religion, though they differ from one another in terms of expressing this belief. Such Odinists are in agreement at certain levels—for instance, with regard to the beliefs that Odinism is exclusively the religion of the northern European peoples to the exclusion of all other gods or traditions and that it should be exclusively observed by those descended from Germanic peoples. But there is often much less comradeship or agreement between them otherwise. Jeffrey Kaplan discusses the discord between the racist and folkish Odinists in his article "The Reconstruction of the Ásatrú and Odinist Traditions."[13] But it is important to note that although both groups define Odinism as an inherited spiritual inclination, folkish Odinists describe themselves as eschewing notions of white supremacy and favoring a sort of multiculturalist tolerance without recourse to what they regard as hurtful bigotry. Nonracialist Odinists say that this is a distinction without a difference. But it is instructive to note the discursive boundaries, especially in that explicitly racist Odinists openly espouse racist ideologies and anti-Semitism.

Nevertheless, this distinction quickly becomes complicated as one engages with the discourses of those who seem firmly within the racist Odinist camp. For example, both David Lane, who was once a member of the white nationalist terrorist organization the Order, and his associate Ron McVan, a former member of the Church of the Creator before coming to Odinism, do not think of themselves as white supremacists. They prefer to think of themselves, like many other white nationalists, as racial separatists. Furthermore, as Gardell points out, antiracist Pagans have accused folkish Odinists of "racializing Ásatrú" in ways that are in their view simply racist. However, Gardell has also said that Stephen McNallen, who by any measure would be described as a folkish Odinist, has made great efforts to keep National Socialist elements and skinheads away from his organization. Gardell concludes that we should therefore not consider all folkish organizations such as AFA, led for a time by Stephen McNallen, and its successor, Ásatrú Alliance, as white supremacist hate groups.[14] However, we should consider, I argue, what the distinction here actually means when we are looking at racialized religions or religions that regard their spiritual power and access to that power as genetically predetermined. Can we say we are dealing with what may be regarded as a measure of virulence in the expression of racialism as the characteristic that distinguishes between folkish and racialist Odinists? Perhaps.

Margot Adler notes in her book concerning Heathenry that within the Pagan movement the general assumption is that "Norse Paganism [is] filled with such people," meaning racists and anti-Semites. Because of what Adler describes as the confusion around this issue for her and many Pagans, she admits that she avoided discussing Heathenry for some time. In subsequent editions of her book, however, she addresses the issue and gives Heathens a chance to clarify their position. She also addresses Ásatrú Alliance and AFA and includes a number of quotes from McNallen, where she found repeated emphasis on "a belief in the primacy of genetics, as well as a belief that certain aspects of the soul are transmitted down the family line, that reincarnation comes within race, tribe, and family." Further, she describes the political discourse in Odinist Fellowship, which was started by Else Christensen, as "frankly racist."[15] So, again, any distinction between folkish and racist Odinists is one that can be asserted but never fully demonstrated to everyone's satisfaction.

We must therefore take a measure of care to distinguish between racialized statements and racist ones in Odinism. It is perhaps productive, then, to establish a sort of racist minimum so that we can distinguish between Odinists in the white nationalist milieu and those outside of it.

For Gardell, the "racist pagans" are defined by the way they "biologize spirituality."[16] Of course, as we have seen from Cosmotheism and Creativity, this biologization of spirituality is not exclusive to Odinism. More to the point, however, we can see how this minimum for understanding "racist paganism" troubles the boundary between racialist and folkish Odinists. Whereas Gardell argues that McNallen and Christensen "represent two separate tendencies within contemporary Norse paganism," contrasting the "more racial and political interpretation" by Christensen and the "more religious and 'ethnic' interpretation" by McNallen, both Christensen and McNallen biologize Odinist spirituality. As I discuss the writings of McNallen, Christensen, David Lane, and others, I apply the terms *folkish* and *racialist* to distinguish those who are operating in terms of a white nationalist project in the way I defined it in the introduction and those who are not, respectively. Whatever troubling biologizing of religion McNallen is doing in his folkish Odinism, he is certainly not in agreement with Christensen or Lane on racial issues. Such differences deserve to be attended to, even if McNallen's voice is present in other forms of specifically white nationalist publications or if we find his folkish bent troublingly racialized.

Odinism in America

The previous section is meant to serve as a primer to understand the internal contests over racialization in Odinism. It also serves as a primer for the history of Odinism in the United States and Odinism's significance to the American white nationalist scene. Both Christensen and McNallen formulated their respective Odinisms at nearly the same time. Else Christensen began to be active in Odinism in America when she established Odinist Fellowship with her husband, Alex, in 1969.[17] Stephen McNallen, as he maintains, began to "follow the gods of the Vikings in either 1968 or 1969" while he was in college and independently of Christensen's influence. For McNallen, the devotion to the northern gods in his early years emerged from his "romanticism" and "desire to do great deeds."[18] After some solitary practice in the beginning, he began to organize others similarly committed to reverence of the Norse gods and what he assumed to be the traditions of his Germanic ancestors.

Such aspirations are situated in a historical moment in America in which European Americans began to seek their roots in projects that mimicked other contemporary identity movements. McNallen in particular makes repeated mention of the similarities, as he sees them, between what he was doing in recovering the ways of his ancestors and what he saw Native Americans and African Americans doing in investigating and practicing their indigenous traditions. He stated fairly recently in his blog, "Just as there is Native American religion and native African religion, so there is native European religion."[19] McNallen also argues in his video *Asatru/Odinism—A Native European Religion* that "beneath" the newer labels *American*, *German*, and *Dane* there "lurks an older and more essential identity" that he seeks to recover by returning to the ways of his European ancestors. He again compares his Ásatrú revival to Native Americans' and African Americans' efforts "in the 1960s and '70s" to return to the "ways of their ancestors" to "express their innate spirituality."[20] For McNallen, then, Odinism is about the recovery of essential, European ethnic identities.

Such projects by Native Americans, African Americans, and other ethnic groups, of course, coincided with more general shifts, realignments, and backlashes that followed the passing of civil rights legislation in the United States in the 1960s. As Mark Noll notes in *God and Race in American Politics*, "The quarter century from 1955 to 1980 witnessed unusually complex connections for the nexus of race, religion, and politics."[21] Noll's observations are focused on the "mobilization of white evangelicals,"[22] but I think we can see that these shifts effected reactions from others, such as McNallen's search for authenticity in his ethnoreligious expression of Odinism. McNallen, however, did not see the empowerment of Native Americans and African Americans by means of a turn to their ethnic roots as a threat to America or to white people, as the white Evangelicals or nationalists did, but rather as an opportunity for European Americans likewise to throw off the imposition of Christianity and return to their own indigenous European religious roots. His Odinism therefore relies not on notions of racial supremacy or imperilment, as do the white nationalist expressions of Odinism, but on a certain understanding of multiculturalism in what he regards as hereditary religious dispositions.

McNallen's folkish Odinism reflects a certain liberalized notion of racial identity, relativized into a schema of tolerance as each supposed people-group finds its true religion in opposition not to other racial groups but to Christianity. McNallen in fact regards aggressive racism as foreign to his project. As Gardell notices, McNallen rejects neo-Nazis and characterizes "national socialism as an unwanted totalitarian philosophy incompatible with freedom-loving Norse paganism."[23]

When McNallen formed the Viking Brotherhood in 1969 and then began publishing his periodical *Runestone* in 1971, his interests were in expressing the romantic notions of Viking lore rather than in pushing for revolution or political action or in advocating the preservation of the white race.[24] His stance against those whom he thought were white supremacist or sympathetic to neo-Nazism in the AFA, which he formed after the Viking Brotherhood, alienated some Odinists in the organization. Most notably, Wyatt Kaldenberg, a well-known racialist Odinist, left the AFA because of what he regarded as McNallen's "soft stance on race."[25] So even by the admission of more racially concerned Odinists, McNallen's brand of Odinism is not racist, at least not in the way that racialist Odinists prefer.

Else Christensen's racialist Odinism, in contrast, has been otherwise perceived by Odinists and scholars alike. Gardell describes her Odinism as political as well as racial in a way that McNallen's is not. It is telling, as I have mentioned, that McNallen directly refutes the claims from an unnamed "Marxist critic" that he was somehow influenced by Christensen or A. R. Mills, whom I discuss more in a moment.[26] Christensen embraced National Socialism, neo-Nazism, and virulent racism, just as she was embraced by white nationalists and especially other racialist Odinists.

One particular influence of Christensen's Odinism was Alexander Rud Mills (1885–1964), an Australian fascist and founder of the Anglecyn Church of Odin. He is still memorialized on the Odinic Rite Australia website as the inspiration for those who introduced Odinism to the English-speaking world—first among them, of course, being Else Christensen.[27] Michael Moynihan, whom I discuss in chapter 6, describes Mills in an entry in the *Encyclopedia of Religion and Nature* as appearing to be the "first person publicly to promote Odinism in the English speaking world" and as someone who advocated "a movement firmly opposed to Christianity."[28] Gardell further describes Mills as a "national socialist and firm believer in old-school Anglo-Saxon supremacy, who like Rudolph von Sebettendorf and the Germanen Orden merged his racial mystical Odinism with Masonic and Rosicrucian elements."[29] Mills did not simply generate a form of racist Odinism but also actively sought to spread it during his travels to Europe and the United States in the 1920s and 1930s before settling back in Australia and founding the Church of Odin in the 1950s.[30]

The ideas that Mills cultivated did catch on, even when his efforts at forming an organization floundered. The affinities between Mills, Christensen, and contemporary racialized Odinism are demonstrated in his influential treatise *The Call of Our Ancient Nordic Religion* (1957), which Odinic Rite reprinted in honor of Mills and Christensen after her death in 2005. In this essay, Mills writes that "contemporary religion has tended to restrict our religious and philosophical thought to that of ancient Judea, two thousand years ago." His goal in constructing his form of Odinism was to reverse this trend. For Mills, the Odinist's goal is to return to the authentic religion of the Germanic peoples, to address the lack of awareness of his people's "racial origins," and to overcome the Christian teachings that he believes instilled in Western man the belief that "race and breeding are of no value so far as mankind is concerned."[31] Odinism, according to Mills, would recover that which was lost to Christianization and would eventually overcome so-called Jewish Christianity to reestablish these ancient connections between members of the race and their ancient racial gods.

Christensen likewise thought of Odinism in this way. Odinism "will replace the alien Christian creed with a religious philosophy based on [the Aryan's] inherent mentality and . . . folkish traditions and culture, in keeping with our folk soul."[32] For her, Odinism is, as it is for Mills, the authentic expression of the Aryan race that directly counters both secularism in the form of Marxism and alien religion in the form of Christianity.

Christensen also agreed with Mills that true Odinism is set deep in the foundation of racial theories that had been popular in the United States and Europe since the nineteenth century. As far as she was concerned, the science of race is confirmation of what she as an Odinist believed to be true. Christensen made explicit references to racial science, particularly in an important essay titled *An Introduction to Odinism*, where she quotes from Hans F. K. Günther's book *Religious Attitudes of the Indo-Europeans* (1967), the thesis of which is that "Indo-European religiosity is always linked with the conviction of the value of birth and pride in heredity, and that man has an unalterable hereditary nature and an inborn nobility which it is his duty to society to maintain."[33] In other words, Christensen's Odinism was tied to racial identity in the form of recovery that places a primacy on heredity. She recommended Günther's book along with *White America* (1923) by Ernest Sevier Cox, *A New Theory of Evolution* (1948) by Sir Arthur Keith, and *The Importance of Race in Civilization* (1968) by Wayne McLeod, calling them books that "every Odinist should read" and that "express Odinist sentiments and form a solid basis for further reading."[34]

These texts are paradigmatic in their expression of race theory and support both racial separation and white racial supremacy. It is important to note that Günther wrote books mostly on the topic of "racial habits," whose titles include *Rassenkunde des deutschen Volkes* (A Raciology of the German Folk, 1930) and *Rassenkunde des judische Volkes* (A Raciology of the Jewish Folk, 1930). He is described as "the most widely read theoretician of race in Nazi Germany," "an exponent of Nordic superiority," and "Heinrich Himmler's mentor."[35] He also held important positions within the Third Reich's university system, establishing, along with Eugen Fischer, the Frankfurt Institute for Research into the Jewish Question. He even received from Nazi Party race ideologue Alfred Rosenberg the Goethe Medal in 1941, whereupon Rosenberg told him, "Your work has been of utmost importance for the safeguarding and development of the National Socialist Weltanschauung."[36]

This connection between Christensen and *Rassenkunde* (raciology) advocates is no mere guilt by association. She based much of her ideology on this work as she decried racial equality and argued for political and religious activity grounded in the "close physical and spiritual similarities" of "all Aryan peoples."[37] In her Odinism, racial differences as described in the race science literature are spiritually significant, political relevant, and determinative of the proper course of action for racial activists.

Despite the similarities between Mills and Christensen, it is important to notice that whereas Mills was for most of his early career a nationalist in the traditional sense, concerned mainly with the English nation and the British Empire, Christensen's Odinist bent was always more transnationally focused. But Mills and Christensen shared a deep racial essentialism and anti-Semitism that informed their opposition to Christianity. Mills also never directly enjoyed much influence in his own time, and he "never found any significant support for his efforts" as his work seemed to fade "into obscurity."[38] But he did have significant influence on Else Christensen and Odinist Fellowship, which went on to have a significant impact on the development of racialist Odinism in America and elsewhere.

Through her publications—namely, *An Introduction to Odinism* and the periodical *The Odinist*—Christensen was able to articulate a vision of a politicized, transnational, racialist Odinism that was very close to what Mills began and that similarly sought to return to the pre-Christian and therefore what was considered the more authentic religion of the white race. But we should keep two things in mind: she did not develop her Odinism in a vacuum, nor was she merely adopting what Mills developed. Some biographical material helps solidify these points.

Else Oscher was born in 1913 on the west coast of Denmark. She married Aage Alex Christensen in 1937, a man who served for a time as a lieutenant in the small Danish National Socialist Workers' Party during the 1930s and early 1940s.[39] When the couple immigrated to the United States, they established Odinist Fellowship, but Else Christensen did not become especially active in it until 1971, after Alex's death.[40] She would in time become known as the "Folk Mother," a nickname that was put on her gravestone after her death in 2005. It is also clear from the little biographical work done on Christensen, primarily by Matthias Gardell and Jeffrey Kaplan, that she had three main influences: Mills, of course, but also her husband, Alex, with whom she helped establish Odinist Fellowship in 1969, and the American Far Right, especially Willis Carto. Both Gardell and Kaplan point out that Christensen was also particularly influenced by that singular document of the Pan-European, postwar moment—*Imperium* by Francis Parker Yockey.[41] Christensen's Odinism therefore must be seen as having emerged from a specific nexus of religioracism that focused multiple notions of the emerging racial nationalist scene through a particular religious lens.

Christensen's own writings also confirm her racial nationalist perspective in her version of Odinism. In *An Introduction to Odinism*, she repeats many themes that should be familiar by now: not only racial essentialism but also most significantly a notion of white racial imperilment. Christensen states plainly that the contest in which she is engaged and that she feels all whites should be aware of is an "age-old fight between opposite, racially-conditioned inner values, reflecting the endless conflict of race vs. race," a conflict she thinks is formative of and expressed in "Western Aryan tribalism with its ideals of personal responsibility and folk identity."[42]

As Christensen describes her view in *Introduction to Odinism*, racial essentialism means an absolute fundamental division between peoples, of course, but it also means that mixing religions is analogous to mixing races in that it leads to confusion and conflict. Moreover, like Ben Klassen, she views discrete racial entities as always in conflict. But rather than enlisting a new religion in this fight, as Klassen did, she aims at recovering the supposed ancient religion of the Aryan peoples of the North. This recovery is then for Christensen a means of racial survival to attack the center of the Jewish strategy to weaken the Aryan will to win—Christianity.

Like Revilo Oliver, who took much of what he says about Christianity's debilitating effects on Western culture from Francis Parker Yockey, Oswald Spengler, and Lawrence R. Brown, Christensen writes a brief historical outline of the collapse of the Roman Empire in the wake of the popularization of Christianity. She says concerning the origins of Christianity that it developed "from an obscure set of universalist-minded Hebrews." She further describes Christianity as the illegitimate progeny of Judaism, which is made up of "stolen" concepts from more ancient traditions, such as Egyptian and Babylonian religions, that the Judaic Hebrews "grafted" into Christianity. Among the most pernicious of these concepts, in her view, is Christianity's "advocacy for equality."[43]

Christensen's verdict regarding the history of the contact between Pagan Rome and this "Jewish" religion is that the Roman Empire was damaged by corruption and "universalism" and was eventually overcome by the "Christian plague" that it was too feeble to resist. Her ultimate point in describing this history is that the same fate awaited the "Teutonic tribes" who first bowed to Rome and then, after coalescing into nations, submitted to the Catholic Church, which was then able to "convert or crush Aryan heathens and 'heretics.'"[44] Like Oliver's treatment, the narrative here is that "Jewish" Christianity corrupted and then destroyed Rome and then set its sights on all of Europe. And the point for Christensen is almost exactly the same—the white race was overcome and corrupted by an alien ideology that must now be rejected. In her telling, however, Christianity must be rejected in favor of the ancestral religion of Odinism, which Oliver, Pierce, and Klassen agreed was not at all the right move.

Christensen restates Lawrence R. Brown's popular racial nationalist thesis that Christianity had a debilitating effect on Europeans resulting from the imposition of a Jewish ideology on the Aryan mind. She calls Christianization an "act of violence" that fundamentally led to the complete destruction of native European "spirituality." She further repeats the frequent accusation that Marxism and Christianity are related in their supposed common Jewish origin. She argues that Christian and Marxist ideals were spread by their respective "missionaries," a claim that is more than simple word play.[45] She is making every effort to connect communism, liberal racial attitudes, and Christianity in order to undermine all three in her efforts to reclaim Odinism as the basis for spiritual and political activity among whites. Christianity and Marxism are for her alien ideologies that imperil the white race via mental and spiritual subversion and that if left unchallenged by a native religion of Europe would eventually lead to the extinction of the white race.

There is very little in Christensen's rejection of Christianity that we are not already familiar with from the discussions of Oliver, Pierce, and Klassen, who were her contemporaries. Yet even though her Odinism expressed common arguments, it was not accepted by her fellow white nationalist ideologues. In his collection of articles on "comparative religion," Klassen incorporates a comparison of Odinism and Creativity and includes in it a letter he wrote to Christensen and her reply. Several points of disagreement are semantic, and yet some are more substantive. Klassen objected to Christensen's use of the phrase "Aryan-soul" and in particular to her notion of deities. Klassen was at his most strident against Odinism on this last point. Although he praised Odinists as fine, intelligent people, whose stance on racial issues is properly pro-white, he was nevertheless concerned about their obsession with "spooks in the sky." He therefore implored them to join him in the Church of the Creator instead of chancing their future on spiritual illusions. His conclusion concerning Odinism was quite harsh. He rhetorically asked, "If Odinism did not have the intellectual and spiritual strength to hold its own against Jewish Christianity a thousand years ago when the Vikings had Europe at its [sic] mercy[,] what would lead any reasonable person to believe it can now reverse the situation under conditions that are a thousand times more unfavorable than they were then?"[46]

Odinism is problematic for Klassen because, of course, there are "spooks in the sky" in its belief system but more importantly because he regarded it as ineffectual in the defense of the white race against Christianity. Christensen replied to these accusations in the letter Klassen included in his publication. She first explained her position vis-à-vis the belief in the gods. She stated that she did not believe in the gods in the same way that she thought a Christian believes in his god. For example, when speaking of Thor, she said she did not think "that the god is traveling across the heavens in the goat-drawn chariot." Rather, her sense of Thor and other gods in Odinism was that they are reminders of the awesome forces of nature.[47]

Christensen set out in this reply to correct a false assumption about what Odinists believe about the gods, but more importantly she wanted to reply to Klassen's question about the efficacy of Odinism. She argued that "most people are driven by their emotions, and not by their logic." The efficacy in Odinism, she contended, is in the way it inspires the kinship and unity of all Aryans rather than in its intellectual soundness. Such an advantage is incredibly important, she thought, because once the emotional aspects promote unity and concern for the folk, political action will then follow.[48]

We can therefore conclude that Christensen was concerned with efficacy in defense of the white race but that efficacy for her meant that one had to consider emotive attachments to one's imagined community embedded in myths of a common spiritual heritage. She wanted to exploit the intangible yet important spiritual communion between all European peoples that she assumed was innate in Odinism. Christensen is clear in *An Introduction to Odinism* that the goal should be to replace alien Christian creeds with beliefs and emotional dispositions that she believes are inherent in the Aryan "folk-soul." To establish a political program for the preservation of the white race, "Western Aryan tribalism" and "folk identity" must be restored to make a future for the white race.[49] In other words, her Odinism is practical and ultimately effective in pursuing racial nationalists' common goal—to secure a future for the white race.

The disagreement between Klassen and Christensen was therefore not about aim but rather about method and in particular about what religion had to offer in that project. Both firmly believed in racial protectionism as the highest calling of the individual white subject but disagreed on the best religious and ideological program that would ensure this outcome. This conversation between Klassen and Christensen again reinforces the centrality of religion as an object of debate and strategy in the emerging white nationalist milieu. It also demonstrates that even though we might see Oliver, Pierce, Klassen, and Christensen in disagreement on specific issues, they all agreed that Christianity has been a serious impediment to the survival of the white race.

The next section discusses how racialist Odinism and Klassen's thought come closer together, particularly in the notion of "race war" and its centrality to white nationalist ideology and in a certain understanding and placement of natural law in articulating a racial philosophy of survival. Other commonalities also become more visible, in particular notions of gender, which are common to white nationalist groups. In these later developments in racialist Odinism first popularized in the United States by Christensen, the admonition to protect white women becomes extremely important and begins to define the way racial protectionism is articulated within a deeply masculinist reimagining of the Viking warrior and his obligations to the imagined white nation.

Wotansvolk and the "Fourteen Words"

Certainly, as Abbey Ferber has ably demonstrated, masculine notions of protectionism and the fear of interracial sexuality are important to racist discourse.[50] I agree with her points on this topic, but it is important to remember that this gendered aspect of white nationalism is best understood as an expression of the more general racial protectionist element that defines American white nationalism. In particular, I want to demonstrate how in the variant of racialist Odinism called "Wotanism" gendered narratives of the protection of white women and children become an ideomotor that is meant to compel men to defend the white race. Furthermore, I want to explain that this command to protect is also linked with the racioreligious identitarian recovery project of racialist Odinism. Particularly in Wotanism, race-war logics are imbued with notions of white racial authenticity as well as with the ubiquitous intersexual anxieties that are common in racist discourses. In Wotanism, fetishized notions of authenticity and anxieties over racial intersexuality are merged in the logic of racial protectionism.

The organization that propagated Wotanism, Wotansvolk, was established by David Lane, his wife, Katja, and longtime associate Ron McVan in 1995 and was headquartered in northern Idaho. They imagined Wotanism as the most pure, effective, and authentic expression of whiteness and revolutionary recovery of what would lead the race back to its true self. In a chapter titled "Wotansvolk: A Revolution in Thought" in his book *Creed of Iron*, McVan states that Wotansvolk and Wotanism are meant to "recharge the folk consciousness of Aryan man, to think with our blood and unite under our common heritage, mythos and indigenous folk religion."[51]

This "creed" is quite close to the stated goal of Christensen's Odinism, but David Lane further described Wotanism as not simply a recovery of the pre-Christian religion but also a "vehicle" by which the followers of this creed can develop and propagate their message of "racial survival."[52] Wotansfolk's mission is not only to recover the European's indigenous religion, long suppressed by the vile forces of Christianity, but to prepare for a violent revolution to preserve the white race. "Be a berserker until the day you depart for Valhalla," wrote Lane.[53] For him, the point of organizing was not simply to create a political base informed by racioreligious ideals gathered from Norse sources but also to use those sources to inspire Aryans to fight as their ancestors did to defend the folk. The fetishization of the imagined Viking past is in Wotanism tied directly to the desire for full race war as the only way the white race can preserve itself. This is a racialist Odinism that takes Christensen's Odinism a step farther in the direction of both masculinism and a love of violence, both of which are imagined as the markers of a true modern Viking warrior.

David Lane, the true founder of Wotansfolk and author of its doctrines, is now remembered as among the most significant ideologues of the
most revolutionary form of white nationalism, within racialist Odinism
in particular. This association in part stems from Lane's earlier affiliations
with the terrorist organization called "the Order" and the legacy he left
that is still seen almost everywhere in the white nationalist milieu. Born
in Colorado in 1951, Lane was a longtime racist activist who subsequently
downplayed the Christian Identity affiliations he had as a younger man.[54]
He died in federal prison in 2007 after having been convicted in 1985 for
his criminal activities in the Order.[55]

Although the Order—also known as the Brüders Schweigen (Silent
Brothers)—is not commonly known today, it is difficult to overstate its
importance to the white nationalist community. The Order has been
memorialized in song, prose, and poetry, and its leader, Robert J. Matthews, has gained martyr status in the global racist context, notably in
the song "Gone with the Breeze" by Saga, a Swedish songwriter and per-
former.[56] The Order and Bob Matthews were even the subjects of an epi-
sode of ABC's news magazine *Turning Point* in 1995 and of a movie titled
Brotherhood of Murder (1999), based on the memoir written by one of the
members, Tom Martinez, who turned informant for the Federal Bureau of
Investigation.[57]

For scholars of domestic criminal terrorism, such as Mark Hamm, "the
Order wrote the book on living in the white underground."[58] The Order's
criminal activity—or revolutionary action, if one adopts its members'
point of view—included counterfeiting US currency to undermine the US
economy, committing armed robbery of three armored cars to fund opera-
tions, bombing a synagogue that killed two people, and, finally, assassinat-
ing radio talk-show host Alan Berg. The group even had an assassination
list that included the names of various "racial enemies," such as Henry
Kissinger and members of the Rockefeller and Rothschild families.[59] However, the Order's revolution was put to an end most spectacularly by the
death of Bob Matthews in a shootout at Whidbey Island off the coast of
Washington in December 1984 and less remarkably by federal authorities'
indictments of key members such as David Lane in 1985.[60] In spite of its
eventual demise, the Order not only served as inspiration for later white

nationalists but also provided some of the groundwork ideology for Lane's Wotanism.

Religion in the Order was a complex affair, as Michael Barkun and Matthias Gardell have noted. According to Barkun, Matthews left behind a "blurred picture of his own religious convictions and loyalties." Matthews's former wife portrayed him as not having any particular religious affiliation, but Zillah Craig, the young girl with whom he fathered a child, maintained that Matthews was a strict Identity believer, and others affirmed that he was an Odinist. Barkun also notes that though the record may be confused in describing what connections Matthews had to Christian Identity, many members of the Order were Identity followers. But it is also true that the organization had members who did not identify as Christian, which, according to Barkun, led later to "tensions . . . between committed Identity believers and others in the organization." Such tensions eventually produced different wings of the organization among the forty members, though clear dissociation between the Identity and non-Identity wings never seemed to materialize.[61]

Of course, some members were devout Identity Christians, but others, such as Richard Scutari, Frank Silva (aka Frank L. DeSilva), and David Lane, took a different religious path in practicing racialist Odinism. Silva, Lane, and Scutari in particular have received attention from racialist Odinists outside the United States.[62] Magnus Söderman, contributor to and editor of the Far Right Swedish nationalist magazine *Nationellt Motstånd* (National Resistance), and Henrik Holappa of Suomen Vastarintaliike (Finnish Resistance Movement) published letters they exchanged with Richard Scutari in a volume titled *Unbroken Warrior* in 2011. Fredrik Vejdeland, a notorious Far Right Swedish nationalist, published this volume through Nationellt Motstånd Förlag (National Resistance Press).[63] So significant was this Odinist wing of the Order that even abroad these members were seen as models for a recovery of a Norse past for the purposes of producing a racial nationalist revolutionary front in other countries.

Lane's own writings, collected in the posthumously published volume *Victory or Valhalla*, a title that speaks to how his admirers saw his life and work, provide significant material to understand Lane's white nationalist, revolutionary religiosity. Much of the content of his bullet-pointed theses in the "88 Precepts" seems to blend notions of natural law similar to Klassen's and Christensen's belief in the need for a return to the spiritual roots of pre-Christian Europe. Speaking to exactly these points, Lane writes, "The white peoples of the earth must collectively understand that they are equally subject to the iron-hard Laws of Nature with every other creature of the Universe, or they will not secure peace, safety, or even their existence." Further, he writes that any true revolution for the preservation of the white race must consider the innate symbolic power that emerges from references to the religion of pre-Christian European peoples and that "multi-racial religion destroys the senses of uniqueness, exclusivity and value necessary to the survival of a race."[64]

The Jungianesque notion of collective symbols in Lane's thought is clear, but what is also significant is his expression of a particular blend of race-war logic and the sense of ethnoreligious identity that he believed Wotanism exclusively supplied in equal measure. The need for an authentic identity is most clear perhaps in Precept 62, in which Lane states that the "organic founding Law of any Nation," referring of course to his notion of racial nationalism, "must start with unmistakable and irrevocable specificity the identity of the homogenous racial, cultural group for whose welfare it was formed."[65] This need for identitarian rootedness is probably more succinctly expressed in another essay titled "Valhalla—Fact or Fiction," in which Lane argues that "as the descendants of the north folk [sic], the offspring of Vikings, face extinction . . . perhaps nothing is more important than to look at our roots, including our indigenous religion." It is clear here that Lane's sense of racial and religious identity and the protection and perpetuation of the white race are linked in Wotanism, not simply as a political project but also in an ethical demand in keeping with the "intent of the Allfather," an epithet for Odin, and with the "Laws of Nature" that Odin allegedly established.[66]

Wotanism's focus on racial survival, the place of gender in its logic, and the important legacy of Lane himself for the white nationalist community are no more evident than in his "Fourteen Words," the sentence "We Must Secure the Existence of Our People and a Future for White Children," which he coined during his time in prison.[67] The Fourteen Words

have become, like RaHoWa, one of the most significant white nationalist slogans shared across religious and organizational affiliations. And for
Lane they encapsulated everything Wotanism is about. In McVan's words,
which echo his previous involvement in the Church of the Creator, "With
Wotansvolk and the 14 Words we can rebuild the foundation towards our
highest potential and our destiny as Nature's finest."[68]

For Lane, the preservation of the race hinges on the purity and beauty
of the white woman, which he pledges to protect for the continuation of
the white race. "I fight to this day for my personal Fourteen Words," he
writes, "BECAUSE THE BEAUTY OF THE WHITE ARYAN WOMAN
MUST NOT PERISH FROM THE EARTH."[69] In the context of his fears
of interracial reproduction and the alleged increasing scarcity of young
white females in the world, Lane argues for the blending of sexual appetites
and violence, writing that "sexual lust is the mother of battle and battle
lust is the mother of nations."[70] So once again we should appreciate that
gender is wedded to violence in the logic of racial protectionism in Wotanism. Gender must therefore be considered a key component of Lane's
thought as he imagines his project, which rests on a recovery of the values
that he thinks are inherent in pre-Christian, northern European religion.

In *White Man Falling*, Ferber argues that "white supremacist discourse
is about redefining masculinity" and that gender "is clearly integral to white
supremacist ideology." She argues further that "key to comprehending the
white supremacist worldview" is understanding the anxieties among white
supremacists regarding interracial sexuality.[71] For the white male, to guard
the white woman is to instantiate masculine control over the white racial
body and thereby to secure his own superior identity. Policing racial intersexuality in this context is always equivalent to policing the boundaries of
white male identity—that is, establishing the white male's racial superiority and his masculine presence as defender of the jealously guarded sexual
and reproductive object.

Ferber's analysis is broadly applicable to the white nationalist perspectives on gender, but it is especially helpful in gaining insight into Lane's
Wotanism in particular. Ferber even uses Lane's "Fourteen Words" as an
epigraph to chapter 9 of her book and argues that faced with "tenuous and
vulnerable borders," racial and gendered, "the white supremacist goal is

to secure these boundaries and guarantee white male domination."[72] On this point, Ferber and I agree. The maintenance of raced and gendered boundaries in the assertion of white male supremacy is certainly at work in Lane's project. But I would add that that this boundary policing is set within a more fundamental project of racial protectionism. The connection between anxieties of interracial sexuality and racial protectionism in Lane's writing is perhaps most apparent in "White Genocide Manifesto."

In this manifesto, Lane prefaces a list of fourteen points with the declaration that has been repeated throughout the contemporary white nationalist scene. He states that the term *racial integration* is a euphemism for *genocide*, a common refrain in white nationalist discourse today.[73] This discourse is of course not new in America, as seen in the segregationist discourse of Mississippi governor Ross Barnett, who in 1962, while opposing racial integration, told the press that Mississippians would not "drink from the cup of genocide."[74] In his manifesto, Lane recalls much of this discourse and goes on to explicitly reference interracial sexuality to argue that the result of racial integration was an increase in "inter-racial matings each year, leading to extinction, as has happened to the White race in numerous areas in the past."[75] But his concern is not simply "matings" in general. Here Lane is rather focused particularly on women as the bearers of white futurity in reproduction—the means by which the race perpetuates itself. Further, he renders this claim as both a biological and a moral imperative, arguing that "the instinct of White men to preserve the beauty of their women and a future for White children on this earth is ordained by Nature and Nature's God."[76] The prevention of the genocide of the white race is thus intimately connected to the assumed imperative of preventing white women from interracial breeding. This is indeed a policing and securing of white male power, but such policing is ultimately set within the larger paradigm of racial protection. The key anxiety regarding intersexuality is racial genocide as it relates to possible miscegenation and the demographic decline of the white race.

From the material quoted earlier, one can certainly affirm Ferber's thesis about the importance of gender and anxieties about interracial sexuality in Lane's project, but there is more to consider. In the fourth point of his manifesto, in which Lane proclaims that the "life of the race is in the wombs of its women," he completes that thought by saying, "Today approximately 2% of the earth's population is White female of childbearing age, this being the essential demographic statistic relative to survival."[77] This seems to bend the discourse in the direction of the demographic anxieties that Arjun Appadurai discusses in *Fear of Small Numbers*. In Appadurai's analysis, these anxieties about population and number are entangled with other insecurities, in particular the material uncertainties in the growth of inequality in the late twentieth and early twenty-first centuries as well as the uncertainty concerning identity that exacerbate such anxieties.[78] That is to say, Lane's anxieties over interracial sexuality are embedded in a demographically articulated concern for the preservation of the white race, not simply in sex. The anxieties over interracial sexuality are entwined with anxieties over a demographic collapse that would signal the end of the white race, a catastrophe that Lane argues only Wotanist ethics can avert.

This analysis of Lane's writings does not disqualify Ferber's argument, but it does bring focus to the contours of racial protectionism drawn in the imbrication of racial and gendered boundary maintenance. Interracial sexual anxieties intersect with demographic anxieties in the primary obligation to defend the white race. To love the white race is to protect its women, to have white children, and to ensure the future for those children. As important as gender and interracial anxieties are in shaping Wotanist logic, racial protectionism is the fundamental concern.

This fear of genocide, which Lane imagines will come through miscegenation, also fuels his hatred for Christianity. From his racial protectionist standpoint, Lane argues in a refrain familiar from others discussed so far that Judeo-Christianity is enthusiastically devoted to what he calls "racial leveling" in its attempt to convince the white race of the oneness of humanity, which he considers to mean genocide for the white race.[79] Christianity not only robbed the white race of its gods, its culture, and its true sense of itself, he argues, but also made the race more inclined to breed itself out of existence. For Lane, to reject Judeo-Christianity is to take an important step in averting the coming white genocide. As we have seen before, this view is logical only in light of the threat posed. The fate of the race—its men, women, and children—is ultimately going to turn on one's ability to recognize these truths embodied in Wotanism.

Other examples of racialist Odinist expressions can, of course, confirm that racial protectionism drove and continues to drive the efforts at the supposed recovery of a pre-Christian Germanic religion. It would also be quite easy to further demonstrate the gendered and demographic anxieties bound up in such projects. But by focusing on Christensen and Lane, we can see most clearly the beginnings of racialist Odinism in American white nationalism and the more modern mutations of it. Most significantly, we can see that two people so significant to white nationalism in the broadest sense were in fact deeply critical of Christianity and advocated nothing short of its full abandonment for the purpose of saving the race from extinction.

Toward the Recoding of Race as Culture

In this chapter, I have tried to describe the complex contours of racialist Odinism and how they shaped the rejection of Christianity for Odinist white nationalists. Furthermore, I have tried to offer a targeted reading of influential white nationalist Odinisms to demonstrate how the problem of Christianity emerges from the beliefs that "Judeo-Christianity" robbed the white race of its will to survive and conquer and that the only way to secure the race from genocide now is to recover its pre-Christian Norse identity. At the conclusion of *Gods of the Blood*, Gardell writes that the "dual attraction" of the Norse mythos and outlaw mystique to contemporary racists "resembles the German national socialist fascination with Norse paganism that appealed to the . . . respective romances with the earth-based yeoman and the barbarian warrior-mystic."[80] In other words, racialist Odinism provides a ferociously racially protective ethic for white nationalists. The place of identity in such a closed morality of communal self-protection would be no surprise to Henri Bergson. "Obligation, which we look upon as a bond between men," he writes, "first binds us to ourselves."[81] The moral force of the command to defend the race pertains, as Ferber states, to "the production of whiteness,"[82] in this case a masculine whiteness that is authentic and strong.

It is significant also that when Nicholas Goodrick-Clarke discusses the emergence of historical fascisms in Europe and the emergence of racialist occult movements in the United States, he echoes some of the demographic anxieties in Lane's writing that I have discussed. In the intro-duction to *Black Sun*, Goodrick-Clarke writes that the United States and European countries are "facing a demographic shift against their historic native stocks" and that the "resulting issue of white identity recapitulates the dilemma of Austrians and Germans fearing a loss of influence in the old Hapsburg Empire."[83] The demographic anxieties that Appadurai ana-lyzes as significant to understanding much of the ethnocidal and genocidal violence of the 1990s comes into play in understanding the discourses of genocide in American white nationalism.

It is also significant that Goodrick-Clarke seems to affirm the timeline I have established thus far—namely, that the new white nationalism in America is a creature of the post–World War II moment, especially in the late 1960s and 1970s. He states that "from the 1970s onward, right-wing extremists began to repackage the old ideology of Aryan racism, elitism and force in new cultic guises involving esotericism and Eastern religions."[84] That is to say, at the same time that other forms of negative responses to Christianity were being developed in the emerging white nationalism in the form of racialized atheism, Cosmotheism, Creativity, racialist Odinism, and Odinism's later variant, Wotanism, other forms of racialized esoteri-cism were being developed and for the same purpose. What I call "esoteric racialism" was in various forms developed and sought to cultivate an ethic of white racial protectionism that would compel whites to defend the race from all that imperiled it, especially so-called Jewish Christianity. It is to these movements I turn in the next chapter.

5

Esoteric Racialism and Christianity

As we embark on another complicated topic in this chapter, we have to carefully consider the terms we use, very much as we had to in the previous chapter. For example, in 2005 Pope Benedict XVI spoke at a synagogue in Germany that was destroyed by Nazis. During the visit, he said to the gathered crowd, "In the 20th century, in the darkest period of German and European history, an insane racist ideology, born of neo-paganism, gave rise to the attempt, planned and systematically carried out by the regime, to exterminate European Jewry."[1] This assertion that "neo-paganism" was responsible for the virulent anti-Semitism that led to one of the worst crimes of the twentieth century of course obscures the deadly history of Christian anti-Semitism that so significantly informed what happened. It also ignores Nazi collaboration with some members of the Catholic Church hierarchy. The pontiff did hint at such culpability but made no clear reference to the Vatican's and Pope Pius XII's inaction during the Holocaust, even as he affirmed the church's commitment to peace and tolerance.

Such distancing rhetoric is common and is readily seen in the United States in a report released in 1954 by the House Un-American Activities Committee (HUAC), *Preliminary Report on Neo-Fascist and Hate Groups.*[2] In this report and indeed elsewhere in American Cold War discourse, Nazism and communism were described together as "totalitarianism" and were regarded as the twin enemies of democracy and the United States. Here, Nazism was signified as the alien source from which racial hatred emerged among American "extremists" who rejected true American principles of democratic equality and tolerance. This report in effect exonerated America for its historical and at the time still very active institutionalized racism in that it presented racism as fundamentally un-American, the result of foreign contamination by alien and even occult totalitarianism.

The rhetoric of the HUAC report, like Pope Benedict's proclamation about "neo-paganism," conceals the true history of anti-Semitism and racism. These two examples also demonstrate how notions of fascism and the occult have been conflated to further obscure the reality of institutional racisms in national and religious institutions, contributing to how the words *occult* and *fascist* have become floating signifiers in rhetorical strategies rather than effective descriptors of actual phenomena. I therefore prefer to use a term native to the white nationalist community, though unfamiliar to most people: *esoteric racialism.*

In the introduction to *Western Esotericism: A Concise History*, Antoine Faivre and Christine Rhone comment that it is less productive to haggle over correct definitions of the term *esoteric* than it is to "inventory the various meanings that it takes according to various speakers."[3] I therefore use the term *esotericism* to signify a diverse group of ideas about accessing sometimes hidden and usually transcendent forms of knowledge that are often imagined to be related to some sense of a primordial tradition.[4] But where the people discussed in this chapter differ from most others in the Western esoteric tradition is that they have adapted esoteric teachings and traditions for the specific purposes of articulating some imagined authentic European or Aryan identity that touches on an alleged indigenous and elusive truth about the white racial self, which they then use to develop political activism aimed at protecting so-called European culture from the degradation of institutional religion (often code for Christianity) and modernity.

In their introduction, Faivre and Rhone come close to addressing this topic when they briefly discuss "Nazi or near Nazi theoreticians" who "have made use of" Western esotericism in what Faivre and Rhone describe as a distortion of esoteric teachings. Faivre and Rhone even go on to describe an "amalgamation" of esotericism proper and "far right" appropriations that are fictive, exemplified for them in Nicholas Goodrick-Clarke's book *The Occult Roots of Nazism.*[5] Their main objectives here seem to be to distance the "true" Western esoteric tradition from what they regard as problematic and politicized appropriations of that tradition and to refute the thesis that there is some esoteric foundation for Nazism and its successor ideologies. Racialist esotericism is for them a distortion, an appropriation, but not really true esotericism.

I am sympathetic to the desire to deny credence to the "extremists" and to the effort to prevent them from defining the Western esoteric tradition, as I am to efforts to refute the conflation of the esoteric tradition and racism, a conflation apparent in the HUAC report and the former pope's statement. But this does not mean that I necessarily agree that the "amalgam" is entirely in the mind of some scholars. I contend that some right-wing ideologues have amalgamated some esoteric ideas with their political positions, but this is not the same as saying that they "distorted" the tradition. Faivre and Rhone's comments reveal their assumption of some point of orthodoxy that positions, applications, and interpretations of the Western esoteric tradition are either true or false—following a similar vein as Pope Benedict's comments or the HUAC report but in the opposite direction. Where the pope and the report want us to see the "true" Western esoteric tradition as racist and affiliated with Nazism, Faivre and Rhone want to define the "true" Western esoteric tradition as untouched by such ambitions. Both positions are defending an assumed inherency and orthodoxy in Western esotericism.

In these cases, proponents are not simply describing the phenomena but policing boundaries by enacting strategies of rhetorical distance to further certain positions on the alleged true tradition. For me, however, the goal is neither to defend the Western esoteric tradition nor to condemn it as an essentially compatible with Nazism, as the former pope would have us believe. For me, the term *esoteric*, here further qualified by racialism, should be used as a descriptor for a milieu in Western thought that has been active in America since at least the 1930s.

In further keeping with this heuristic, *esoteric racialism* is the general term I use for a trend within white nationalism in America that neither impugns nor defends esoteric traditions but rather seeks to understand their importance to white nationalist religious thought and specifically how they have described Christianity. Both William Pelley and James Madole in particular adapted a reading of theosophy and narratives of Atlantis as the ancient homeland of the Aryan race for relatively similar purposes. The sources for their forms of esoteric thought are therefore more recognizable to those familiar with esoteric traditions, which places them as part of that tradition even if they are not in any way a majority representation of it.

Other forms of esoteric racialism are less obviously sourced in esoteric traditions and further require terminology to identify them. Some racial nationalist activists, especially Seth Kippoth and his organization, the Order of the Black Ram, were influenced by esoteric Satanism in their racialism. But as Jesper Petersen, Kennet Granholm, and others have pointed out, the name "Satanism" is more complex and fraught with difficulties than many assume and is furthermore not accepted by everyone as a part of the esoteric tradition. To address this difficulty, Granholm argues for the use of the name "Left-Hand Path to denote the milieu of 'dark spirituality' that includes many forms of modern Satanism." For him, those "dark spiritualties" compose a "distinct esoteric current" that tends to emphasize individuality, self-deification, and an "antinomian stance."[6] "Left-Hand Path," especially because it is a term emergent from that community, though differently understood in relation to modern forms of Satanism, is a useful name to use to think about the eclectic borrowings from Satanism and other racialized interpretations of antinomian esoteric traditions by white nationalists in the late 1960s onward and as a subcategory within esoteric racialism more broadly. But again, as we had to consider with racialist Paganism, not all who follow a "Left-Hand Path" are white nationalists. And as we had to consider in our discussion of racialist Paganism, those esotericists who are nonracialist in orientation are not the subject of this chapter.

In thinking about how esoteric racialism has actually been articulated, we have to consider the complex and diffuse ways that white nationalists define their positions rather than focus on looking for an orthodox center where none exists. The point is to try to capture as much as possible that has defined this milieu of racist activist currents in America. In so doing, we can better contextualize and find relationships between racialist esoteric movements and individual contributors and thereby more accurately understand why people influenced by this trend have rejected Christianity. And it is to that end that I now turn to William Pelley and his esoteric racialist politics.

William Pelley and "Occult Fascism" in the 1930s

In *The Western Esoteric Traditions*, Goodrick-Clarke states that "it is notable that esoteric ideas often attend the breakdown of settled religious orthodoxies and socioeconomic orders."[7] This is no less true for the esoteric racialist ideas that emerged in the early to middle twentieth century in the United States. For example, William Pelley's esoteric racialism and his organization the Silver Legion of America, emerged at a moment of particular social and economic crisis in the 1920s and 1930s. Arthur Schlesinger Jr. certainly confirms for us in his classic political history of the Roosevelt years, *The Politics of Upheaval*, that this period was rife with religious and political demagoguery. From yellow journalism and Red scaring under Hearst to the popularity of racist and anti-Semitic demagogues such as Father William Coughlin, Gerald Winrod, and Gerald L. K. Smith as well as the political machinations of Huey P. Long, this period was indeed one of social upheaval and economic uncertainty that inspired some of the most infamous voices in America. Schlesinger notes that the "followers of demagogues mostly came from the old lower-middle classes, now in an unprecedented stage of frustration and fear, menaced by humiliation, dispossession, and poverty."[8] It seemed a time that uniquely shaped the general receptivity of radical thinking and populism.

In this context, emerging fascisms from Europe seemed to offer solutions for some, such as poet Ezra Pound, who saw in Benito Mussolini's example a remedy to "usury" and the "cultural degeneracy" that he perceived to be causing strife and degeneracy America.[9] Leo Ribuffo confirms Schlesinger's conclusions in his classic study of the older American Right and states further that "by the mid-1930s, visions of literal or metaphorical apocalypse had become commonplace."[10] To many Americans of this era, it seemed that the world order was not working for them, that the nation was imperiled by the elites, often a code for Jews, and that there was no future in hoping that any established institutions could set right what was wrong. In this context, radical solutions seemed to be the obvious measure for the task at hand.

One figure of significance in this moment of turmoil, both Schlesinger and Ribuffo agree, is William Dudley Pelley (1890–1965). Much has already been written about Pelley's life, from his childhood in a religiously puritanical home to his early successes as a screenwriter in Hollywood to his efforts as a novelist. But it is his populist political activism, developed from his spiritual assessment of the Christian Church and American society, that is our focus here.[11] And though Pelley was deeply influenced by the progressive politics of Edward Bellamy and what Pelley regarded as humanitarian Christian virtue in Bellamy's ideas, the story of Pelley's mystical politics begins with an experience that Ribuffo and Scott Beekman, Pelley's more recent biographer, liken to William James's description of the experience of the "sick soul" who finds solace through "self-surrender."[12] In Pelley's case, one simply must define his explorations as esoteric.

To understand Pelley's religious and esoteric thought, we have to go further than the existing biographical sources, though they are certainly informative. We can do better in reading his own words. Pelley recorded what one might define as his foundational mystical experience in a tract titled "My Seven Minutes in Eternity—The Amazing Experience That Made Me Over," published in 1929. In this article, Pelley describes being taken from his physical body and transported in the spirit to a wondrous palace made of white and luminous marble, where he is tended by two male beings possessed of exceptional "virility" and "strong and friendly personalities."[13]

Among the things revealed to him during this experience, as Pelley records it, is the "need of experiences" in a "mortal life," which creates the need for one to live many lives. He goes on to describe how he came to understand how this need relates to the "races" on earth and more particularly to how reincarnation is implicated in these racial divisions. He writes concerning races that they are "great classifications of humanity epitomizing gradations of spiritual development, starting with the black man and proceeding upward in cycles to the white." Pelley claims that he learned that this was part of the "Earthly classroom" wherein the soul is perfected throughout multiple lives in a spiritual evolution as one is embodied in different races.[14] Race is therefore, for Pelley, not only a biological fact but also a spiritual reality that contributes to the development of the soul through multiple lives in racial embodiment, as in William Pierce's Cosmotheism.

Though such ideas are not completely unique to Pelley, he thought his experiences were. As scholars who have written on Pelley have noted, he always rejected the assertion that he acquired his ideas through previous contact with esoteric movements, though it is known, too, that he already had a deep interest in esoteric thought before he recorded this experience. Beekman specifically argues that there was a similarity between Pelley's thought and the teachings of Rudolph Steiner and Alice Bailey, though Pelley had not mentioned either in his writings before 1929. "Given Pelley's voluminous appetite for metaphysical books," Beekman further notes, "it seems unlikely that he did not possess at least a rudimentary knowledge of these groups."[15] Ribuffo also writes that Pelley was aware of the popularity of the occult and spiritualism in the late 1920s and the 1930s and from that realization "built his own eclectic theology" from a bricolage of spiritualism, Christian Science, Rosicrucianism, and elements of theosophical speculation.[16] But wherever Pelley got his source material or however conscious he was, in any case, of the similarities his ideas had with other forms of esotericism, his vision of a spiritualist evolutionary hierarchy in which the "races" develop was synthesized with his notions of populism in a political program fronted by an organization that he called the Silver Legion of America, also known as the Silver Shirts.

In 1933, Pelley announced the Silver Legion and published his populist political tract *No More Hunger*. He had dissolved his former association, the League for the Liberation, but kept alive the organization's paper, *Liberation*, subtitled *A Journal of Prophecy and Higher Fraternity*, which then became the publication for the Silver Shirts.[17] In *No More Hunger*, Pelley set out to define the program the Silver Shirts would attempt to enact. He argued for a "Christian Commonwealth" that would create a utopian state in America, patterned quite closely on early American socialist Edward Bellamy's vision in the futuristic romance *Looking Backward, 2000–1887*, published in 1888. But Pelley's utopianism was enmeshed with a deep anti-Semitism that had developed in his writing since the 1920s.

In issues of *Liberation*, for example, Pelley's vilification of the Jews was obvious; he blamed them for America's problems, especially the Depression. In *No More Hunger*, Pelley further expounded upon his anti-Semitic populism by contrasting his utopian economic system to the present mode of commerce, which he said was "introduced by Levantines and Orientals."[18] In a later article, referring to Hitler's chancellorship, Pelley confessed both admiration for and moral support of Hitler as a strong nationalist leader for Germany and a "political philosopher."[19]

Pelly's support for Hitler, his own deep-seated anti-Semitism, and his utopic visions of the future informed by alleged mystical experiences defined his efforts as the founder and leader of the Silver Shirts. But as divergent as his activities were from the religious norms of his day, his ideas and his organization were not as explicitly anti-Christian as much as they were anti–Christian Church. As is often the case for those who proclaim new religious visions or revelations, the dominant organized religion at that moment is often described as both the thing that needs to be reformed and the thing that stands in the way of the new message. Pelley commented that religious orthodoxy and "man-made concepts of the 'here-after,'" a clear reference to organized Christianity, kept people from full preparedness to hear such truths as he would reveal.[20] His disposition toward Christianity was then not one of rejection but of reform. He saw institutionalized Christianity as obfuscating the message of spiritual evolution through a racial embodiment that he claimed to learn of from his spiritual masters but not as completely corrupt and beyond hope of reform per se. What he offered was what he thought of as a clearer and more accurate account of the Christian message.

Pelley's early esoteric racialism, politically organized in the Silver Shirts, represented a trend of racist activism in America that is all but completely unfamiliar to most people today. Although his movement predates white nationalism properly speaking, it set a precedent for later activism. Also, Pelly never fully rejected Christianity as incompatible with white racial survival, and his concerns were more American nationalist in the traditional sense. Something much closer to contemporary white nationalism that included the rejection of Christianity, not just of the Christian Church, became stronger in the later American esotericism of the National Renaissance Party.

James Madole, the National Renaissance Party, and the Aryan Eden

Like William Pelley and the Silver Shirts, members of the National Renaissance Party (NRP), formed by James Madole, were uniformed in the manner of fascist movements in Europe. This is in part why the NRP and

Madole himself captured the attention of the public and federal authorities in the 1950s. Catching such attention was certainly by design in that the NRP and Madole made frequent appearances on the streets of New York City to protest what they regarded as the corruption of American society and Western civilization by Jews. Like Pelley's politics, Madole's politics were deeply influenced by a certain approach to and understanding of eso- teric traditions, especially theosophy. Founded in 1949, the NRP was, as Betty Dobratz puts it, "the first neo-Nazi party," preceding the American Nazi Party by nearly a decade.[21] And though, as Jeffrey Kaplan and Leon- ard Weinberg have noted, Madole was almost forgotten after his death in 1979, by the 1990s he experienced "something of a renaissance . . . on both sides of the Atlantic as a visionary whose thought was decades ahead of its time."[22] For these reasons, a discussion of Madole, the NRP, and their critique of Christianity is important to understanding the development of esoteric racialism in America.

The most thorough treatment of Madole, his esoteric racialism, and his self-described National Socialist politics is in Goodrick-Clarke's book *Black Sun*. It is not necessary to reproduce everything Goodrick-Clarke discusses therein, but it is useful for the reader to be quickly introduced to Madole and the NRP before I continue. James Madole was born in 1927 in New York City and from a relatively early age was influenced by sci- ence fiction and occultism. He later became deeply interested in American interpretations of European forms of fascism. One of his chief influences was science fiction writer Charles B. Hudson. An American supporter of Italian fascism and German National Socialism, Hudson was, like William Pelley, a defendant in what came to be called the "Great Sedition Trial of 1944."[23] It was the largest sedition trial in the United States, in which forty individuals were tried for Nazi sympathies under the Alien Sedition Act of 1940 (otherwise known as the Smith Act).[24] Goodrick-Clarke notes that Madole was also influenced in significant ways by Francis Parker Yockey and the German émigré Fredrick Charles Weiss.[25]

In short, the milieu of American "third-way" political activity, with its opposition to Franklin D. Roosevelt, its admiration of fascism, and its often virulent anti-Semitism from the 1920s through the 1950s, formed the background for Madole's activism. These influences, alongside Madole's early interest in the writings of Madame Helena Pertovna Blavatsky (1831–91) and the story of Atlantis as the homeland of the Aryans, which deeply fascinated him throughout his adult life, shaped what the NRP eventually came to teach as the foundations for its street activism and to propagate through its publications.

As important as Madole was for the NRP's later development, the party was not exclusively his creation. Goodrick-Clarke notes that it actually began in 1949 under the leadership of Kurt Mertig, a longtime right-wing activist and affiliate of openly Nazi sympathetic organizations in America in the period leading up to and during World War II. Mertig was particularly noted for his leadership in the Citizens Protective League, headquartered in the Yorkville neighborhood of Manhattan.[26] He later began the NRP, which he named after a line in Hitler's last "political testament," a letter in which Hitler articulated the hope for a "renaissance" of National Socialism after the war.[27]

Mertig was, however, not energetic enough to found a vibrant National Socialism in America by himself. He had grown quite old by 1949 and looked to the much younger James Madole as his successor. Madole quickly took leadership of the NRP and began to make an impression on the general public and the federal government, as the prevalence of his name in the HUAC report demonstrates. From this point on, the NRP began to evidence Madole's theosophical influences, especially in the NRP mouthpiece, the *National Renaissance Bulletin*. This influence was no more clear than in a series that ran in the paper beginning in 1973 and that Madole titled "'The New Atlantis': A Blueprint for an Aryan Garden of Eden."[28]

This series amounted to a blending of theosophical works, primarily *The Secret Doctrine* by Helena Blavatsky, with National Socialism as a program for change in the United States and for the creation of godlike Aryans who would eventually rule the world from America.[29] I discuss this important series in a moment, but it is important to note that it was not the first time Madole had synthesized occult notions of the Aryan with his politics, nor was he the only one to do so in the bulletin.

The NRP described itself on the banner of its paper as a "political party devoted to the restoration of the American Republic, the preservation of American Sovereignty and the establishment of an American

regime based on the principles of racial nationalism and social justice."
The paper always presented itself as the voice of the Aryan in America
and tied all the problems in America of whatever period to race. In a later
article titled "The Leadership Principle: A Heritage of Aryan Man" (1970),
Madole attacked in particular "Liberal Democrats, apostles of human
equality, Jews and the enemies of ARYAN MAN" and extoled the virtues
and promise of a racial dictatorship over democracy in the United States.[30]
For him, both political equality and the denial of race as a reality had
caused the general breakdown of social order in America, typified by illicit
drugs and anarchy in the streets, all of which demonstrated the need for
Aryan rule. In this article, for example, he pointed to the Chicago Seven,
who were on trial at the time, as evidence of a Jewish and Marxist plot to
use "Black terrorists" and disaffected youths to destroy America and the
white race. Madole then went on to rhetorically ask what the "democratic
form of government" had done to "curb any of these evils" and answered,
"Absolutely nothing!"[31] The only way to preserve the civilization that he
conceived as Aryan civilization in America was to look to the imagined
mythical supermen, the Aryans, to rule unencumbered by liberal notions
of equality and democracy.

Angered by the successes of the civil rights movement and fueled by
memories of the tumultuous 1960s, all persistently accompanied by conspiracy theorizing about Jewish forces operating behind general social disorder, Madole proposed an American national socialism as the solution.
He found examples of such solutions to social disorder in the "authoritar-
ian idealists" of the past, men such as Léon Degrelle, founder of the Nazi-
aligned Rexist Party in Belgium; Vidkun Quisling, cofounder of Nasjonal
Samling, the Norwegian National Socialist Party; and, of course, Adolf
Hitler, whom Madole held up as the model of Aryan leadership. Madole attempted to offer a political alternative to democracy in the form of
National Socialist dictatorship set in esoteric terms. He wrote that the
"mission of Aryan man" is to gain mastery over the human race and to
"purge HOMO SAPIENS of its more bestial and sub-human elements"
so that the "highest racial elements will become as Gods among mortal
men." These rulers whom he admired were to him "demigods" and the

"natural rulers of humanity," an ideal depicted in the "glorious saga of the Aryan race."[32]

For Madole, then, the NRP's mission was an extension of a longer history of the Aryan race's mission to build civilization, a mission that had begun in Atlantis—or what Christians falsely identified as the Garden of Eden. In Madole's outline of this history, after the loss of Atlantis, this mission of civilization building was continued by Aryan survivors in Mesoamerica, Egypt, and the Iranian plateau; was carried out through European history; and finally now had been taken on in America. Through all of this mythologized history, he argued, the "Aryan masses followed [the] heroic leadership" of such figures as Alexander the Great, Julius Caesar, Charlemagne, Napoleon Bonaparte, Otto von Bismarck, and finally Adolf Hitler.[33] Dictatorial leadership was therefore a necessity for Madole, not simply a pragmatic goal, because it was in harmony with "Natural Law," to which democracy, communism, parliamentarianism, and other forms of government were opposed.[34] As such, it was also in harmony with the mythologized Aryan race's final destiny.

If some of this historical outline sounds like Ben Klassen's statements in *Nature's Eternal Religion*, it may be because Klassen had a relationship with the NRP, and Madole warmly welcomed Klassen's opus upon its publication. In the *National Renaissance Bulletin* of January and February 1973, Madole praised Klassen's book as "the new 'Mein Kampf' of the NRP" and lauded it as the "most vital text on the topic of racial nationalism ever to appear on the North American Continent." In this same article, Madole listed some other influences, specifically Plato and Heraclitus, Friedrich Nietzsche, Johann Gottlieb Fichte, G. F. W. Hegel, Eugen Karl Dühring, and Oswald Spengler as well as Madison Grant, author of *The Passing of the Great Race* (1916), Grant's protégé Lothrop Stoddard, and, of course, Francis Parker Yockey. Madole then named other influences that he described as "occultists"—Aleister Crowley, Helena Blavatsky, Grigori Rasputin, and Anton Szandor LaVey, founder of the then very new Church of Satan. Madole described each of those whom he named as great thinkers who both understood human nature and were, he thought, "exponents of an 'elitist society.'"[35] In other words, Madole was a bricoleur who combined multiple esoteric influences with historical fascism, racial scientism, as well as the emerging American white nationalist movement to create a racial activist party dedicated to realizing Aryan rule in America as both a political and a spiritual ambition.

As one might suspect given his influences, Madole was deeply critical of Christianity, a view that created problems for the NRP, as it did for William Pierce and National Alliance. In an article titled "A Stern Rebuke to the Critics of the National Renaissance Party" (1971), Madole responded to those concerned about his position on Christianity. He argued that all significant Christian leaders were "committed to breaking down all racial barriers between Aryans and Stone Age primitives" and that he had no choice but to oppose Christianity as an alien and Semitic spiritual creed that propagated a "morality of slaves" and had "subjugated the minds of our healthy pagan ancestors!" For Madole, as for the other white nationalists I have discussed so far, Christianity had caused Aryan people to abandon their relationship with their own native spirituality and reason and therefore had to be rejected in favor of trying to return to the imagined "Aryan heritage."[36]

Other NRP members contributed to the organization's position on religion as well. In particular, Robert Bayer wrote a series for the *National Renaissance Bulletin* titled "The Aryan Concept of Race, Religion, and History." In it, Bayer compared Christianity and the NRP's Aryanism and stated that whereas Christianity was in defiance of nature in its belief in equality, "we National Socialists demand of ourselves that we live . . . in accordance with the laws of life."[37] Here we can see that the objection to Christianity is based on its allegedly unnatural attitudes toward race and equality. Bayer further argued that the "heresy of Semitic Judeo-Christianity" tried to eradicate truths about the Aryan race and nature that still reside in "the racial memory of the Aryan Race."[38] Similar to the goals of Cosmotheism and racialist Odinism, the NRP's mission was to rediscover the hidden and suppressed truths about the ancient Aryan past and apply them to the present political situation.

Bayer's series was a significant expression of the way in which political ambitions and esoteric ideas were mixed in the NRP, especially as the organization made a stand in opposition to both democracy and Christianity.

However, Madole's "New Atlantis" series, which he began not long after Bayer published the last installment of "The Aryan Concept of Race" in 1973, is the most complete discussion of the NRP's esoteric racialism. Madole repeats himself quite a bit in this series and quotes other sources at length, so I will not exhaustively reference each essay in the series. It is sufficient for my purposes here to analyze the first article in it and to make some references to material in other articles to discuss how Madole articulated his vision of racial political activism.

The first installment of the series significantly begins with Madole presenting a contrast between what he called the "metaphysical heritage" of Atlantis and the "Hebraic fairy tales known as 'The Holy Bible.'" Very much like Bayer, Madole here presented an absolute dichotomy between the NRP and Christianity. But Madole went a step further in his claim by arguing that the United States was the inheritor of an unusually high concentration of esoteric movements and teachings and finally that it was the place previous occultists had prophesied as the land from which the Aryan god-men would emerge to rule the world. He argued that Madame Blavatsky was the first to predict in *The Secret Doctrine* that America would become the "cradle" of a new and immensely greater race of humanity. He further referenced Blavatsky to argue that the mixing of other mythical races with the "Aryans" had produced a progeny that had since come to populate America; the "pure Anglo-Saxon stock" had mixed with other Aryans and had since become "a race apart, and strongly separated from all other now existing races." That is to say, there was an occult historical parallel for the new and dynamic Aryan mixing ongoing in the United States that had come to make America that place of prophecy, the land in which the new Aryan supermen would be born. For Madole, America had become the most significant melting pot of "various Aryan strains from Europe," which had created that peculiar strain of Aryan in America and had prepared these Aryans uniquely for worldwide rule.[39]

This narrative was finally the justification Madole used for his argument that the "New Atlantis" is the United States. This view, of course, positions Madole as someone who was still an American nationalist and who still saw white America as the hope for eventual Pan-Aryan rule. Although he was a self-described racial nationalist, he was not quite a

Pan-European in the way Yockey was. At the conclusion of this first article in the "New Atlantis" series, Madole described the NRP's goal as the creation of an earthly paradise that will emerge in America from the party's racial nationalist philosophy: "A rebellion of Aryan Man upon the North American continent will save the New Race from destruction and bring about the glorious fulfillment of Madame Blavatsky's prophecy."[40]

Madole was indeed a racial nationalist, though perhaps not quite like the others I have discussed so far. His goals were ultimately framed by a notion of racial protectionism, but his racial esoteric schema, inspired by an eclectic reading of Blavatsky, still placed a priority on America as the so-called New Atlantis. He believed that from America would eventually come a global movement inspired by an awakened racial consciousness that would save the Aryan race from ruin. So he shared the racial protectionist vision of his fellow racial nationalists but differed with them slightly in his American-focused Aryanism. It is important to note, too, that both Madole's and Bayer's series came out at the same time as Klassen, Pierce, Oliver, and racialist Odinists were forming their responses to a perceived white racial imperilment. Although they seemed to be more Pan-European like Yockey than Madole was, they all shared a particular dislike for Christianity.

Madole, much like Pierce, viewed Christianity as inhibiting what he saw as Aryan man's progress of spiritual evolution and thereby also the sense of duty to bring the world under Aryan subjection, a goal to which the NRP was committed. He wrote in a later installment of the "New Atlantis" series that the NRP's aim was not simply to describe the incredibly destructive effects of the "Afro-Semitic impact on Western Aryan Civilization" but also to remind Aryan peoples of the "glorious racial heritage which they inherited from common ancestors."[41] Such a claim referenced a number of things for Madole, but the most significant among them was that the "Semitic" ideology of Christianity had allegedly blinded most Aryans to their own spiritual legacy. The rejection of Christianity was then, for Madole, an obvious first step for anyone committed to the attainment of the white man's destiny. So long as Aryans in America accepted Christianity, he contended, there would be no emergence of the godlike figures fated to rule the world. Rejecting Christianity and teaching others to do so would hasten the apotheosis of the American Aryan, who would lead the white race into its bright future. The NRP thus had at its foundation an esoteric racialist critique of all non-Aryan ideologies, especially Christianity.

By the time Madole died in 1979, National Socialist activism had diffused throughout several organizations. During his leadership of the NRP, he had seen the rise of the ANP and its transformation into the World Union of National Socialists. He had also seen other esoteric interpretations of Hitler and National Socialism from abroad become important in the American scene. But, as Kaplan notes, though "National Socialist occultism is not for everyone," Madole's thought and activism indicated that he was "simply ahead of his time."[42] The National Renaissance Party faded from public memory, but before doing so it set a particular tone in racialist activism in the coming decades and tapped into an energy that existed later in a number of different organizations and outlets. What we see in Madole's thought and its embodiment in the NRP is one of the first real developments of a white nationalist esotericism committed to countering the false teachings of Christianity to help the race preserve itself and to realize its allegedly prophetic mission of deification and worldwide conquest.

Racial Esotericism beyond Madole

Almost a decade after Kurt Mertig founded the NRP, George Lincoln Rockwell founded the American Nazi Party as yet another uniformed fascist organization. Rockwell formed the ANP in part because of his frustration with the John Birch Society, *National Review*, and the National States Rights Party, which he had a hand in founding.[43] According to Fredrick Simonelli, Rockwell regarded *National Review*—for which he had done some contract work promoting subscriptions at college campuses in the magazine's early days—and these organizations, in particular the anti-Communist JBS, as "too tame" or otherwise insufficient.[44] In much the same spirit as Oliver, Klassen, and Pierce, Rockwell abandoned any hope of using conservative politics to achieve his desired end of beginning a racialist organization that he thought would finally embody what he regarded as the most efficacious methodologies and ideas of racial protectionism. As it was with Madole, Rockwell's notions of what that embodiment of racialist principles meant were laden with mystical ideas concerning the Aryan race and Hitler.

In his autobiography, *This Time the World*, Rockwell describes his embrace of aggressively racist politics in terms of a spiritual conversion that happened when he first read *Mein Kampf*. Hitler's book provided him with "mental sunshine" as "word after word, sentence after sentence stabbed into the darkness like thunderclaps and lightning bolts of revelation . . . brilliantly illuminating the 'mysteries' of the heretofore impenetrable murk in a world gone mad." In 1951, he felt alone in his inspiration, but for the "GOOD OF THE WHOLE RACE" and to subvert the efforts of the "Destroyers of Mankind," his code for Jews, he would throw himself at the challenge and become an "Apostle of Adolph Hitler [*sic*]," whom he regarded as "the greatest world savior in two thousand years."[45] From this inspiration and commitment, he founded the ANP in 1958 and in the style of Madole and the NRP took to the streets surrounded by uniformed troopers to agitate for National Socialism as the salvation of white America and eventually of white people everywhere.

Rockwell's ANP, like Madole's NRP, was focused mostly on America. But Rockwell's ambitions for what he could eventually do for the Aryan race quickly became truly global. As early as 1959, Rockwell sought to internationalize his Nazi movement when he formulated what he originally called the World Union of Free Enterprise National Socialists, a name he then shortened to World Union of National Socialists, or WUNS.[46]

The purpose of WUNS was to bring together various neofascists in the United States and Europe, and it was partially successful in doing that. Rockwell's contacts abroad included Colin Jordan, a revivalist of Oswald Mosley's wartime British Union of Fascists in England, and Savitri Devi, who was, as discussed in chapter 2, a significant force in post–World War II admiration of Hitler as an "avatar" or "world savior" of the Aryan people and who was an inspirational figure for William Pierce while he was still working with the ANP.[47] It was through WUNS, with significant help from Pierce's reproductions of Devi's writings, that her esoteric ideas about Hitler and the Aryan quickly spread throughout the emerging racial nationalist scene in America.

Here I would like to take a moment to elaborate on Devi's ideas because they were so significant for the ANP, William Pierce, and the general post–World War II environment of racialized esotericism. Goodrick-Clarke describes Devi as "a leading light of the neo-Nazi underground from the 1960s onward" and a significant popularizer of mystical National Socialism and the "divinization of Adolph Hitler."[48] To form what we can call "esoteric Hitlerism," she intentionally blended the most occult interpretations of Nazism with a racialized reading of Hindu mythology and adoration of the person of Adolf Hitler to develop a political and spiritual ideology of the history and future destiny of the Aryan race. She was convinced by her early journeys to India that, in Goodrick-Clarke's words, "Hinduism was the only living Aryan heritage in the modern world."[49] Devi's own words also help us understand exactly what she taught in this regard. In particular, in her book *Defiance*, published in 1951, she describes Germany's loss in World War II as evidence of the "Kali Yuga," the final age in the cyclical cosmology of Hinduism. With this time of decay and decadence in mind, Devi writes:

> It is the superior man's business to feel happy in the service of the highest purpose of Nature which is the return to original perfection,—to supermanhood. It is the business of every man to be happy to serve that purpose, directly or indirectly, from his natural place, which is the place his race gives him in the scheme of creation. And if he cannot be? Let him not be. Who cares? Time rolls on, just the same, marked by the great Individuals who have understood the true meaning of history, and striven to remold the earth according to the standards of the eternal Order, against the downward rush of decay, result of life in falsehood;— the Men against Time.[50]

So it is clear that Devi thought esoteric National Socialism should provide a political and spiritual basis of political activity for the purpose of preparing the emergence of Aryan god-men. And like Madole, she regarded her esoteric National Socialism and Christianity as incompatible.

For Devi, Hitler's teachings and the Aryan mythology that she developed during her time in India defied everything she had learned in what she called her "Judeo-Christian democratic education."[51] Christianity's teachings of universal brotherly love and equality before God were, for her, as for the other figures I have discussed, against natural law and a poison in the minds of Aryans. But more fundamentally they were contrary to the aims and teachings of her racialist esotericism.

This sort of synthesis of esotericism and National Socialism was prevalent among the international neo-Nazis whom WUNS sought to unite. Another enigmatic figure, Miguel Serrano (1917–2009), a former Chilean diplomat and friend of Hermann Hesse and Carl Jung, also developed a synthesis of Aryanist interpretations of Hinduism and National Socialism that was in some ways similar to Devi's. He similarly thought of Hitler as a racial savior, the restorer of order in Hindu mythology—"el ultimo avatāra," the final avatar.[52] Like Madole and Devi, Serrano was sure that the best chance of survival for the Aryan race was to cultivate awareness among the Aryan people of the esoteric principles of Aryan mythological history and the power and proper political organization that Christianity had convinced them to deny.

Many of these figures are all but completely unheard of outside the very racialist circles upon which they exerted influence, and I would contend that they were not as broadly influential, apart from Rockwell, for the development of American white nationalism as Oliver, Pierce, and Klassen. And even the ANP's significance seems to have been organizational rather than ideological. But these very brief discussions of Madole, Rockwell, Devi, and Serrano are meant simply to indicate their rejection of Christianity in favor of particularly occult readings of Hitler as an avatar and of the Aryan race itself and to show how they established an early racialist esotericism that still has a place in the longer history of American white nationalism. Though the impact that Devi's and Serrano's books and essays, for example, had on that history is somewhat less direct than that of others, they are still easily found on white nationalist websites; indeed, that is where they can in general be accessed.

I should also note that the connections between Rockwell and Devi through WUNS and the ultimate influence Devi had on Pierce show how this moment in the late 1950s through the 1970s was a time in which what we now recognize as white nationalism—critical of established conservative political ideologies, deeply suspicious of Christianity's influence,

Pan-European in orientation, and focused on broader white racial survival—came about. I contend that Oliver, Klassen, and Pierce, more so than other figures, played significant roles in shaping the religious and intellectual basis of American white nationalism. If that is the case, we then can consider these earlier figures as transitional forms, to borrow evolutionary language, that marked this period of transformation of the old racist Right into the new white nationalism in America.

I wish to be clear in saying that though I regard the influence of early racial esotericists as less direct than the influence of those figures discussed in the first three chapters, the former still have had a deep influence in those quarters of American white nationalism that are fascinated by such occult ideas as Aryan origins in Atlantis and Hindu notions of the avatar. Some racial esotericists have also become important in the general intersections of new religions, especially those that seem to straddle the line between antinomianism, cultural criticism of democracy, and fascism. One of those places of intersection is Satanism and other forms of "Left-Hand" esotericism, to which I now turn.

The Left-Hand Path and Racialist Activism
in the 1980s and 1990s

The most obvious place to begin this inquiry into contacts between Left-Hand practitioners, to use Granholm's term, and racialist activists is to discuss the contact between James Madole and the founder of the Church of Satan, Anton LaVey (1930–97), in the 1970s. Madole referenced LaVey in his list of people who had been inspirational for him, as I mentioned, and in the back of some editions of *National Renaissance Bulletin* he even recommended LaVey's books *Satanic Bible* (1969) and *Satanic Rituals* (1976).[53] Madole regarded LaVey highly because he thought LaVey offered important occult insights into the laws of nature and the human psyche, especially in his diatribes against Christian teachings.

LaVey for his own part, however, seemed not to care too much for Madole. According to the biography written by his longtime companion Blanche Barton, LaVey's attitude toward racial "extremists" was one of disdain for anything as lazy as race prejudice.[54] Further, in an interview with Gavin Baddeley, LaVey specifically rejected racism, stating, "My own prejudices are not ethnic but ethical—somebody's race or background really has nothing to do with it."[55] Furthermore, in *The Satanic Scriptures*, a compilation of essays written by LaVey's successor in the Church of Satan, Peter Gilmore, the question of racism and fascism is addressed directly. Gilmore states that the Church of Satan was in no way compatible with racist thinking or political fascism because of the strong emphasis on individuality in LaVey's teachings.[56] So we can say that although the contact between Madole and LaVey is verifiable, it can easily be misconstrued. It is true that Madole and LaVey corresponded and even met, but these exchanges were never fully collaborative.[57] Whatever Madole saw in LaVey's Satanic teachings, LaVey very much seemed to regard their interaction as a one-sided exchange of ideas.

For some racialist activists, the connections between Satanism and white nationalism were more significant, even if LaVey and Gilmore dismissed them. For example, Seth Kippoth, an NRP organizer in Michigan, founded the Satanist and white nationalist organization Order of the Black Ram with other NRP members and a former Church of Satan member.[58] As Goodrick-Clarke further argues, these early contacts between LaVey and the NRP as well as the founding of the Order of the Black Ram anticipated later coalitions between neo-Nazis and Satanists in the 1990s.[59] Furthermore, such an alliance was not so farfetched and was certainly not diminished by LaVey, Gilmore, and Barton's claims that Satanism is neither fascist nor racist. I would argue that Satanism was indeed attractive for some white nationalists because of its overt antiegalitarianism, its embrace of social Darwinism, and its rejection of Christianity as the source of liberal values that were seen as violations of natural law and debilitating for those who wished to advance in esoteric, spiritual understanding.

The intersections of Satanism and extremism are quite tangled indeed. For us to follow these pathways requires that we separate forms of influence so as not simply to imply guilt by association. It is known, for example, that Charles Manson and his "family" were linked to all manner of occult conspiracies during the maelstrom of media attention that resulted from the grotesque and public murders they committed. Such speculation was fueled by the fact that before these crimes were committed, Anton LaVey had employed Susan Adkins, one of the Manson Family members, to play the role of a topless female vampire in a performance in San Francisco, but this hardly counts as proof of complicity, as some would have it.[60] So I have to be cautious with my claims here. There nevertheless are more direct links between Satanism and white nationalism that I would like to explore.

One of the most notable and I think overlooked intersections of Satanism and white nationalist ideology occurred when Nicholas Schreck, spouse to LaVey's daughter Zeena LaVey-Schreck, and longtime member of the Church of Satan breakaway group Temple of Set, appeared on Tom Metzger's public-access program *Race and Reason* in 1988 to discuss his newly released book, *The Manson File*.[61] Schreck described this book as a revisionist history of Charles Manson as a creator of a "white colony . . . akin to National Socialism." For him, Manson served as a teacher of esoteric wisdom that defied the Judeo-Christian weakness Schreck saw engulfing the Western world. This meeting between Metzger and Schreck and their discussion of Manson's alleged "white colony" should be considered an important moment in which avant-garde Left-Hand esotericism met organized white nationalism on mutual, if manufactured, ground—a significant part of which was a mutual disdain for the Judeo-Christian tradition because it was imagined to dull the presumed natural instincts of European man.

In the interview, Schreck described his other projects, including his gothic music band Radio Werewolf, as efforts to conduct "cultural war on every front" to bring about a "resurgence of the Western European tradition" and "to awaken the wolf in man." He said these efforts were attempts to "unleash the beast" in European man in opposition to the "Judeo-Christian values" that he thought had repressed the so-called natural instincts in European people. Calling upon the Norse myth of Ragnarök— the end of the age—he compared releasing the wolf in European man as synonymous with releasing "the ancient wolf god" Fenrir and, in his words, bringing about the "Götterdämmerung," or the end of the present egalitarian order. Schreck therefore stated in no uncertain terms that the goal of his occult projects was to bring about a "new order" in the wake of the destruction of the present corrupt one.

When Metzger asked Schreck how this project related specifically to race, Schreck affirmed that race held a significant place in his efforts. Moments later, after quoting Hitler to describe his project as an attempt to create a "youth without pity" who would be opposed to humanistic and Judeo-Christian values, and after offering praise for the skinhead movement, Schreck identified "race-mixing" as "genetic suicide" and described it as "inimical to the natural order." In other words, he adopted the language of white nationalism as well as the racialist Odinists' mythological references to describe his project to create a superior human species that would directly oppose the "drug culture, race mixing, equality" of the 1960s as well as "everything that Judeo-Christianity has succored."

The culturally chauvinist elements in Schreck's thinking are clearly seen in this interview as well. He argued that he and his collaborators were in their various projects exclusively concerned with the "Western European tradition" and what he regarded as essential to that culture in its opposition to non-European cultural influences, which trap Western peoples in "a nightmare of racial confusion." Referencing Francis Parker Yockey, Schreck professed a firm belief in the creation of an "Imperium" as "the Western man, the Faustian man[,] seeks to dominate the world." Further deploying the white nationalist discourse of imperilment, he said that European peoples were losing the fight to preserve their culture and could no longer let their culture and history "die out in the face of this dysgenic ocean of mud that has swept the world." Furthermore, echoing the esoteric Hitlerism of Madole, Rockwell, Devi, and Serrano, Schreck compared Manson and Hitler and claimed that both were "shaman[s]" and "spiritual" spokesmen of European culture for their time.

In this interaction between Schreck and Metzger, we have one of the most succinct examples of a certain interpretation of Satanism situated in relation to white racial activism in the 1980s, adorned with the very terms of white nationalism. But it is important to address the fact that not everyone sees such intersections as a wedding of Satanism and white nationalism. Jesper Petersen argues that Schreck's and others' use of "Nazi aesthetics" seems "more in tune with a general program of situationist 'culture jamming' . . . than a political statement."[62]

It is possible that this sort of activity among Left-Hand Path practitioners can be seen as a "radicalization of LaVey's tongue-in-cheek cultural critique rather than an ideological investment in the Far Right as a political project."[63] I have my doubts, however, about this interpretation of Schreck's intentions in this interview, given the vociferousness of his racialist language and professed concern for "the movement" in subsequent interviews with Metzger. The interview seems to indicate that there is something heartfelt in Schreck's Euro-chauvinism. In any case, it demonstrates the degree to which the "culture jamming" of Satanism is so easily incorporated within the paradigm of American white nationalism.

The point for me here is not whether Schreck was a white nationalist or not but rather that his Left-Hand esotericism was racialized and ultimately listened to and taken seriously enough that he made multiple appearances on Metzger's program. What seems of further significance to me is that Metzger and Schreck shared a critique of Christianity posited along social Darwinist lines and that for Schreck this critique was embedded in the alleged mystical truth of the European folk-soul and had as its purpose the preservation of Western European-ness. That is to say, regardless of Schreck's internal disposition toward race or his perhaps hidden intentions in these interviews, it is clear that Tom Metzger, one of the most important white nationalist leaders in America, listened to and regarded well the Left-Hand esoteric racialism that Schreck articulated. More importantly, this is just a case in point.

Such intersections of Left-Hand esotericism and white nationalism are not entirely anomalous. Esotericists who are not seemingly or confessedly white nationalist will participate in congenial conversations with confessed white nationalists and find agreement with them. This is particularly true of racial esotericists, who tend to recode racial protectionist language in terms of cultural preservation. In such cases, the critique of Christianity that is plainly anti-Semitic in the writings of Oliver, Pierce, Klassen, and others is fashioned instead as non-European (i.e., nonwhite) ideologies' "cultural incompatibility" in the goal of preserving the authentic expression of European folkways that are imagined to have some genetic import. In other words, the biological narrative of race is recoded in terms of culture. But what remains is the essential narrative of preservation of things imagined to be white in the face of an imagined persecution and distortion of a Europeanness that is imagined to be innate and contradictory to Semitic Christianity.

Esoteric Racialism and a European Cultural Renaissance

This chapter was meant to describe racialist esotericism in American white nationalism as one of the strains of religiosity in the movement and how Christianity was understood by some of this strain's formative figures. We can see, for example, that with Pelley's Silver Shirts and what he called "Soul-Craft" before World War II, the rejection of Christianity was not the point but rather the reformation of it. With the NRP after the war, however, there was more of a critique of Christianity as an ideology that had detracted from American Aryans' full awakening to esoteric truths. With the ANP, Rockwell's esoteric Hitlerism took on the messianic trope of Christianity. In all of these cases, there was a particular emphasis on Americanism rather than the more thoroughly global outlook held by later racial nationalists.

We also saw the development of racial esotericisms directly after World War II that drew explicitly from non-Christian sources from abroad, especially Hinduism. Both Serrano and Devi used these sources to articulate an understanding of Hitler as an avatar and a sharp critique of Christianity as non-Aryan and therefore detrimental to a possible future Aryan awakening. These sources pointed to the later development of white nationalism as something that would be more transnational as American white nationalists cultivated relationships with ideologues from outside the United States. And, of course, the founding of WUNS was a significant starting point for the development that Oliver, Pierce, Klassen, and racialist Odinists would see as the signature of their political activity.

This chapter was also meant to establish some of the esoteric thought that serves as part of the background for the latest developments in American white nationalism. I argue that in esoteric racialism directly after World War II we see the development of an undercurrent in racial nationalism as it was becoming what we now understand as white nationalism. This undercurrent was influential for thinkers such as Pierce and some in the North American New Right, providing them with the inspiration for articulating a plan for preserving the white race. Esoteric racialism also helped shape the more general white nationalist critique of Christianity—that it poisoned the mind of Aryan man, robbing him of his full spiritual potential and will to conquer.

This critique is of course also found in nonesoteric sources such as Yockey's *Imperium* (1948) and Lawrence R. Brown's *Might of the West* (1963), both of which were important foundational texts for what became white nationalism, especially as Oliver articulated it. For both Yockey and Brown as well as for the racialist esotericists, the notion of European culture was important and tied to certain understanding of what it means to be white—though Yockey, Brown, and even Oliver seem to be more broadly and directly significant for the development of white nationalism in America from the 1970s to the present. That is to say, the particular relationship between race and culture in white nationalism is held in common between racialist esotericism and the broader white nationalist community, particularly the view that different races produce certain cultures and that this linkage between biology and culture is not simply natural but also supernatural. Furthermore, this connection between race and culture is significant for how white nationalists have come to see Christianity as a problem for white racial survival.

We should therefore acknowledge that a certain notion of culture has always been at stake in white nationalist ideation. However, I argue that in esoteric racialism there seems to be particular emphasis on what we might call cultural salvation through the teachings of a racially enlightened elite, an emphasis that was in some ways an innovation after the defeat of state fascisms.

The next chapter discusses how in the most recent developments in American white nationalist thought, particularly in the North American New Right, especially where adaptations of the European New Right and esoteric racialism intersect, the preservation of an idealized representation of European culture has become an extremely important component in strategies to popularize white nationalist ideas in an effort to secure the future of the white race. I therefore emphasize that in the New Right—in both Europe and now the United States—*"culture can function like a nature* [*sic*]," to quote Étienne Balibar, and "can in particular function as a way of locking individuals and groups a priori into a genealogy, into a determination that is immutable and intangible in origin."[64] That is to say, racialization in this context takes the form of a cultural essentialism that is imagined to determine social belonging that maintains the contours of racial identification.

Racial esotericism, the entrenched antipathy toward Christianity among American white nationalists, and the more pragmatic and accommodating religious attitudes in the North American New Right come together to inform what has been described as a metapolitical project for the preservation of European culture and the future existence of the white race. Where there was once a deep antagonism between American white nationalists who reject Christianity outright and those who still hold to an Aryanized version of Christianity, we are seeing now a move toward religious tolerance within the white nationalist movement to bring about political solidarity among white Americans in order to accomplish a deeper cultural change in favor of the white nationalist cause and thereby to exert political pressure in the conservative mainstream.

6

The North American New Right and Contemporary White Nationalism's Latest Religious Adaptations

I began this book by describing Revilo Oliver's parallel criticism of Christianity and rejection of conservative politics, both of which evolved with his innovative racial nationalist ideas. At the same time as Oliver's critique of Christianity sharpened to eventual rejection, Else Christensen began preaching her racist brand of Odinism, and groups such as the National Renaissance Party, the Church of the Creator, and National Alliance were active in constructing slightly differing views about how and with what ideology they would save the white race from its imagined perils. In these case studies, what I have called "racial protectionism" drove such criticisms of Christianity and the development of alternative religious points of view and in some cases new religious organizations. At this time, too, various esoteric interpretations of National Socialism, like those by Savitri Devi and Miguel Serrano, were circulating in the new American white nationalist scene and helped shape white nationalist perceptions about religion.

These various thinkers and movements sometimes cooperated but were often in competition or outright disagreement with one another, as we saw with Ben Klassen's criticism of Odinism and William Pierce's criticism of Creativity. But as differentiated and complexly diverse as these expressions were, they all were equally committed to overcoming what they regarded as the imposition of "Jewish Christianity" on the minds of European peoples, which they believed was responsible for the white race's present imperilment.

A shared commitment to the protection of the white race across the world, not just in the United States, defined this new racialist activism and differentiated it from the older, more narrowly patriotic right-wing activism. These new white nationalists were looking to secure a future for white people everywhere, often in opposition to the US government and mainstream political conservatism in America. In this context, Pan-European racial protectionism had become the primary obligation in the new imagined racial community, and the religious outlook of American white nationalists reflected that commitment.

Transatlantic ambitions and established connections became emblematic of this new racialist activism in the United States at the beginning of its development, especially in the correspondence between Oliver and Alain de Benoist, in Devi's influence on Pierce, and in the World Union of National Socialists. After that, Pan-European connections among racial activists were sought out and cultivated on online forums such as Storm-front, established in 1995, along with other sites for National Alliance, Church of the Creator, and several racialist Odinist organizations. But nowhere is the connection between the European Right and the American white nationalists more overt and purposeful than in the more recent development of what has been called the "North American New Right" (NANR).

The name "North American New Right" as I use it here refers to both a general trend of thought within contemporary American white nationalism that makes use of the innovations in cultural politics formulated by the European New Right (ENR) and a specific organization with its own journal and other publication outlets designed to introduce and popularize ENR ideas in the American context.

The NANR in both senses represents one of the more intellectual trends of American white nationalism today, often drawing university-trained individuals to contribute work to its publishing firm, Counter-Currents Publishing, established in 2010, and its journal, the *North American New Right*, first released in 2012—both under the leadership of Greg Johnson. Johnson states plainly that the "entire project is motivated by consciousness of an existential threat" that confronts "European peoples," who "now live under a cultural and economic system that has set our race on the path to cultural decadence and demographic decline."[1]

Driven by that conviction, the NANR engages with and draws explicitly from the work of European rightists such as Benoist but is nevertheless, according to Johnson, a new movement, unique in its orientation to the American context. Johnson therefore describes the NANR as a cultural movement that transcends party politics in an effort to effect broader change, arguing that its "primary metapolitical project . . . is to challenge and replace the hegemony of anti-white ideas throughout our culture and political system."[2] That is to say, NANR activism is focused not simply on white separatism but also on a project to influence the broader culture for the benefit of European peoples who live in North America. Just as earlier manifestations of American white nationalism were the result of a disillusionment with and separation from the dominant American culture and politics, those who form the NANR are seeking to access and change both culture and politics.

The focus on Pan-European racial protectionism in the NANR is therefore consistent with white nationalism as I have discussed it so far, but in the NANR's metapolitical project some aspects common to all white nationalists in America are approached differently. This is especially true in the case of religion. Where there has typically been in most cases an overt rejection of Christianity, in the case of the NANR responses to Christianity are more complex. Identity Christians' rejection of Pierce and Oliver, for example, has caused friction between Christian and anti-Christian racial activists in America. For the NANR, this friction has presented a particular problem, especially in that some of the most important articulators of New Right ideology in America are not ready to relinquish European Christianity as incompatible with their metapolitical project, and others still view religious conflict among racial activists as something that threatens the white racial movement's larger political ambitions. Not only are the responses to Christianity more complex than simply rejecting or accepting Christianity, but also some within the NANR are concerned that the very debate about Christianity's place in the scheme of racial protectionism may imperil that scheme even further.

In the NANR, responses to Christianity can range from uncompromised rejection to apologetics if Christianity is presented in certain racialized terms and even to a pragmatic accommodation of it to avoid allowing the problem it poses to become too divisive. The problem of Christianity that confronts the NANR is the result of the same logic of racial protectionism that produced the rejection of Christianity among the figures I have discussed so far. That is to say, just as the logic of racial protectionism has produced a hostile response to so-called Jewish Christianity, it has also produced the need to develop new approaches to religion more generally for the sake of unity between non-Christian and Christian racialists.

This chapter is thus about the various discussions that have given shape to the NANR, how this intellectual trend has been institutionalized, and what the NANR has done to restate and adapt to the problem of Christianity in American white nationalism.

The Emergence of the Transatlantic New Right

The North American New Right developed in the context of American white nationalism, but its deeper roots are in the European Right, especially the Right that developed from the French New Right (FNR) after 1968. The individuals most responsible for the NANR's emergence either were in fact European themselves or were educated in part at European universities. Those Americans who have become a part of the NANR but were not trained in European universities, such as Stephen Edred Flowers, looked to the ENR for inspiration, identity, and intellectual resources to formulate their activism in the United States. More than any other current in American white nationalism, the NANR therefore owes its existence to contact with Europe and Europeans, especially the ENR, and is in this way the fullest expression of Pan-Europeanism even as it focuses on the American context. We therefore must start with a discussion of the ENR's history and basic ideology to contextualize the NANR's development.

The first thing to mention is that when discussing the history of the ENR, one has to keep in mind that it is, as Tamir Bar-On has stated, "a coherent 'cultural school of thought' with historical origins in ultranationalism, the revolutionary right and fascism" and that those within it "consciously separate themselves from both the parliamentary and extra-parliamentary wings of the revolutionary right milieu."[3] Although ENR theorists agree that they stand apart from mainstream right-wing politics in Europe, many of them also contest that they emerged from the fascist groups that came before them, most likely because such affiliations present specific legal difficulties for them in the European context—not to mention that one of the strategies within the ENR has been to shun state fascisms on ideological grounds. Nevertheless, scholars such as Bar-On have made the case that the ENR did grow out of the older, failed fascisms of the pre–World War II era.

It is appropriate in any case to say that the New Right in Europe and by extension in America has a specific common origin in the founding of the Groupement de recherche et d'études pour la civilisation européenne (GRECE, Group for the Study and Research of European Civilization) in 1968.[4] Founded "not as a political movement, but as a school of thought," GRECE has become synonymous with la Nouvelle Droite, or the FNR, which since its founding has become the nexus for intellectual activity that spread New Right thought throughout Europe and later found a place in North America.[5]

Among the founding members of GRECE were Oliver's onetime interlocutor Alain de Benoist (who often used the nom de plume Fabrice Laroche), Guillaume Faye, and Pierre Vial. Their purpose was to create the ideological foundations, in the words from the title of a book Vial published in 1979, "for a cultural renaissance."[6] They were not simply looking, as many French nationalists were, to deal with the political upheavals of the 1960s by preserving control over colonies or by acquiring political control of existing parties, nor were they interested in seeking office per se. They were looking to rethink the political situation in France at the time, often through the adaptation of ideas from the New Left and certain readings of the Marxist theorist Antonio Gramsci, to address what they regarded as fundamental problems facing European cultures.

The Nouvelle Droite, as the GRECEists came to be called in the French press, was characterized by antiegalitarianism, antiliberalism, and an "overwhelming fixation on cultural identity and 'rootedness.'"[7] It further came to distance itself from other right-wing movements, such as the later emergent and much better known Front National, particularly because of contrary views on economics and religion. Where most nation-alist parties in western Europe tended to be comparatively both pro-Chris-tian and pro-capitalism, the FNR was critical of both Christianity and capitalism and considered them sources of cultural decline in Europe.[8] To formulate critiques of both, the FNR came to associate itself with New Left thinking in the 1960s, particular with theorists such as Gramsci and the American Left philosopher Herbert Marcuse. In fact, so important was this form of leftist thought to GRECE that its approach came to be called the "gramscism of the right."[9]

The use and adaptation of Marcuse's and Gramsci's work did not, how-ever, signal a turn to the left in all respects. In his book on the New Right, *Against Democracy and Equality: The European New Right*, Tomislav Sunic, a former Croatian cultural attaché and one of the more significant inter-preters and discussants of the ENR from within it, argues that Gramscian thought among the New Right emerged from the position that reverses the "Marxian theorem" and that for the New Right "ideas, and not eco-nomic infrastructure, constitute the base of each polity."[10] In other words, GRECE was not interested in promoting socialism or communism in its criticism of capitalism. In the late 1960s and 1970s, it was doing something rather different from both the normative Right and the normative Left in France. GRECEists were attempting to decrease the political influence of socialism and liberalism and at the same time to improve the more tra-ditional Right's approaches by proposing "a scheme for cultural battle by simply readapting the message of Antonio Gramsci."[11]

Michael O'Meara, another significant white nationalist interpreter of the ENR and contributor to the journal *North American New Right*, con-curs with Sunic in his sympathetic treatment of GRECE and the Nouvelle Droite in his book *New Culture, New Right: Anti-liberalism in Postmodern Europe*. O'Meara credits Benoist with having "reversed the relationship" between ideas and economics à la Gramsci by asserting that "ideology dic-tates politics," not economics.[12] Whatever else this adaptation of Gramsci meant for GRECE, it helps us see the focus on "culture" in the New Right-ists' politics of ideology and articulation of their project. In pursuing a "renaissance culturelle," the New Right in Europe and then in North America has had as its focus neither the salvation of capitalism nor the

establishment of a socialist utopia but rather the resurgence and application of a presumed authentic European cultural order.

Two main influences apart from the New Left and possibly earlier fascist
movements that contributed to the formation of GRECE were the general
workers' strike and student protests against the Gaullist regime that took
place in May 1968 and the war in and eventual loss of Algérie française.
Bar-On comments that many of the New Right thinkers had their origins
in ultranationalist movements prior to 1968 and were shaped by the legacies of French politics in this period. But he goes on to note that although
FNR thinkers were "firmly rooted in the ultra-nationalist, anticommunist
camp," "the events of May 1968 still represented a critical turning point
in the school of thought's cultural and political evolution and appraisal of
modernity."[13] The Nouvelle Droite neither emerged from a vacuum nor was
unaffected by the massive political and social challenges of 1968.

Although those involved in founding GRECE were hostile to what
they considered the hedonism of the leftists of 1968, these thinkers shared
the leftists' dislike of Gaullism and capitalism. GRECEists eventually came
to regard themselves as the custodians of the true revolutionary spirit of
May 1968 and regarded liberals, socialists, and the New Left as having
abandoned the revolution to become "bourgeois socialists" and thus part
of the status quo they once vehemently rejected.[14] In particular, as Bar-On
argues, the failure to maintain French Algeria presented thinkers associated with the Nouvelle Droite as an opportunity to interject an alternative
to traditional French nationalism in the form of a Pan-European nationalism that was critical of the "fallacy of colonialism."[15]

Colonialism was for Benoist both the root of French cultural decline
and evidence of "the irreconcilable differences between world cultures."[16] For Benoist in particular and the ENR in general, there was a
turn away from colonialism and militarism and toward what came to be
called "the right to difference"—the right for cultures to live separately
and unencumbered by miscegenationist interference. The crisis in Algeria therefore allowed the FNR the opportunity to specifically recode the
old biological and paternalistic racism of colonialism in terms of cultural
difference and to critique colonialism and immigration alike as destroyers of cultural integrity.

To whatever degree one may be familiar with midcentury French politics or the New Left ideas that the Nouvelle Droite adapted for itself, one can still recognize that the Nouvelle Droite had formulated a new critique of both the political Right and the political Left. Such critiques inspired the broader ENR and more recently the NANR. New Rightists in these other contexts still agree with the FNR's basic points, although they have either adapted or omitted French-specific aspects of these politics in their application. Moreover, Benoist and others have continued to influence New Right ideas as they have emerged in Europe and the United States. This influence from abroad is most important for understanding how the NANR developed its ideas about race and religion.

Race and Religion in the European New Right

In the development of what the ENR calls its "metapolitics," which focuses on cultural change rather than political office to accomplish its goals, arguments concerning race and religion are at once important to understand and difficult to state in simple terms. We have, of course, differences of opinion to consider, especially where Christianity is concerned. But we also have to think about how race and religion are linked in New Right discourse to a European cultural identity that is imagined to be timeless and innate. That is to say, religion in the New Right is deeply tied to what Étienne Balibar calls "cultural racism."[17]

FNR and ENR thinkers have been very aware of their vulnerability to accusations of racism, fascism, and anti-Semitism. In the European context, such labels can be legally damaging, which is in part why ENR theorists have had to be strategic in expressing their views, often coding racist language in other terms. They thus often present a Nietzschean critique of Christian morality and a Dumézilian Indo-Europeanism to articulate religion as properly belonging to a naturalized understanding of the relationship between social structure, biological identity, and myths that define the relationships between the two. It is thus common for some in the ENR to imagine their metapolitical project to include a rejection of Christianity in an appeal to imagined pre-Christian European social structures. In this way, ENR theorists think of race and religion together in both their critique of modern society and their construction of a supposedly authentic European identity within a purely European cultural arrangement.

The New Right in Europe, as Pierre-André Taguieff argues, offers a reformulation of nationalism that references Indo-Europeanness as both an origin of the peoples of Europe and a model for the ideal organizational scheme for the "imperial unification of Europe."[18] In New Right discourse, the various peoples of the world are organized together as belonging to a specific region and culture and ultimately defined as a group by a supposed common origin and essence. Alberto Spektorowski calls this ideology a "differentialist ethno-pluralism," which, he argues, informs an "ethno-regionalism" that shapes how ENR theorists imagine "culture" as a biologically informed sense of cultural identity.[19] In this way, the so-called right to difference in ENR discourse reifies exclusivist notions of cultural belonging, the contours of which are drawn along the lines established by older narratives of biological race.

When dealing with the ENR, we therefore cannot assume that simply because it has abandoned discourses of hierarchy for a discourse of difference that the latter is not racist and fundamentally xenophobic. In the context of contemporary American white nationalism, where accusations of white supremacy are rebuffed with claims that white nationalists actually want racial separatism, not supremacy, the lesson is the same. To quote Balibar, "At the cost of abandoning the hierarchical model . . . *culture can also function like a nature* [sic], and it can in particular function as a way of locking individuals and groups a priori into a genealogy, into a determination that is immutable and intangible in origin." He argues further that the "*return of the biological theme* is permitted and with it the elaboration of new variants of the biological 'myth' within the framework of a cultural racism."[20]

Religion for the New Right in Europe is therefore deeply tied to essentialism of religion as a cultural expression of a people and to anxieties over imagined cultural/racial imperilment owing to the imagined threat to European biological and cultural particularism posed by cultural/racial mixing. Such anxieties have compelled many of those in the ENR to reject Christianity as alien to Europeans' supposedly natural sensibilities and the predecessor of liberal universalism and modernity in general, which they imagine to threaten European distinctiveness and therefore to threaten the future of European peoples. And as we will see in more detail in a moment, this notion has found a ready audience in the United States through translations of the works by ENR authors. But complicating the picture of religion in the ENR and the NANR is the fact that some in both movements have not deemed the full rejection of Christianity as necessary or even wise. They worry that religious tensions might split white nationalist communities along religious lines and consequently weaken efforts to effectively protect the white race. We can therefore observe how religion is a central concern in negotiating tensions between the need for unity and the desire for authenticity, both of which are important in the logic of racial protectionism. It is for this reason that a significant amount of the work of translating ENR ideas into the American context has been focused on religion.

Translating the New Right in America

To discuss the place of religion in the Pan-European New Right and particularly how it has taken shape in the United States, the writings of Alain de Benoist seem the most obvious place to begin both because of his prominence in the founding of GRECE and because of the important role his translated works have played in introducing ENR thought to American white nationalists. The most significant of his works related to religion and the rejection of Christianity is *Comment peut-on être païen?*—written under the nom de plume Albin Michel in 1981 and translated in 2004 as *On Being a Pagan*. Stephen Edred Flowers, an important figure in racialized Odinism, a member of the Temple of Set, and one of the intellectual contributors to the New Right in America, wrote the preface to the English edition, and Greg Johnson, the founder of the NANR organization, edited it. This text is therefore not only an important commentary on "paganism," which Benoist describes as "the original religion of Europe and . . . an ever-central component of its present day,"[21] but also, as Flowers puts it, "a sobering reflection on the true difficulties of undertaking a revival of [European] ancient heritage."[22]

On Being a Pagan was written, according to Benoist, to present an opposition to modern society and "to recall the possibility of a landscape and a spiritual *re-presentation* that would resonate with the beauty of a painting, a face, a harmony—with the face of a people uplifted by hope and the will to live another beginning." He further describes his argument as fundamentally Nietzschean, with an admixture of Evolian Traditionalism designed to evaluate the history of Western metaphysics as a "slow unmasking of a Christian aspiration to nothingness." From this position, he argues for a break with the secularization or desacrilization of society that he blames "Judeo-Christian discourse" for creating. He further argues in familiar tones that the establishment of Christianity in Europe was the starting point for a process of alienation of European peoples from their true selves and for traditions that shattered the social order, which he contends resulted in the neuroses of modern liberalism, capitalism, and consumerist decadence.[23]

Much of this view is of course quite familiar from Lawrence R. Brown's and, by adoption, Revilo Oliver's analyses. In Benoist's approach, however, there is the addition of a specific reference to Herbert Marcuse's cultural criticism of the one-dimensional man of late capitalism, the politically dominated and alienated consumer in a vacant industrial society. Here the common white nationalist argument concerning the psychological damage that Christianization has allegedly inflicted on Europeans is merged with the New Left criticism of industrial capitalist society in a social-psychological critique of both Christianity and capitalism. Indeed, the latter are for him the twin monsters of modern society that have destroyed the more meaningful, authentically European social frame by extinguishing the mythical bases of European culture through the devastating introduction of universalism and individualism. He blames Christianity primarily, however, for the psychological and social circumstances of European decline and considers it the root of the alienation that made European peoples vulnerable to industrial capitalist exploitation.

To reverse these processes, Benoist argues for the reversal of Christianization through the transcendence of the current social conditions that it created. He contends that what is required is nothing less than, first, the full abandonment of a metaphysics based on a God who created the "world *ex nihilo*" and, second, the creation of the intellectual space for making truth out of "a new system of values" through a more authentically

European Neopaganism. The latter means for him beginning a process of rebirth of older European systems of metaphysics that are tied to one's rootedness to place and thinking from the standpoint of being a European. The fundamental struggle, for Benoist, is therefore defined as an effort to "break the *language*" of Christianization—namely, two millennia of "Judeo-Christian egalitarianism"—to begin the process of becoming more fully and authentically European.[24]

This argument against egalitarianism is fundamentally an argument about antiuniversalism, positing that one's cultural roots are in fact determinative of one's way of thinking. For Benoist, all cultures are unique and fundamentally incompatible and interchangeable. Hierarchy is implied in what he says, but his particular argument is about an absolute difference between what are imagined to be different peoples' inalienable cultural inheritances. Because Christianity is an alien ideology produced by non-European peoples, he argues, it can only ever produce the alienation and social damage he describes. Only in becoming rooted in one's alleged native, authentic, and particular culture and allowing that rooted identity to shape one's thought over and against Christianity can that damage be undone.

Though there are some similarities with Odinism, Benoist's Paganism is not the same as the Paganism discussed in connection with racialist Odinism. He argues that his Paganism is not a regression or recovery, in the sense that Else Christensen imagined, though he does assert that it requires a certain familiarity with older Indo-European religions—what he describes as a "scholarly familiarity" as well as a "spiritual" and "intuitive familiarity."[25] His Paganism is more diversely understood and more inflected toward classical Greco-Roman influences. Moreover, he is interested in a sacrilization of social life in the opposite direction of Judeo-Christianity that will reform Europe to its supposedly rightful metaphysical disposition and not perhaps simply recover the worship of the old gods. What he means by "Paganism" is a metaphysical and philosophical Paganism that would create the space for imaginative thought unfettered by the chains of Christian references to the commands of the Christian God.

We can therefore say that Benoist's Paganism is not the same as racialist Odinism, in which full recovery of the Pagan and specifically Germanic past is desired for the purposes of racial identity and the reclamation of a devotion to the gods of the Northern Tradition. His project is more of a futurist social project in the sense that he is looking back only to classical Paganism to provide for future innovation. But in this project, perhaps by necessity, Benoist never quite relinquishes attachment to an imagined Euro-Pagan past, either. In seeking something authentically European, he is very close to the Odinists, indeed to all the American white nationalists I have discussed so far. It is important, however, to remember that his way of looking back at pre-Christian traditions is still a futurism. His Paganism is fundamentally about new modes of creative thought to put Europe and Europeans back in the metaphysical space where they can detach themselves from Christianity and the effects of Christianization so that they can create a new Europe.

In another work titled *Démocratie: Le probléme* (1985), translated as *The Problem of Democracy* for the English-speaking market in 2011 and published by Arktos Media, a publisher of many New Right materials in the United States, we see once again Benoist's argument for the rejection of Christianity in favor of imagined pre-Christian, Indo-European values to shape a new society. Here he contrasts Christian and pre-Christian societies in Europe and argues that they offer "two different conceptions of man, two different views of the world and of social ties." In this book, his focus is on "re-appropriating" and "adapting to the modern world" a notion of community that he argues has been obscured by two millennia of egalitarianism, rationalism, and individualism—all of which he blames on the Christianization of Europe. Above all, Benoist is concerned with what he calls an "organic democracy" based on one's "belonging to a given folk—that is a culture, history and destiny."[26]

In *The Problem of Democracy*, we can specifically see a biological/cultural essentialism that indicates a "cultural racism" in that it reifies all supposed natural relations along the lines of one's belonging to a people, who in turn belong in a place where they have produced a distinct culture. This cultural racism then substantiates a critique of Christianity as an imposed, foreign ideology that has corrupted "Indo-European" traditions that are regarded as organic to European peoples. Like Brown, Yockey, Oliver, and others, Benoist, though he is always careful not to articulate directly a biological racism in the same way these others did, produces a racialized metanarrative of cultural difference that is marshalled to confront what he considers a perverse universalism and egalitarianism generated by a totally un-European Christianity.

It is important, however, to note in light of Benoist's outspoken anti-Christianity that not all GRECEists agreed with the outright rejection of Christianity that he repeatedly advocates in these books. A principle example of this dissenting voice is Guillaume Faye. A onetime associate of Benoist and a cofounder of GRECE, Faye has been also influential among English-speaking New Rightists. In particular, his work *Archeofuturism: European Visions of the Post-catastrophic Age*, released in English in 2010 with a foreword written by Michael O'Meara, offers the same critiques of modernity, democracy, and egalitarianism that we have seen from Benoist.

"Archeofuturism" is described as an all-out assault on modernity and egalitarianism and a forward-looking replacement of the present order, something like a reconciliation between "[Julius] Evola and [Filippo] Marinetti"—that is, a reconciliation of Traditionalism and old Italian Futurism. Faye also argues that archeofuturism helps nationalism today understand the necessity for the defense of the "native members of a people" but also emphasizes the need for a separation from the "traditional idea of a nation and citizenship" inherited "from the egalitarian philosophy of the Enlightenment." He therefore advocates a nationalism that will view citizenship as rooted in the concept of a people, in particular a concept that embraces the notion of a "European people," which he argues "is under threat, but is not yet politically organized for its self-defense." To organize for this defense, argues Faye, European peoples—"whether in Toulouse, Rennes, Milan, Prague, Munich, Antwerp or Moscow"—necessarily should "revert to and embrace [their] ancestral virility."[27] Here we see a Pan-European nationalism that is perfectly recognizable from Yockey's work and from ideas espoused by the American white nationalists after him, in particular their shared Pan-European racial protectionism.

In almost all ways, Faye—his Pan-Europeanism, his hatred of egalitarianism, his attacks on modern capitalist society, and his sense of Europe's imperilment—is in agreement with Benoist, except in the area of religion. Faye does not think that a revival of pre-Christian past is what is needed, or at least not in the way Benoist articulates it. So what religious outlook does Faye consider best for his goals? "The Archeofuturist answer might be," he argues, "a neo-medieval, quasi-polytheistic, superstitious and ritualized Christianity for the masses and a pagan agnosticism—a 'religion of the philosophers'—for the elite."[28] That is to say, a form of Christianity is needed for the common people, but the philosophers who rule would be more inspired by the kind of philosophical metaphysical Paganism that attracts Benoist. This archeofuturist model contains more than a passing reference to Plato's *Republic*, but it also signals how Faye's antiegalitarianism cuts through the idealized European society to reveal stratification of religious practice for the commoners and the philosopher kings. Faye argues, again like Benoist, that imperiled European peoples have been overcome by egalitarianism and monetarism, which he regards as legacies of an ineffectual and universalist Christianity.

Contrary to Benoist, therefore, Faye does not see the need for the complete removal of Christianity. Rather, he argues that Christianity can be reformed to perform a useful, unifying function in the future European republic. But more than this, he worries that the outright rejection of Christianity is a tactical error because it is likely to alienate support from Christians who would otherwise be amenable to the ENR program. "I believe that this insistence on paganism," he argues, "has been a huge propaganda mistake, which has distanced the Nouvelle Droite from many Catholic milieus initially favorable to it."[29] In other words, for Faye the problem of Christianity is not its origins per se but the way in which it has been shaped to serve the needs of a modern, egalitarian society instead of maintaining the mediaeval ritualism and European particularism that might serve once again as a unifier of the European peoples. Moreover, abandoning or attacking Christianity is a fundamental strategic error that has alienated an otherwise sympathetic public from the New Right cause, or so Faye argues.

For these two founding members of the New Right, Benoist and Faye, Christianity presented very specific problems, but they disagreed somewhat on what to do about it. Others among the New Right have continued this discussion, and this issue is of course no longer localized to the French context where it began. The debates about religion have continued

elsewhere in the ENR in much the same way as described for Benoist and
Faye. For example, in *Fighting for the Essence: Western Ethnosuicide or European Renaissance?* Pierre Krebs—a French-born German theorist described
as a major figure in the Neue Kultur, or German New Right—echoes much
of what Benoist articulated.

In this book, Krebs makes an appeal for "organic democracy" as
opposed to the "cycle of egalitarian madness" of modern liberal democra-
cies. In keeping with the ENR neoracist notion of "a right to difference"
within the frame of cultural racism, he argues that "peoples" are "biologically definable, sociologically identifiable and geographically localizable."
Like Benoist and others, he blames the "plague" of humanitarianism and
equality on the "monster of Judeo-Christianity." Diagnostically, he is
nearly identical to Benoist but perhaps more directly ties the biological
and culturalist narratives of race together to describe Christianity as alien
and destructive to European social consciousness. In any case, Christianity is for him the root of the existential problem European peoples face.
To address this situation, Krebs argues for a return to "bio-cultural reality,"
the refusal of any compromise with anything derived from "the Judeo-
Christian root," and a "return to [the] *pagan Indo-European tradition.*"[30]

In Krebs's book, we see again a strong cultural critique of Christianity in the ENR, one that is closer to that of Benoist than to that of Faye,
but a critique nonetheless. As such, there are obviously affinities between
all three of these ENR theorists, not the least of which is that their intellectual projects are motivated by a deep anxiety over the imperilment of
European culture and Europeans themselves. But more significantly for our
purposes, each of these works has been translated into English, primarily for the American market, and each deals heavily with the problem
of Christianity and how religious reforms must play a part in the larger
metapolitical project. There are, however, subtle differences in how these
ENR theorists think about religion and Christianity and how one ought to
navigate questions concerning the place of Christianity in creating a supposedly bioculturally rational society. In particular, there is the difference
between the majority of ENR theorists, who, like Krebs and Benoist, argue
for an outright rejection of Christianity, and the minority of theorists,
who, like Faye, feel that Christianity can be reformed and that an outright

rejection of it is dangerously divisive. This difference of opinion is also significant because these questions and debates continue in the New Right in America, whose members look to both camps as they think about the role of religion and the place of Christianity for an American New Right.

In this section, I have looked more closely at selected works that have been translated into English for the specific purpose of introducing Americans to ENR ideas. That Greg Johnson, Stephen Flowers, and Tomislav Sunic, all of whom are significant to the NANR, have been involved in the distribution of such translated works or the writing of introductions to them or both demonstrates the importance of the content of these works to the NANR. In particular, it demonstrates how important Christianity is in shaping the fundamental arguments of both the ENR and the NANR. That is to say, in this recent intellectual formation of American white nationalism, the Pan-European connections become more explicit, the emphasis on racial preservation—though now coded as "cultural survival"—remains, and the problem of Christianity is to be resolved not simply by rejection but by complex strategic and intellectual negotiation.

The New Right in North America

The vision of an authentic European identity as the basis for a revolt against the modern world and against Christianity as both alien and alienating is, as we have seen thus far, common among white nationalists, though perhaps expressed in various ways. But now with the purposeful infusion of European New Right ideas into the United States, American white nationalists have developed their own New Right. This new North American Right is itself quite diverse, which is certainly in keeping with the general milieu of American white nationalism, but it is nevertheless like its European predecessor a coherent school of thought. Although Flowers and some other contributors to the NANR do not call themselves white nationalists—and it should be noted that neither Oliver nor Benoist ever used the term to describe themselves—ideological similarities and cooperation among those associated with the NANR call for an examination that goes well beyond simple guilt by association. We should think of confessed white nationalists and those in the NANR who eschew the term *white nationalism* as connected by common ideation and collaboration toward similar goals—the revivification of so-called "European culture" and the preservation of the white race.

The journal *TYR*, for example, is exactly the meeting place for the ideas held in common by Flowers, Benoist, Johnson, and others. But also significant is the fact that Flowers wrote the prefaces to the English translations of *On Being a Pagan* by Benoist and *Manifesto for a European Renaissance*, which Benoist coauthored with Charles Champetier and Flowers published through the now defunct Runa-Raven Press.[31] Such relationships point to specific associations that are consequential beyond mere association. So the NANR not only presents an evolution of white nationalist ideation in dialogue with ENR ideas but also represents challenges to identifying white nationalist racism both in that race is coded in terms of culture and that the label *white nationalist* is itself sometimes rejected by those who otherwise seem to be perfectly described by this term. As we will see later, this opaqueness also becomes extremely important to understanding the ways in which white nationalists have more recently interacted with mainstream political movements.

There are connections between this newer movement within American white nationalism and racial esotericism as North American New Rightists incorporate aspects of the ENR into their political thought and criticisms of the modern world and Christianity. In the first instance, figures such as Stephen Flowers and Michael Moynihan are deeply involved in the NANR and are themselves best classified as "esoteric racialists." I discuss this classification in a moment, but I first want to claim that we can describe the notion that the soul of a people is expressed in their culture as an esoteric notion that is itself deeply racialized. It is a "cultural racism," as Balibar describes it—one that justifies racism but allows an alibi for it in that it can deny being biologically racist while still preserving racial segregation through the definition of "culture" as a marker of insurmountable differences between groups of people. Such notions are important especially for those associated with the intellectual project exemplified by the journal *TYR: Myth–Culture–Tradition*.

The first volume of *TYR* was published in 2002 and was edited by Joshua Buckley, Michael Moynihan, and Collin Cleary. In volumes 2 and 3, Cleary is not listed as an editor, most likely because of his work on an independent project, *Summoning the Gods*, a collection of essays concerning the primordial, pre-Christian tradition in Europe and its place in the revival of European racial awareness.[32] The full careers of Buckley, about whom little public knowledge is available, and Moynihan, who has a complex history with publishing and the musical group Blood Axis, cannot be easily discussed in a short space.[33] What is important, however, is how they, along with Cleary, define their project in *TYR*. In the editorial preface to volume 1, they state that they are committed to "resacraliz[ing] . . . the world"; upholding "folk/traditional culture versus mass culture"; emphasizing a "Natural hierarchy," which would be "based, perhaps, on [Georges] Dumézil's 'three functions'"; prioritizing the "tribal community versus the nation-state," an ecological attitude described as "stewardship of the earth," a "harmonious relationship between men and women versus the 'war between the sexes'"; and emphasizing "handicrafts and artisanship versus industrial mass culture."[34]

These ideals, as the editors remark, share a close relationship with what Flowers has called "integral culture," which he describes in the first article in volume 1. He argues for a reintegration of culture, which he understands as ethnic, ethical, symbolic, and material. For him, tradition follows these "pathways" through "genetic, mythic, linguistic, and material" means. The proper cultural expression is rooted deep in the integration of the four elements to "*become who we are*," in Flowers's paraphrasing of Fichte.[35] We should note that the so-called Alt-Right and specifically the organization Identity Europa, which has significant connections to the National Policy Institute (NPI), a white nationalist political think tank, uses this phrase in advocating for a reclamation of European cultural identity.[36]

There are two points I want to note before moving forward. First, the relationships between racial esoteric trends and white nationalism, though complicated and often diffuse, are important to the continued development of white nationalism in America, particularly among the NANR. Second, particular articulations coming from racial esoteric thinkers such as Nicholas Schreck, discussed in the previous chapter, and Flowers, among others associated with *TYR* and the NANR, have used culture to reframe racist and racial protectionist discourses and from that have produced related criticism of Christianity. For Schreck, Flowers, the editors of

TYR, and others in the NANR, Christianity has interrupted Europeans' primordial harmony, which seems to be a repeated theme in early white nationalism and in the ENR, and, they claim, Christianity's role was later taken up by "modernity."[37] Integral culture, as described by Flowers, is thus about the mystical connection to one's ancestors and the endeavor from that connection to live in a fashion that is imagined as more authentically European than what Christianity can provide and modernity allows. Each of these individuals shares the ambition to look for "a return to origins" in the recovery of metaphysical Europeanness defined through racialized notions of culture.[38]

These more recent developments in American white nationalist thought help us understand not only the problem that Christianity presents to American white nationalism now but also how racist discourses of difference have shifted within white nationalism. Coding racist ideology in terms of "culture" has become important for the efforts of some white nationalists in America, particularly in the NANR and the more recent Alt-Right. This coding of racism in terms of cultural difference has been both the dominant expression within these movements and a significant part of a larger metapolitical strategy to mainstream their ideas without being obligated to fully disclose their ideology.

Such efforts are clearly not easy. As the New Right in Europe did, the NANR has had to navigate charges of fascism and racism. In the second issue of *TYR*, the editors specifically rebuff any accusation of fascism, which they connect with modernity. In his work, Flowers also tries to avoid accusations of fascism and racism, which he thinks of in strictly supremacist terms and not related to his and his fellow NANR ideologues' cultural separatist attitudes.[39] This racialism, like Benoist's "right to difference," is exactly the differentialist and culturalist racism that typifies what Balibar calls "neoracism." But I do not accuse Flowers or anyone else affiliated with *TYR* of fascism in the Italian or Nazi tradition, nor do I simply accuse them of being white supremacists. Such a charge obscures the racialized particularism they express and does not completely describe what they are doing in their metapolitics. I do, however, argue that they advocate a cultural racism in that they recode the biological narrative of "race as culture" as a heritable trait to argue for what is in that sense racial separatism and that this recoding is key to how they formulate the ethical demand to preserve the white race. As such, they fear mixing, ideological or otherwise, of what they imagine to be racially discrete essences because they believe it will lead to biocultural genocide of the white race. It is in this sense that they are racists, though I hesitate to call them white supremacists.

On the basis of an assumed esoteric connection of all peoples within racially specific groupings to their respective folk and cultures, many in the NANR, as did many in the ENR, articulate the need to reject Christianity as a foreign, Jewish imposition that destroyed what they imagine to be the natural European social order and "thought-life." But others associated with the NANR think that such a rigid rejection is possibly divisive and therefore unwise.

Tomislav Sunic was the first of the New Right theorists to write about the ENR in English for English-speaking audiences, and he has become one of the most important New Right theorists in America. In 1990, he adapted his PhD dissertation on the history of the Nouvelle Droite into his opus on the topic, *Against Democracy and Equality: The European New Right*.[40] The stated purpose of the book is to describe the "resurgent conservative movements in Europe and their intellectual heritage," as discussed earlier.[41] However, Sunic's treatment here differs from treatments in French up to 1990 in that Sunic focuses on the "differences between the European New Right and the American 'new right.'"[42] Of course, he is here drawing a distinction between the New Right in Europe, on the one hand, and the Right in America that evolved during the Reagan years as well as the rise of what eventually came to be called "neoconservatism," on the other, and he particularly focuses on how they differ on the topic of religion.

Very early in *Against Democracy and Equality*, Sunic identifies some of these differences—most significantly, the American Right's liberal heritage, with a focus on individual rights and its accompanying economic liberalism, and the fact that many conservatives in the United States view their politics as "inseparable from Roman Catholic and Protestant beliefs."[43] In Sunic's description of the differences between the Nouvelle Droite and the American Right, there is not only an implied contrarian position toward Christianity but also a latent anti-Semitism. He critiques neoconservatives such as Norman Podhertz and Irving Kristol, for example, by claiming that they are less focused on the United States than they are concerned with the defense of Israel and that they view the defense of Israel as a means of defending the United States—a critique that is heavy with the suggestion that their position follows from their Jewish heritage.[44] Such descriptions insinuate a corrupting effect by supposedly Jewish thought in American politics, as much as Christianity is likewise thought to be a corrupting Jewish ideology itself.

Some of Sunic's own thought does make it into the analysis he offers, but the purpose of the book is mainly to describe the New Right for the American audience in the hopes that the book will be instructive as they begin rethinking rightist politics. His book therefore reads as both an introduction to ENR thought and a political comparison between the ENR and American conservatism. It also reads in places as less of a reportage of New Right history and thought than a commentary on how ENR ideologies can better influence the American Right. This is apparent in his comments in the conclusion, where he states that the New Right in France has "made a path-breaking effort in probing the roots of the modern crisis" and in drawing "our attention" to critiques of liberal democratic societies.[45] One can certainly read the term *our* as referring to fellow political scientists because Sunic is ostensibly writing as an academic, but I think one should say that it refers to the Euro-American audience as well.

Such ambiguity and the pretense that Sunic is commenting simply as an academic evaporate when one looks at his comments elsewhere—for example, when one looks at his website, and more specifically when one listens to a talk he gave in 2011 at a meeting organized by the NPI, whose banner on its website homepage reads "For Our People, Our Culture, Our Future."[46] Founded by Samuel Francis and William Regnery II, both of them longtime racialist activists, the NPI describes itself as "an independent research and educational foundation" that represents "White Americans—our country's historic majority and founding population—the people that bears [sic] the unique heritage of Europe, Christianity, cultural excellence, and the scientific awakening," and that works to counter "the dispossession of White Americans," which is seen as immanent and as leading to "catastrophic effects for the entire world, not just [white] people."[47]

The context of Sunic's talk at the NPI meeting in 2011 positions his statements as being directed to those on the racialist right in America who still look to Christianity as the basis of the more mainstream political position. The NPI is also one of the organizations that helped to create what is now called the "Alt-Right." Before the NPI audience, Sunic described himself as a member of the ENR, a proponent of white nationalism in the tradition of Francis Parker Yockey's Pan-European vision, and a member of the American Third Position Party (often written as "American 3rd Position"), which has since changed its name to the American Freedom Party and describes itself as a "nationalist party that shares the customs and heritage of the European American People."[48] Sunic sits as the party's director, along with other notables such as longtime friend and associate Kevin MacDonald, a professor at California State University, Long Beach, whom the party website describes as an "expert in evolutionary psychology."[49]

MacDonald has been a significant contributor to the American racial nationalist milieu for some time. In particular, he has written several articles and books, the most significant of which is A People That Shall Dwell Alone: Judaism as a Group Evolutionary Strategy, with Diaspora Peoples.[50] In his review of the book, Sander Gilman writes, "It is evident that MacDonald recasts all of the hoary old myths about Jewish psychological difference and its presumed link to Jewish superior intelligence in contemporary sociobiological garb."[51] Indeed, that same thing can be said of MacDonald's subsequent books on the "Jewish Question" in America. At the time Sunic gave his NPI talk in 2011, he was therefore positioned as occupying the center of the contemporary white nationalist intelligentsia, not simply by association but also by affiliation and self-description. He was no mere historian of the New Right by this point, but a major force within it.

The title of Sunic's talk, "Prospects for the Nationalist Right in America," suggests his main point: America offers the best opportunity for a "rebirth and revival" of revolutionary, Pan-European nationalism.[52] He argued that although Europe had been plagued with narrow territorial nationalist concerns that produced, for example, World War I, World War II, and the Balkan conflict, all described as racially suicidal, fraternal wars, America's white population has a sense of identity that mitigates this kind of conflict. Some white Americans, he asserted, are therefore already prepared for a Pan-Europeanism that assumes a unity in race that transcends geographical and historical conditions in a way that Europeans are not.

This argument certainly points to why Sunic is so active in the American white nationalist scene: he seems to regard it as the germ community from which a transnational Europeanist future might emerge. But Sunic went on in his talk to describe other elements that define this coming community he imagines and therefore those things that deserve the American Right's attention. In this talk, as he does elsewhere, Sunic argued that there is a spiritual essence that defines the basic identity of every member of a race, one that is, as it is for Benoist, at odds with Christian notions of liberal inclusiveness and equality. In other places, Sunic is more confrontational in discussing what he regards as Christianity's role in cultural decline and racial endangerment through ideological mixing, but in this particular talk Sunic was guarded about such criticisms of Christianity. He only briefly mentioned at the end of the talk that Christianity presents an obstacle to an emerging racial consciousness but came short of advocating for its rejection. He has added some introductory remarks to the recorded NPI talk on his website, where he is more candid about his criticisms of both Christianity and, in keeping with the New Right in Europe, capitalism. But in the talk itself, both perspectives were muted as he focused on themes that were likely better received by the particular audience to whom he was speaking.

Sunic states on his website comments introducing the talk that he is not necessarily anti-Christian, but he then goes on to discuss at length the support that Cardinal John Joseph O'Connor and the pope displayed for migrant peoples who Sunic perceives as "swamping" European lands—support that he derides as "sentimental double-talk." He states that because of limited time he was unable to get into this discussion at the NPI gathering, but I think if one looks at the NPI's general attitude toward Christianity, we may conclude that he was aware of the political inefficacy of such statements in that particular context.

Sunic's performance of the talk at NPI and his later discussion of it are particularly valuable in that they demonstrate both the difference between him and the NPI and further highlight the tension between the ENR and the majority American Right on the topic of religion. Sunic's criticism of Christianity, as I said, is elsewhere more apparent. In his foreword to the English edition of Krebs's book *Fighting for the Essence*, Sunic lauds the book as one that "urges the reader to decolonize his mindset, purging it from the images and concepts that have been contaminating White European brains over the last two millennia which resulted in in a distorted perception of objective reality and a perverse form of White identity." For Sunic, Krebs "correctly traces the problem of White racial decay and cultural decadence not to liberalism and multiculturalism, but to the Judeo-Christian tradition."[53] Here Sunic sounds much more like Brown, Oliver, and Benoist: a harsh critic of Christianity without much, if any, qualification. Where Sunic has no reason to assume there will be a political consequence of his criticism of Christianity, as on his website or in his comments in Krebs's book, he is much more candid on this topic. But before a certain other kind of audience, such as the one at the NPI, he presents Christianity not as a corrupter of white brains but as a part of the matrix of Euro-American identity that has helped shape a future Pan-European unity.

More discussion of Christianity and its role in Pan-European nationalism appears again in Sunic's book *Homo Americanus: Child of the Postmodern Age* (2007), in which he is focused on criticism of "Americanism" while offering a redefinition of rightist ideas and providing a "different meaning for those concepts." In particular, he wants to address the shortcomings in American racialist thought by incorporating ENR analysis of Americanism and the American white nationalists, such as Francis P. Yockey and Revilo P. Oliver, who he claims have pointed to the "contradictions among American racialists." Among those contradictions Sunic targets is what he calls "Judeo-American monotheism." The fundamental problem he identifies in this regard is an "absence of a common cultural identity among white Americans," which seems to him a "fundamental weakness of postmodern American nationalists, racialists, and conservatives." Like others in the ENR, Sunic points to "Judeo-Christian universalism" practiced in America as the ideology that "set the stage for the rise of postmodern egalitarian aberrations and the complete promiscuity of all values."[54]

In this regard, Sunic is clearly in line with Benoist concerning Judeo-Christianity. But, once again, in his talk before the nominally Christian and more American nationalist NPI, Sunic was notably different in tone. His rhetorical shift concerning Christianity, Americanism, and capitalism at the NPI conference signals something I see as key to understanding positions on Christianity among the New Right in America. So in taking Sunic as an example of how New Right theorists in the American context deal with Christianity and American nationalism, we can see that the tensions between tendencies toward ideological purity and tendencies toward organizational efficacy in the logic of racial protectionism in American white nationalism are pulling some activists toward a softened position concerning Christianity rather than toward an insistence on the rejection of it.

Nevertheless, Sunic was hopeful in his talk as he wondered if "the death of communism and the exhaustion of postmodern Americanism" may lead to "the dawn of a new American culture and a return to ancient European heritage,"[55] though he is clear elsewhere that he does not think Christianity has been or can be compatible with that aim. But, as in the ENR, not all those involved in shaping a New Right in America agree. In *New Culture, New Right: Anti-liberalism in Postmodern Europe*, Michael O'Meara, another extremely important interpreter of the ENR for Americans, repeats much of what Sunic says in his study of the Nouvelle Droite.

O'Meara was a student at Berkeley in the 1960s and later went to France to study at the École des hautes études en sciences sociales in Paris.[56] Since the publication of *New Culture, New Right* in 2004, O'Meara has come to be known as one of the foremost contributors to the emerging New Right in America by writing articles and reviews of books, in particular the works of Guillaume Faye. He has also become a significant theorist of white nationalism in his own right, contributing to several white nationalist journals and websites.[57] But *New Culture, New Right* and his collection of articles in the volume *Toward the White Republic*, published by Counter-Currents in 2010, have been the most significant of his works to date.

In *New Culture, New Right*, O'Meara outlines a history of the New Right in Europe, primarily through an examination of the French scene. But O'Meara's account is more prescriptive of the American white nationalist scene than Sunic's more descriptive account of the ENR. O'Meara's commentary further reveals a different interpretation of the role of Christianity in white nationalist metapolitics. Whereas Sunic sees Christianity as the predecessor of liberalism and egalitarianism, O'Meara seems closer in his analysis to Revilo Oliver's earlier defense of Christianity in the late 1960s before he rejected it outright.

O'Meara fundamentally argues for two different Christian traditions in the West—one that is liberal and alien and another that is thoroughly Europeanized and expressive of the European consciousness. He therefore argues that ENR anti-Christianity results from the misrecognition of the historical divergence between what he calls "historical Christianity" and "modern Christianity." O'Meara states in clear terms that "Christianity is Europe's religion." He, however, qualifies this statement very carefully in chapter 4 of *New Culture, New Right*. He admits that Christianity did not emerge "as an organic offshoot of the European spirit" but, drawing from James C. Russell's book *The Germanization of Early Medieval Christianity* (1994), he argues that "Catholicism was compelled to make so many concessions to paganism that it ended up transforming itself from a universal salvation religion [into] a Germanic, and eventually European, folk religion."[58]

But this position is again not one that O'Meara takes on all forms of Christianity. He contrasts this traditionalist form of European Christianity with Protestantism, in particular Calvinism, which he argues undid this Europeanization by "re-rooting North Europeans in the Hebraic forms of the early church." O'Meara therefore argues that not all Christianity is responsible for egalitarianism but rather only that wing that later came to be "profaned" and united with the "modernist project" and the "secularizing forces" that this project unleashed. He does not argue that white nationalists should return to paganism in the way he sees the GRECEists hoping for such a return but rather that they should embrace a racialized, traditionalist Christianity that will revive a "historical Christianity" that conserves European Pagan elements that had endured and become part of a specifically European Christianity.[59]

In spite of these differences between Sunic and O'Meara where Christianity is concerned, both are still committed to the white nationalist cause. In a later article, O'Meara writes in clear terms that the "threat to white existence is profound, rooted in the civilizational, ontological, and spiritual disorders undergirding the Judaification" that he marks as currently pervading the lives of white Americans. The solution he proposes is a metapolitical project in which white Americans "return to the ancient practices that formed [white Europeans]" in order to produce a more ancient and authentic white identity.[60]

Here the two poles of ENR responses to Christianity become visible in the American context. Sunic is selective in how he presents his argument at times, but he rejects Christianity on almost exactly the same grounds as Benoist. O'Meara, however, as Oliver did at one time, rejects only liberalized Christianity and argues for a traditionalist and ritualized European Christianity. Furthermore, O'Meara, like Faye in responding to Benoist's anti-Christianity, argues that a rejection of Christianity is a tactical mistake. So once again there is less of a clear New Right position on Christianity than there is a debate that takes into account a number of issues, in particular efficacy in relation to white nationalism's larger metapolitical project and political aims.

These antagonisms and debates, not to mention the discrepancies in presentation that depend on audience, point to the tension that Sunic noticed in comparing the American Right and the ENR. They also point to the way that the difference of opinion concerning religion between Faye and Benoist is alive and well in the American context. Nonetheless, it is important to keep in mind that though prescriptions differ, rightists in this lineage agree that Christianity in some sense presents a problem for those concerned with white racial survival, even as they recode that discourse in terms of cultural preservation. In the NANR, this problem of Christianity is negotiated in sometimes novel ways. What has been emerging in American white nationalism since the mid-2000s in part because of the influence of NANR theorists is a multireligious toleration for the purposes of white racial unity to preserve Euro-America and to advance white nationalist political ambitions.

The North American New Right Proper

As I mentioned, the NANR can be understood as an intellectual trend, represented by the kinds of theorizing led by Sunic and O'Meara, as they in turn were influenced by the New Right in Europe. But the NANR can also mean a recently institutionalized and specific organization in American white nationalism led by Greg Johnson, who gave the organization its name and headed up the initiatives that made it an online resource for New Right ideas. Although the first and to date the only issue of the journal *North American New Right* was not released until 2012, prior to this publication the NANR organization established Counter-Currents/North American New Right as an online entity on June 11, 2010.[61] In fact, much of the content in the journal's first volume was drawn from the website that predated it. So we can mark the official beginning of the organization known as the North American New Right as happening in 2010, when Greg Johnson established it and named it, though its roots are in the first systemic and purposeful exposure of American racialists to the ENR's ideas in the early 1990s.

In an interview by Tomislav Sunic in 2011, Greg Johnson discussed his naming of the NANR organization and his work at Counter-Currents, both as a publisher and administrator of the website and as the base for a metapolitical project that seeks to "get enough of our fellow white people" to begin to believe that an ethnic state can be constructed.[62] In the interview, Johnson was quite self-deprecating about his role in starting the NANR movement, and he deflected the idea that he is a leader of the movement in any official capacity. Nevertheless, it is clear that he sits in a very influential position within this community of white nationalists that is, for lack of a better description, at the cutting edge of an emerging racialist ideological trend. Johnson is then rightly seen not simply as another figure popularizing ENR ideology in American white nationalism but also as someone who is working to develop a distinct intellectual movement within white nationalism in North America through publishing and establishing online resources for the white nationalist community.

One important thing to consider when discussing Johnson's ambitions for his organization is the relationship between the NANR as a movement and organization and the ENR as he describes it. In an article titled "New Right vs. Old Right," Johnson is clear that the NANR is "indebted to" thinkers such as Alain de Benoist and Guillaume Faye, among others, but he quickly adds that there are important differences.[63] First, there are the differences between Europeans and Americans in racial identity, which he describes in terms similar to the ones Sunic used in his talk at the NPI conference. So the NANR movement and organization see themselves as unique in that they are set, as Sunic believes, in a context where white people possess a unique racial consciousness that awaits an awakening and direction.

Second, also something discussed briefly during the interview, Johnson describes in "New Right vs. Old Right" the need for the NANR movement to more directly address "the Jewish Question" "because of the leading role of the organized Jewish community in engineering the destruction of European peoples, and because the United States is the citadel of Jewish power."[64] Johnson further argues that the NANR has this unique and paramount responsibility that his European counterparts do not because of the unique proximity that Americans have to these alleged centers of Jewish power. Such a claim is also distinctive because ENR thinkers, for reasons already discussed, avoided putting their positions in those clearly anti-Semitic terms. In the article, Johnson even remarks on American rightists' specific ability to address so-called Jewish power because of the legal differences between the free-speech statutes in the United States and the stern hate-speech statutes in Europe. For Johnson, one of the distinctive features of the NANR is its approach to addressing the role of Jews as a specific threat to the white race.

Concerning religion, Johnson argues for a nondoctrinaire position: "We have atheists, and we have representatives of all schools of religion, Christian and pagan, Eastern and Western."[65] He writes on the Counter-Currents website that the NANR has no established religious doctrine but that it does not avoid the question of religion, either. He goes a bit further, suggesting that most white nationalists agree that Christianity needs reform concerning its positions on race if it is going to help with the cause of ensuring the future survival of the white race, though he does not elaborate on exactly what he means. He does, however, suggest other articles for further reading on this issue.[66] Among them is his article "The Christian Question and White Nationalism," originally published online in the *Occidental Observer* in 2010.[67]

The *Occidental Observer* article begins with a summarization white nationalism's attitude toward Christianity:

> Christianity is one of the primary causes of the decline of the White race for two reasons. First, it gives the Jews a privileged place in the sacred history of mankind, a role that they have used to gain their enormous power over us today. Second, Christian moral teachings—inborn collective guilt, magical redemption, universalism, altruism, humility, meekness, turning the other check, etc.—are the primary cause of the White race's ongoing suicide and the main impediment to turning the tide. . . . The usual conclusion is that the White race will not be able to save itself unless it rejects Christianity.

Johnson explains that he agrees that Christianity is indeed one of the foremost causes of the deterioration of racial consciousness among white Americans, for the reasons he describes. But he disagrees with those who argue from these points that white nationalists need to reject Christianity, offering three main reasons for his disagreement. First, he regards white nationalism as a political movement rather than a religious one. This is truly the most significant reason, and it motivates for him an accommodation with racialist Christians so as to not alienate potential allies. The goal, Johnson argues, is a homeland for whites in North America, and such a "political goal is shared by Christians and non-Christians alike."

There seems, then, some similarity of opinion between him, O'Meara, and Faye on this point, though Johnson states clearly in "The Christian Question" that he is not favorable toward Christianity. His position is best understood as an accommodationist stance toward religion driven by the political goal of lebensraum for whites and the deeper concern of racial protectionism. This position, though opinions of Johnson's view vary, is one of the key features of his engagement with religion in the NANR movement. Religion and concerns about religious difference are always subordinated to the goal of a white North American homeland where the survival of the white race can be assured.

The second reason Johnson gives in "The Christian Question" for not taking an outright anti-Christian position is that although Christianity is in his view culpable for weakening the white race, it is not in the final analysis "the driving force" behind "racial suicide." This position is fundamentally based on his understanding of the historical relationship between the Christian Church and political power. The Christian Church, he argues, has always "trimmed its sails to the winds of political expediency." He reasons, therefore, that because Christian leadership has always reflected the power dynamics of the societies in which it has existed, it is not responsible for white people's subservience to Jewish power, influence, or interests and is therefore not necessarily precluded from playing a part in the white republic's imagined future. In this sense, he regards the church as a victim of Jewish power, though not completely innocent either. He argues that organized Christianity will resist the establishment of the white republic and other NANR aims "less fervently than those whose aims are primarily secular, such as Jewish organizations, non-White ethnic organizations, and the secular left." So, for Johnson, whites beholden to institutionalized Christianity will inevitably accept the new regime when the old regime of Jewish power is overthrown. In his view, the Christian Church is malleable to white nationalist interests because of its lack of political conviction.

The third reason Johnson gives for not rejecting all Christianity is certainly related to the first. He is concerned here with the political efficacy of maintaining unity among the diverse community of white nationalists. He argues that a split in the community would inhibit achieving the ultimate goal of a white nationalist state but that the mere presence of Christians within white nationalism will not weaken the movement. On the contrary, he thinks their presence would fragment Christians along racial lines and soften resistance within churches toward the white nationalist cause.

Johnson's hope, as articulated in "The Christian Question," is that white nationalist Christians will be significant allies who will perhaps bring racially unaware white Christians into agreement with the white nationalist cause so that they will eventually form part of the coming white republic. That being said, Johnson maintains that the white nationalist movement needs to remain a political movement that is set toward the goal of establishing a white homeland to ensure the survival of the white race, one that makes political decisions based on "secular reason" and not on religious dogma.

The way in which Johnson addresses religion demonstrates a specific recognition of the problem that Christianity poses for American white nationalists—a problem that in his opinion is not solved by outright rejection. In fact, he claims, overt rejection of Christianity may exacerbate the difficulties it presents. In this case, the anxieties of imperilment and the perceived need to preserve the white race via some holistic program that permeates the white nationalist milieu have produced a slightly different take on religion in general. A sense of expediency is now fashioning a sense of religious tolerance to bolster the political aspiration of white home rule in a Pan-European white ethnostate.

To further his intellectual and political agenda, Johnson took up various publishing and online projects. But the most concentrated and personal of these projects is the journal he started, which he clearly patterned after academic journals and is not dissimilar from *TYR*. The journal *North American New Right* certainly reflects Johnson's religious tolerance, eclecticism, and sense of political expediency. The first volume combines translations of works by Julius Evola, Guillaume Faye, and others, along with interviews with Alain de Benoist and Harold Covington, who is best known for the "Northwest quartet," a series of novels that tell the "fictional story of White Nationalists who consciously and deliberately set out to form an independent homeland for Whites in the American Northwest."[68] And perhaps most significantly, the journal's first volume contains a section of five articles dedicated to the memory of Francis Parker Yockey, thus tying it to the older white nationalist movement. In short, to define the newer white nationalism that NANR wants to represent, this first volume of *North American New Right* brings together some of the most influential voices in contemporary white nationalism with theorists from the ENR, Evola's esoteric thought, and the longer-lived and influential dream of a Pan-European imperium as articulated by Yockey.

In both the inclusive structure of *North American New Right* and how Johnson describes the NANR's project in the journal, there is a conscious effort to construct a platform for unity among white nationalists. In the introductory essay in volume 1, "Toward a North American New Right," Johnson affirms both a place for diverse opinions and an emphasis on the political solution to the "existential threat" to the white race. The

NANR, he argues, focuses on identity, which he qualifies as the "deep roots" of a "common European identity" that includes biological notions of race, history, and prehistory focusing on Indo-European development and contributions to civilization as well as "various diffusions . . . revealed by comparative linguistics and mythology." This imagined rootedness in a common heritage is, for him, a baseline for white nationalist identity from which all other opinions are derived. All other concerns, including those of religious preference, are negotiable. Although he personally sees the Traditionalism of Rene Guénon and Julius Evola as key elements to discuss in relation to this claim to an authentic and politically useful white identity, he still insists that the NANR is a "pluralistic movement" that seeks to bring commonality to bear in the prosecution of the metapolitical project at hand.[69]

Unlike what we have seen among racialist Odinists, esoteric racialist, Creators, Cosmotheists, and even racialist atheists such as Revilo Oliver and Tom Metzger, anti-Christianity is not the defining position of the North American New Right. Though some of those involved in the NANR have strong objections to even racialist Christianities, the NANR, according to Johnson, strives for accommodation of religious difference within white nationalism for the greater goal of white racial survival. We can say, then, that in the NANR the pragmatics of racial protectionism have created a space for tolerance, wherein the problem of Christianity in American white nationalism is dealt with via accommodation and not rejection.

White Nationalist Tolerance

Greg Johnson is hardly alone in wanting to make space for religious difference in contemporary white nationalism. A simple search of threads on the topic of white nationalism and religion on the website Stormfront reveals that a number of white nationalists agree that, in the words of Stormfront member folkabovedogma, "yes, you will find the atheist, the pagan and the agnostic amongst the adherents of WN [white nationalism], our common cause is the preservation of our Race."[70] Another Stormfront member, Some American, writes, "I don't care if people believe in the Flying Spaghetti Monster if they can manage to spin it to be pro-white."[71] And perhaps more directly addressing this accommodationist stance,

WhiteNationalist writes, "Whatever ism a WN [white nationalist] believes matters not. The key, in my opinion, is does the person put the survival of his race ahead of his religious belief?"[72] Another participant, Grey Fang, posted on this same topic, "Whatever religion we are, we all seek the same thing: the preservation of the white race."[73] For a growing number of white nationalists, the impulse to preserve the white race is motivating not simply either the acceptance or the rejection of Christianity but rather efforts to create unity among all racialists of various religious perspectives to realize the fulfillment of their primary obligation—racial protectionism.

Racialist Odinism, Creativity, and other white nationalist religions that define themselves as opposed to Christianity have not ceased to be important. Nonetheless, we can see in the posted comments on religion and the preservation of the white race that the NANR may be on the cutting edge of complex and still evolving responses by white nationalists to the problem of Christianity in American white nationalism. With the NANR, we have perhaps the most significant meeting point between the most intellectualized trends in white nationalism and European New Rightism and possibly the ideological vanguard of future transformations of racial nationalism in the United States. With the emergence of the Alt-Right during the election of 2016 in the United States and the prominent position held by Steve Bannon of the online news magazine *Breitbart* in the Trump administration, we will have to be observant to how white nationalist influences within the "Alt-Right" may shape policy positions within the administration and how the white nationalist movement's openly hostile attitudes toward conservatives may play a part in those positions. We should also be especially attentive to how white nationalism's evolving relationship with white Christians will shape political and religious discourses and even campaign strategies for the next four years and beyond.

As racial nationalists seek to have a broader appeal to white conservatives through strategic repackaging of their racialist ideology, mostly through anti-immigration, antimulticulturalism, and anti-Islamism, we can expect also a dual trajectory for American white nationalism. One the one hand, we can expect a transformation of the public face of white nationalism for the sake of political expediency. On the other, we can expect a private holding of the line in regard to racial protectionism, which is still ill at ease with some aspects of the American conservative mainstream and American Christianity. As a number of white nationalists continue to be concerned about Christianity's place in their efforts to secure a future for the white race and even establish a white homeland in North America, it is clear that the reference to the Religious Right in America now encompasses much more in the American experience than we previously thought.

Conclusion

Making White Nationalism Familiar

In an interview in 1940, Henri Bergson claimed that the events Hitler put in motion had confirmed his thesis in *The Two Sources*.[1] By the time he gave this interview, the Third Reich had become Bergson's paradigmatic example of all that he had written in the early 1930s. It was inarguably a society organized for war, concerned only for self-defense and racial nationalist advancement, and obsessed with purging its internal enemies, with all of these elements situated in the construction of a restrictive social identity that relied on the fiction of Aryan specificity and superiority. But far from simply regarding Nazi Germany as an expression of either aberrant racism or illogical romanticism, Bergson thought that it was the best and perhaps the purest example of the tendency inherent in any closed nationalist social structure.

In Bergson's view, the genocidal ethnocentricity that the Third Reich demonstrated was a part, at least latently if not overtly, of all nationalisms in that they all are expressions of closed societies to some degree. For him, the xenophobia and violence of Nazism might be the dark destiny of any closed society, even ones that regard themselves as relatively democratic. Societies easily go in this violent direction when they adhere too closely to mythologies of exclusivity and exceptionalism and, out of this adherence, aggressively police borders, become fixated on self-defense, and command obedience to defend the imagined national community against equally imaginary alien others at all cost. That is to say, for Bergson, Nazism was proof of what he had tried to demonstrate in *The Two Sources*: that all closed societies are potentially genocidal.

Nazism is further instructive in the arena of religion as well. Religion in the Third Reich was complex, more so than even Bergson himself recognized. It was certainly much more complicated than some commentators would have us believe when describing the Reich as predominantly anti-Christian and "pagan." As Uriel Tal, Doris Bergen, and more recently Susannah Heschel have demonstrated,[2] Aryan paganism was far from the only religious influence or even the most significant one in Nazi Germany. Christian anti-Semitism, especially as expressed in the Glaubensbewegung Deutsche Christen (German Christian Movement), was deeply implicated in the popular expression of religious ideology in Nazi Germany. In contrast, members of the Bekennende Kirche (Confessing Church) actively resisted the Aryanizing of Jesus and the de-Judaizing of Christianity propagated by the virulently anti-Semitic German Christians. In addition, there was significant strain between the German Christians and those who wanted to retrieve a pre-Christian and supposedly more authentically German spiritual and esoteric Aryan past. Just as we saw in more recent discussions concerning religion in American white nationalism, caution was exercised in criticizing Christianity under the Third Reich.

Uriel Tal, for example, mentions that although Heinrich Himmler and his Schutzstaffel (Protection Squadron) were deeply invested in developing "a clearly defined historical consciousness" that employed notions of the pre-Christian German past in terms of myth and history, they nevertheless had to moderate their outspokenness on the subject.[3] Religious differences between Christian and non-Christian party members was not to be allowed to distract from the broader political mission of the preservation of the Aryan Volk in the German state. Religion of any kind could be tolerated insofar only as it supported the program of Aryan racial survival and advancement, which was after all the goal of the Third Reich's closed racial society.

This should bring to mind the debates about religion I have explored in contemporary white nationalism in this book. There is certainly much that the Third Reich and contemporary white nationalism do not share, but they do share similar internal debates about the place of Christianity in the larger project of protecting whoever is imagined to be situated within the imagined racial community. In that regard, we can see clearly that religion in both instances is a significant site of contest and political strategy to the end of preserving the closed racial society. Individual commitment is of course important, but that individuality is always related to an individual's choice to be a functional and "good" member of the imagined community. It is crucially important, therefore, to understand that the closed society requires and enacts the construction of a certain kind of individual who properly believes himself to be a part of the grand project of communal protection and to be morally good in believing that.

The point is that in the paradigm of nationalism, especially in the case of Nazi Germany, Bergson's paradigmatic closed society, and in American white nationalism all interests are subordinated to the primary ethical demand of communal self-defense. As we have seen, religious preferences and commitments can strain that obligation and thereby present a challenge to the project of protectionism, especially if those religious traditions are imagined to teach universal solidarity beyond the immediate communal group. When that happens, potentially disruptive religiosities are either cast as alien and dangerous ideologies or somehow subordinated to or subsumed within the larger demands of the racial protectionist project. This is why Christianity is a problem for American white nationalism. Where it makes demands seemingly contrary to racial protectionism, it must be rejected. Where it is regarded as having been "Europeanized," it may be accepted. Where it is too Jewish or modern, it may be reformed. Where it is seen as entrenched in European and American cultures, it must be managed. The problem of Christianity is thus multivalent. But the racial protectionist logic inherent in American white nationalism has nevertheless made Christianity a problem for that nationalism.

"How about You?" The Obligation One Feels

In this book, I have tried to answer one basic question: Why have a significant number of white nationalists in America seen Christianity as a problem? As noted time and again, Christianity is a problem because it in some ways presents a threat to the imagined white racial community. This answer is of course adapted from Benedict Anderson's classic study on nationalism, *Imagined Communities*, but more fundamentally it is adapted from Bergson's description of the closed society and what that means in terms of the "force" of moral obligation placed upon the individual to defend the white race.[4]

Anthony Parel elucidates this basic Bergsonian point in positing three "headings" under which we may situate the "content of social obligation" that Bergson describes in *The Two Sources*: the preservation and survival of one's group; "hostility toward other groups and loyalty to one's hostility toward others [as] an integral part of the love of one's own [group]"; and "the desire for the expansion of one's group through domination and imperialism, violence and war."[5] By way of example, we can look at a selection from an article titled "Why We Hate," posted on White Aryan Resistance's website, resist.com: "I will not apologize for wanting to protect my race from the rest of the world or from our enemies. I will continue to love those that deserve it, and I will continue to hate those that deserve it, and no amount of legislation by my enemies can ever stop me, or my race from doing so."[6] For white nationalists, the highest form of love is connected to hatred of anything that threatens the imagined racial community. The one cannot be separated from the other. Love in this case justifies hate. The desire to preserve leads to the desire to eradicate. In white nationalism, they are the twin elements that animate the movement.

Because white nationalism is a variant of ethnonationalism, the conclusions arrived at here should go beyond the question of Christianity in American white nationalism to shed light on the social dimensions of racisms in other contexts. In this sense, racism is more than the irrational hatred of a sexually repressed or resentful failed subject. In the various forms of ethnonationalism and particularly in American white nationalism, racism is an expression of *amor patriae*. This definition then presents us with an all too human puzzle: How do we reconcile love and hate in something such as white nationalism? As Bergson remarks near the end of *The Two Sources*, "Let us only say that the two opposing maxims, *Homo homini deus* [man is a god to man] and *Homo homini lupus* [man is a wolf to man], are easily reconcilable. . . . When we formulate the first, we are thinking of some fellow countrymen. The other applies to foreigners."[7]

Final Remarks

The final chapter on American white nationalism and religion is far from having been written. Some points are nevertheless worthy of note by way of conclusion. As I discussed in chapter 6, there is a strong pragmatist move among some white nationalist organizations to attract broader attention from white Americans. Regarding Christianity, one might say that the racial protectionist imperative in white nationalism may yet produce a broad religious tolerance similar to what we saw from the Stormfront blog posts quoted in chapter 6, claiming that they do not care what religions other white people follow as long as white people are pro-white and work to preserve the white race. This change indicates a change in political strategy as well. As the initial rejection of Christianity by Revilo Oliver, William Pierce, and Ben Klassen paralleled their withdrawal from conservative politics, so religious toleration among the newer white nationalists, aimed mainly at reconciling white nationalism with Christianity, signals renewed interest in participation in American conservativism. With the rise of the Alt-Right to public awareness, we are witnessing an effort by American white nationalists to appeal to the conservative mainstream, particularly on the issues of immigration and multiculturalism. Like everything else I have discussed concerning American white nationalism, this shift did not happen in a vacuum.

Even before Donald Trump became infamous for attracting the likes of David Duke to support his bid for the presidency and found himself embroiled in scandals for retweeting white nationalist memes and quotes from Mussolini, white racist activists have been seeking reentry into right-wing politics. The Conservative Political Action Convention (CPAC), the most widely attended meeting of American conservatives, has in recent years made room for white nationalists, wittingly or not. At the meeting in 2012, a panel titled "The Failure of Multiculturalism: How the Pursuit of Diversity Is Weakening American Identity" featured the likes of John Derbyshire and Peter Brimelow.[8] Derbyshire, known for his controversial views on race, was let go by *National Review* after publishing deeply racist remarks in an online magazine in 2012.[9] He now writes independently, but he has most significantly become quite close to the white nationalist website V-Dare.[10]

Peter Brimelow established V-Dare, which was named for Virginia Dare, "the first English child to be born in the New World, in August 1587," specifically to provide a voice for those who wish to battle "multiculturalism."[11] Brimelow is also the author of *Alien Nation: Common Sense about America's Immigration Disaster*, the central thesis of which is that the "racial and ethnic balance of America is being radically altered through public policy" and that this bodes ill for American society.[12] That Derbyshire and Brimelow had an entire panel to present their views to attendees at CPAC should be reason enough for attention to how immigration policy and the specter of "multiculturalism" in particular can be a rhetorical and ideological point of access for white nationalist ideologues to appeal to the conservative political mainstream. The subtext of racist anxiety in such discourses is more than enough to offer rhetorically skillful white nationalists entrée into what is an increasingly reactionary American political Right.

At the CPAC meeting in 2014, the NPI was present to appeal to white America. Though Senator Ted Cruz said of Richard Spencer, director of the white nationalist think tank NPI and the person credited with coining the name "Alt-Right," that Spencer was simply "using white angst" for his own "career advancement," Spencer himself was confident that many at CPAC were supportive of his ideas and the aims of his organization.[13] In light of the recent election, we have to consider that Spencer was not far from the mark. Senator Cruz was in a certain sense correct, even if he seemed to be interested in explaining away the presence of white nationalists at CPAC. White angst is exactly what white nationalists depend on to make their ideas resonant at CPAC and elsewhere in conservative politics.

Notwithstanding the efforts by many in the conservative mainstream to distance themselves from the "extremists," there is little daylight between their positions on immigration and multiculturalism and the position held by the white nationalists in the Alt-Right. Again, even before Trump's electoral victory, the revelation that Republican House Majority Whip Steve Scalise spoke at a white nationalist meeting in 2002 made it clear that it is far more than simple conjecture to say that some connections exist between the new white nationalism in America and the established Right.[14]

Of course, it is far too simple to suggest absolute collusion between large numbers of conservatives and white nationalist leadership. The point I want to make is more subtle. White nationalists, especially those who associate themselves with the Alt-Right, are seeking points of overlap between their ideation and the talking points and political strategies of the mainstream conservative movement. Key among these points are immigration, especially now with the politicization of the Syrian refugee crisis; anxieties over multiculturalism's perceived (and often hoped for) failure; and more recently the often violent backlashes against the Black Lives Matter movement. Moreover, Trump's comments about Mexicans and Muslims during the presidential campaign and his generally virulent bellicosity, which of course drew support from David Duke, various white nationalist organizations, and the Alt-Right, signal the acceptance of such ideology and rhetoric among a certain segment of the mainstream voting public.

Such overlap of support for Trump's ideas between a large portion of the American public and white nationalists should signal the importance of studying the internal logics of white nationalism. Although it is true, as Michael Barkun argues, that the respectability of any given system of thought should neither qualify nor disqualify it for study,[15] American white nationalists' efforts to access the political mainstream through popular racialized discourses on multiculturalism and immigration may point to the importance of studying the racist Right as more than an outlier in American public life. Certainly in the wake of the shootings committed by the self-confessed white nationalist Dylann Roof at the historic Emanuel African Methodist Episcopal Church in Charleston, South Carolina, in the summer of 2014, we must realize we do not live in a world in which the "extremist" is unimportant.

Finally, I want to state that continued study of these kinds of protectionist logics is warranted as the complex relationship between race and religion continues to be a source of debate in many contexts. In an era of increased border control of human migration, we cannot afford to discount the power of European identity politics both to shape and to take advantage of demographic anxiety and fear. The recent Syrian crisis, for example, has displaced many thousands of people and made Europeans and North Americans take stock of their own sense of nationalism. Widespread Islamophobia in Western nations such as Germany, France, and the United States presents what promises to be continued debate over what those nations' verbalized commitment to tolerance actually means. In addition, the continued statelessness of Rohingya Muslims in western Myanmar on the grounds of protecting the nation's Buddhist demographic superiority and religious integrity presents a modern case of regional ethnic cleansing and possible genocide where religion is deeply implicated. More generally, xenophobia has proven to be continually effective in political campaigns in modern liberal countries where state resources are shrinking under austerity and jobs have become scarce. All of this of course demonstrates the need for just the kind of inquiry that I have tried to engage in here. To ignore the logic of the so-called extremists is not only foolish but also neglectful of the fact that extremism can easily become the norm if we are not vigilant in valuing human lives beyond our own closed notions of society.

Epilogue

The "Alt-Right," Trumpian Populism,
and White Religious America

On Saturday, November 19, 2016, the National Policy Institute held a conference at the Ronald Reagan Pavilion on Pennsylvania Avenue in Washington, DC, to discuss the electoral victory of Donald Trump and to celebrate the influence that the Alt-Right had during the campaign as well as the increased interest and membership in the movement in part because of that influence.[1] The conference was titled "Become What We Are," and it included, besides Richard Spencer, such speakers as Kevin MacDonald and Peter Brimelow, among others from the less-well-known Alt-Right and white nationalist community. Media attention to this event was assured, in part because of the steady stream of stories describing Spencer, the man credited with coining the name "Alt-Right," and Stephen Bannon of the online news magazine *Breitbart*, which he calls the platform for the Alt-Right.[2] Bannon, of course, was the latest strategist to come to the Trump campaign and at the time of the conference had just recently been appointed as senior policy adviser to the incoming president.

At this event, the public's suspicions that the Alt-Right simply was simply a bunch of neo-Nazis appeared to be resoundingly confirmed. At the conclusion of his talk before the audience, Spencer proclaimed, "Hail Trump! Hail our people! Hail victory!"—at which time some in attendance stood and repeated his sentiment while giving the "Roman Salute," better known as the Nazi Salute.[3]

What is less well known and publicized is the controversy that this incident caused among Spencer's fellow Alt-Rightists. Paul Ramsey, also known by his Twitter handle "RAMZPAUL," a very significant advocate of the Alt-Right and white identity politics, decried the use of the Roman Salute and the vocal presence of white nationalists in the Alt-Right, saying in particular that Spencer himself had damaged the "Alt-Right brand."[4] Even Greg Johnson referred to the incident as a "public relations disaster."[5] In his Twitter video post, Ramsey even questioned the further use of the name "Alt-Right" to continue opposition to globalism, antinationalism, and open borders, especially considering that the Alt-Right's man, Trump, had been elected to office. Responses from within the community to Ramsey's tweet varied between full support and absolute derision wherein some of his Twitter respondents accused him of turning his back on the movement and even of having abandoned his defense of the white race.

But the movement had somewhat complicated beginnings. The term *alternative Right* has its origins in the writings and speeches of a Jewish intellectual and political philosopher who is credited with inventing the term *paleoconservative* in the 1980s and indeed gave it much of its meaning: Paul Gottfried. Gottfried began to describe this new alternative within the nonestablishment Right in 2008 as a movement of the youth who were doing what the rightists of the previous generation were never able to: overcome the neoconservative establishment of the Republican Party to establish conservativism in their own image.

Gottfried first used the term *alternative Right* in this sense in a talk he delivered before the H. L. Mencken Club in the very year the club was founded, 2008, in part by Gottfried himself. A transcript of the talk was published in *Taki's Magazine*, an online news and opinion medium for the alternative Right.[6] It should be noted that at the time Spencer, who was also scheduled to speak at this event, was described as a managing editor for *Taki's Magazine*. Also scheduled to talk were Peter Brimelow, John Derbyshire, and other academics—namely, the coauthor of *The Bell Curve*, Charles Murray; James Madison University professor emeritus Lee Cogdon; and James Kurth, the Claude Smith Professor of Political Science at Swarthmore College—all of whom were in attendance to discuss the meeting's theme, "the egalitarian temptation."[7]

Gottfried opened his talk with a description of the Mencken Club's efforts to put together a movement of the "independent intellectual Right" and to do so apart from "establishment funding." Significantly, he noted that the movement had attracted young people, whom he hoped would become the leaders of the independent Right in the near future. Referencing *Taki's Magazine* and the website V-Dare, he pointed to the generation of "postpaleos" who would come to form the alternative Right on the web.

Gottfried typified the alternative Right as a youth movement emergent from the paleoconservatives with a significant presence on the Internet. He also described it as carrying forward the standards of the paleos of Gottfried's generation—antiliberalism and antiestablishment attitudes toward conservatives. But I should note that although Gottfried was indeed harsh in his criticism of equality, feminism, and open borders, he was directly aiming the youthful alternative Right revolutionaries' ambitions squarely at the neoconservative establishment itself. He envisioned the alternative Right as young, computer savvy, focused on antiegalitarianism, and taking on the moneyed conservative establishment, who are called "cuckservatives" in the alternative Right movement.

In 2009, Gottfried once again addressed the alternative Right in an article published in *Taki's Magazine*, where once again he praised the young people who had come to form the vanguard of the "non-authorized Right" and to continue the fight against mainstream conservatives as they "stand outside of," as Gottfried put it, "the egalitarian, managerial-state consensus," a stance that had only led conservatives further to the left.[8] Gottfried's main target beyond social liberalism in general was the conservative mainstream itself. The so-called Alt-Right had its naissance in this milieu, and its grandfather is in fact Gottfried and his associates in the Menken Club. These discussions were the point of origin for the Alt-Right, but changes were afoot that would make it more closely associated with Spencer and white nationalism.

In 2010, Spencer founded the website Alternative Right (www.alter native-right.blogspot.com). On this site, one can read articles by figures familiar from *Counter-Currents* and other New Right venues as well as commentary by Ramsey and other Alt-Right figures. More importantly, the website was the fulfillment of Gottfried's vision expressed two years earlier:

a web-based youth movement taking on the establishment. Even though there is new controversy over Spencer's speech at the NPI in Washington, DC, in November 2016, he is viewed as one of the most significant leaders of the movement.

The Alt-Right's other outlets, in particular the online news magazine *Breitbart*, have been as influential in sharing and popularizing the movement's agenda. But *Breitbart*'s presentation of the Alt-Right has made evident some differences within the movement exactly around the issue of white nationalists under the larger umbrella "Alt-Right." Notably, in an article for *Breitbart* titled "A Conservative's Guide to the Alt-Right" in March 2016, Allum Bokhari and Milo Yiannopoulos point to several distinctions between the different kinds of groups that make up the movement: anti-free-market and antiglobalization conservatives, or what they call "Natural" or "cultural" conservatives; white identity activists; men's rights advocates, which is to say antifeminists; so-called race realists; disaffected libertarians; self-described "radical free speech advocates"; as well as overtly neo-Nazi and white nationalist elements within the Alt-Right, whom Bokhari and Yiannopoulos call "14/88ers" (a reference to David Lane's "14 Words," the eighty-eight precepts of white nationalism, and the number 88's connection to the acronym HH, "Heil Hitler"—all used to self-signify in white nationalist communities).[9]

Bokhari and Yiannopoulos present the movement as more diverse than being simply white nationalist, but critics on one side have described such a position as simply a white washing of the racism in the movement, and critics on the other side have condemned it as a betrayal of the movement. It should be noted that the *Daily Stormer*, a strongly neo-Nazi periodical, described Bokhari as a "half-Paki" and Yiannopoulos as a "half-Jew" and a "Homosexualist [sic]," in clear disapproval of their inclusion in the conversation, and ascribed the origin of the name "14/88er" to Paul Ramsey, arguing that the point of the name is to insult "white activists who talk about Jews."[10] Also, as I mentioned earlier, Greg Johnson wrote a piece in *Counter-Currents* in August 2016 in which he claimed that "the Alternative Right means White Nationalism—or it means nothing at all." And in recounting the very lineage of the term *alternative Right*, he stated that Spencer founded the website Alternative Right "simply as a vehicle for

White Nationalist entryism," and the principle funders and writers of the project "would have blown it up rather than see it become anything else."[11] For Johnson, the whole point of the Alt-Right is to become the vehicle for moving white nationalism into the political mainstream in spite of those who may wish it would not be moved there.

In this sense, the Alt-Right as it exists today is relatively ill at ease with itself and perhaps struggling to find a clear identity as we enter what proponents and detractors alike have called "Trump's America." Nevertheless, the racism so common in the movement cannot be papered over with a discussion of its diversity. The best advice so far for thinking through this issue has come from John Daniszewski, the Associated Press vice president for standards, who writes that when using the name "Alt-Right" in a story, authors should include a definition that clarifies that the Alt-Right is "'an offshoot of conservatism mixing racism, white nationalism and populism,' or, more simply, 'a white nationalist movement.'" He further explains that writers who discuss the movement should offer sound evidence for their characterizations of the Alt-Right and should not simply allow the Alt-Right to "define themselves" but rather focus on reporting "their actions, associations, history and positions to reveal their actual beliefs and philosophy, as well as how others see them."[12]

This very dilemma is one that I have wrestled with throughout this project: How does one define these individuals and their communities in such a way that neither simplistically reduces their impact or significance nor whitewashes their racist discourse? In addition, I continue to think about how we should look at different forms of racist discourse and describe them without relying too much on terms such as *white supremacist, Nazi,* and *extremist,* which may distract us from the damage that less-obvious forms of racism can cause. This last point seems of paramount significance as we move into whatever awaits us in the next four years.

Trump's electoral victory was cheered by nationalists from around the world, including France's National Front and Germany's overtly anti-Muslim Alternative für Deutschland (Alternative for Germany) Party.[13] Hindu nationalists, too, felt a particular sort of pride in Trump's victory, some of them even praising candidate Trump as the only person capable of saving humanity from Islam because of his strong stance on Muslim immigration and the need to create a Muslim registry.[14] The reason for such widespread support from the global Far Right is of course what drew support for Trump from David Duke, Jared Taylor, and those associated with the Alt-Right in the first place—his anti-immigration and antiglobalization rhetoric and his very strongly racialized and bigoted language about Mexicans and Muslims. What is perhaps of concern, too, especially for students of American religious history, is that white Evangelicals flocked to the polls for Trump for very similar reasons.

According to the Pew Research Center, white Evangelical voters voted for Trump (81 percent) by a larger margin that they did for George W. Bush in 2004 (78 percent), John McCain in 2008 (74 percent), and Mitt Romney in 2012 (78 percent). According to the same survey, white Catholics voted for Trump in slightly higher numbers as well, as did a majority of Mormons in spite of their stated concerns about his personal life.[15] Postelection studies from the Public Religion Research Institute (PRRI) seem to confirm the Pew findings: white Christians voted heavily for Trump and did not disqualify his personal failings, multiple marriages, lack of transparency about his business and tax dealings, lewd language, or multiple accusations of sexual assault that threatened to confirm that he did in fact grope women without consent, as he bragged in the infamous leaked audio.[16]

There are, of course, a number of variables to consider when quantifying voting patterns among any group. And, of course, there is little space here to embark on a full explanation. But a postelection survey conducted by PRRI and the *Atlantic* in December 2016 demonstrated that party affiliation and race were big factors, as was the fact that white Evangelicals are largely Republican voters. But what is more, the survey indicated that the majority of white Americans looked at this election as an opportunity to stave off what they considered to be America's decline. With respect to immigration, the survey found that "Whites (54%) are considerably more likely than Hispanics (40%) and blacks (28%) to believe Trump's position on immigration was a boon to his campaign."[17] In another report by the PRRI issued before the election, we learn that 56 percent of white Americans said American society had changed for the worse since the 1950s and that 74 percent of white Evangelical Protestants agreed.[18]

In *The End of White Christian America*, released a few months before the election, Robert P. Jones, CEO of the PRRI, wrote that white Evangelical Christians find themselves in the position of "having lost much cultural power while still retaining—at least in the southern enclaves—the remnants of significant political clout."[19] Such a statement resonates strongly after the election, considering the nostalgia that many white Americans, especially white Evangelicals, expressed in the PRRI surveys. Indeed, this is why Jones describes white Evangelicals not as values voters, but as nostalgia voters. In an interview by Jennifer Rubin published in the *Washington Post* on November 17, 2016, Jones expressed a measure of surprise about how thorough the conversion from values voters to nostalgia voters actually was. He explained further in the interview that white Evangelicals' support for Trump had "completely upended their political ethics" in that just five years earlier only 30 percent of them had claimed that "a public official who commits immoral acts in their private life could still fulfill their public duties ethically," whereas in 2016, "with Trump at the top of the ticket, 72% of white evangelicals [*sic*] agree that this bifurcation is possible."[20]

These results should be read as evidence that white Evangelicals are animated by other issues and not just by their moral convictions and that some of those issues intersect with the reasons why members of the Alt-Right saw Trump as their candidate. These findings also perhaps point to the susceptibility of white Americans, white Evangelicals in particular, to Far Right ideology expressed by the Alt-Right and white nationalists such as Brimelow. As demographics continue to trend toward the decline of the white majority in the United States, a demographic decline of white Evangelicals in particular, we may see the increasing appeal of protectionist rhetoric as a radicalizing element for some white Americans, Christian and non-Christian alike.

I hasten to add that those who would oppose the kinds of policies proposed by President Trump, which won him support from the Far Right, including white nationalists, should be aware that the winds of history are not necessarily at their back. Even now, the new generation of white nationalists has taken aim at university campuses to influence a new generation of would-be racial activists. For example, the group Identity Europa, a white nationalist youth organization with deep ties to Spencer and the NPI, has begun an initiative called Project Siege in which their activists post stickers and posters on college campuses and speak with students.[21]

Such organizations are trying to recruit the next generation of white nationalists. But perhaps more immediately our concern should be the incredible jump in reports of hate crimes and harassment after the election. Even as it seems that Trump is stocking his cabinet with Wall Street insiders who will no doubt push policies that will harm the very white working-class voters who trusted he would protect them from the ravages of global capitalism, people of color, Muslims, LGBTQI (lesbian, gay, bisexual, transgender, queer, and intersex) citizens have been harassed and assaulted and had their residences and vehicles vandalized. We should keep in mind that, as Thomas Frank writes in *What's the Matter with Kansas*, the white working class's resentment has found its expression in a "backlash conservativism" that does not hold the forces of capitalism in check but is advantageous to certain political ends.[22] If the economic policies of the new administration do indeed end up hurting the white working class that voted Trump into office, we should not expect the administration to automatically receive the blame. Rather, we should expect scapegoating, so the most vulnerable among us will have to face even further hardship and violence. The same accusatory politics that brought Trump to electoral victory will be mobilized to keep him from accountability.

Those who would oppose racism and religious bigotry will have a tough task in confronting the policies of the new administration and the popular sentiments around and within it. Those who regard themselves as progressives and those who want an equal, open, and tolerant society are going to have to be smart, attentive, and responsive. A society based on those values is not guaranteed to us. It never was. We are going to have to construct it. In the final account, doing so is up to us, we the people.

Notes

Bibliography

Index

Notes

Introduction

1. Kelly Baker, *Gospel according to the Klan: The KKK's Appeal to Protestant America, 1915–1930* (Lawrence: Univ. Press of Kansas, 2011).

2. Michael Barkun, *Religion and the Racist Right: The Origins of the Christian Identity Movement*, rev. ed. (Chapel Hill: Univ. of North Carolina Press, 1997).

3. Betty Dobratz, "The Role of Religion in the Collective Identity of the White Racialist Movement," *Journal for the Scientific Study of Religion* 40, no. 2 (2001): 299.

4. See, for example, Matthias Gardell, *Gods of the Blood: The Pagan Revival and White Separatism* (Durham, NC: Duke Univ. Press, 2003); Nicholas Goodrick-Clarke, *Black Sun: Aryan Cults, Esoteric Nazism, and the Politics of Identity* (New York: New York Univ. Press, 2003); and George Michael, *Theology of Hate: A History of the World Church of the Creator* (Gainesville: Univ. of Florida Press, 2009).

5. Barkun, *Religion and the Racist Right*, xiii.

6. Michael O'Meara, "Toward the White Republic," in *Toward the White Republic, and Other Essays*, ed. Greg Johnson (San Francisco: Counter-Currents, 2010), 1.

7. Ibid., 3.

8. Carol Swain, *The New White Nationalism in America: Its Challenge to Integration* (New York: Cambridge Univ. Press, 2002), 1.

9. Ibid., 3, 16–17.

10. Jeffery Kaplan and Leonard Weinberg, *The Emergence of a Euro-American Right* (New Brunswick, NJ: Rutgers Univ. Press, 1998), 23.

11. The quote "rising tide of color" is from Lothrop Stoddard's infamous work on race titled *The Rising Tide of Colour against White World-Supremacy* (New York: Scribner's, 1920). The book that his mentor, Madison Grant, wrote, *The Passing of the Great Race, or The Racial Basis of European History* (1916; reprint, New York: Scribner's, 1936), was influential because Adolf Hitler wrote to Grant to express his admiration for the book, stating, "Your book is my Bible" (quoted in Jonathan Spiro, *Defending the Master Race: Conservation, Eugenics, and the Legacy of Madison Grant* [Burlington: Univ. of Vermont Press, 2008], 357).

12. Kaplan and Weinberg, *Emergence of a Euro-American Right*, 105.

13. Ibid.

14. Ibid., 106.

15. Francis Parker Yockey, *Imperium: The Philosophy of History and Politics* (1948; reprint, Costa Mesa, CA: Noontide Press, 1991), xlvii, 63–64.

16. Ibid., 619.

17. Ibid., 616, emphasis in original.

18. Ibid., 591, 595.

19. Ibid., 595.

20. Ibid., 594–95.

21. Pete Simi and Robert Futrell, *American Swastika: Inside the White Power Movement's Hidden Spaces of Hate* (Lanham, MD: Rowman and Littlefield, 2010), 17.

22. James Aho, *This Thing of Darkness: A Sociology of the Enemy* (Seattle: Univ. of Washington Press, 1994), 69.

23. Bruce Lincoln, *Discourse and the Construction of Society: Comparative Studies of Myth, Ritual, and Classification* (New York: Oxford Univ. Press, 1989), 25.

24. Ibid., 53.

25. Benedict Anderson, *Imagined Communities: Reflections on the Origins and Spread of Nationalism*, rev. ed. (New York: Verso, 1991), 6–7.

26. Henry Bergson, *Two Sources of Morality and Religion*, trans. Ashley Audra and Cloudesley Brereton, with W. Horsfall Carter (Garden City, NY: Doubleday Anchor Books, 1935), 15.

27. Alexandre Lefebvre and Melanie White, "Introduction: Bergson, Politics, and Religion," in *Bergson, Politics, and Religion*, ed. Alexandre Lefebvre and Melanie White (Durham, NC: Duke Univ. Press, 2012), 3.

28. Gilles Deleuze, *Bergsonism*, trans. Hugh Tomlinson and Barbara Habberjam (1966; reprint, Brooklyn, NY: Zone Books, 1990); Gilles Deleuze and Félix Guattari, *Anti-Oedipus: Capitalism and Schizophrenia*, trans. Robert Hurley, 1972, new ed. (New York: Penguin Classics, 2009), and *Thousand Plateaus: Capitalism and Schizophrenia*, trans. Brian Massumi (1980; reprint, New York: Continuum, 2002).

29. Lefebvre and White, "Introduction," 1, 3, 5, emphasis in original.

30. Philippe Soulez, "Bergson as Philosopher of War and Theorist of the Political," trans. Melissa McMahon, in *Bergson, Politics, and Religion*, ed. Lefebvre and White, 110.

31. Bergson, *Two Sources*, 266–77.

32. Greg Johnson, "Toward a North American New Right," *North American New Right* 1 (2012): 1.

1. Revilo Oliver and the Emerging Racialist Critique of Christianity

1. Oliver provides this information in his autobiographical note in *The Jewish Strategy* (Earlysville, VA: Kevin Alfred Strom, 2002), v, but George Michael gives 1911 as Oliver's

birth date in *Willis Carto and the American Far Right* (Gainesville: Univ. of Florida Press, 2008), 97.

2. Oliver, *The Jewish Strategy*, v, vi.

3. Carl T. Bogus, *William F. Buckley Jr. and the Rise of the American Conservative Movement* (New York: Bloomsbury, 2011), 183–84.

4. Barbra A. Stone, "A Profile of the John Birch Society," *Journal of Politics* 36, no. 1 (1974): 191.

5. Robert Welch, *The Blue Book of the John Birch Society*, 8th printing (Belmont, MA: John Birch Society, 1961), 39.

6. Oliver's testimony before the Warren Commission regarding the Kennedy assassination is, of course, a matter of public record, but it is also discussed in J. Allen Broyels, *The John Birch Society: Anatomy of a Protest* (Boston: Beacon Press, 1964), 33–34, and is given in full on a website established in Oliver's honor: see Revilo P. Oliver, "The Testimony of Professor Revilo Pendleton Oliver before the Warren Commission," Sept. 9, 1964, at http://www.revilo-oliver.com/rpo/Warren_Commission_Testimony.html.

7. Robert Welch, *The Neutralizers* (Belmont, MA: John Birch Society, 1963), 5.

8. Ibid., 15–16.

9. Seymour Martin Lipset and Earl Raab, *The Politics of Unreason: Right Wing Extremism in America from 1790–1977*, 2nd ed. (Chicago: Univ. of Chicago Press, 1978), 266.

10. Oliver, *The Jewish Strategy*, viii.

11. Ibid.

12. Martin Durham, *White Rage: The Extreme Right and American Politics* (New York: Routledge, 2007), 116.

13. Revilo P. Oliver, *America's Decline: The Education of a Conservative* (London: Londinium Press, 1981), and *Against the Grain: The Writings of Professor Revilo Pendleton Oliver* (York, SC: Liberty Bell, 1995).

14. For quotations from "After Fifty Years," I use Revilo P. Oliver, *After Fifty Years*, advance offprint (Washington, DC: National Youth Alliance, 1970); this offprint is unpaginated, so the page numbers I cite represent my count of pages. In this version, the National Youth Alliance notes Oliver's interest in the organization and offers that as the reason for its distribution of the article in advance of the talk. The film of his talk can be easily viewed at https://www.youtube.com/watch?v=oQoH6KOvBGA. Reproductions of the article are also available on white nationalist websites, including http://www.revilo-oliver.com/news/1969/09/after-fifty-years/.

15. Oliver, *After Fifty Years*, 1, 2.

16. Ibid., 2, emphasis in original.

17. Ibid.

18. Ibid., 4.

19. Revilo Oliver, "America after the Holy War," in *America's Decline*, 107.

20. Oliver, *After Fifty Years*, 4.

21. Pierre-André Taguieff, "Origines et métamorphoses de la Nouvelle Droite," *Vingtième Siècle: Revue d'histoire*, no. 40 (Oct.–Dec. 1993): 3.

22. Alain de Benoist to Revilo Oliver, June 15, 1970, at http://www.revilo-oliver.com /papers/De%20Benoist,%20Alain/19700615_from_DeBenoist.jpg. The letters referenced in this chapter have since been removed from Kevin Alfred Strom's website recording Oliver's correspondence, but they can be accessed through the Internet Archive at http://archive .org/web/. This letter introduces Benoist to Oliver as the man behind the pen name for his "political studies," under which, he states, he had sent Oliver materials before this time. This clarification, of course, pushes the date of initial contact, though it may have been unidirectional at first, between the French New Right and American rightists to a time near the formation of Groupement de recherche. This letter also demonstrates Benoist's overtures to establish an alliance, as he states clearly in the letter, "In . . . general point of view, we are very [close] to what is expressed in the American-review, WESTERN DESTINY, published some years ago by Noontide Press," the publisher of *Imperium* in the United States.

23. Revilo Oliver to Alain de Benoist, April 6, 1971, at http://www.revilo-oliver.com /papers/De%20Benoist,%20Alain/19710406_to_DeBenoist_page1.jpg.

24. Robert S. Griffin, *Fame of a Dead Man's Deeds: An Up-close Portrait of White Nationalist William Pierce* (Bloomington, IN: 1st Books, 2001), 142–43, 143–44. Most sources list *The Franklin Letters* as written anonymously because its authorship cannot be confirmed. Griffin records that Pierce told him that though he believed Oliver wrote the book, Oliver never confirmed it. Griffin himself seems more convinced of Oliver's authorship of the book.

25. Ibid., 162.

26. Revilo P. Oliver, "Aftermath," in *America's Decline*, 333, 334, 337.

27. Ibid., 338, 339.

28. Revilo P. Oliver, "*Which Way Western Man*, a Book Review," in *Against the Grain*, 153.

29. Will Herberg, *Protestant, Catholic, Jew: An Essay on American Religious Sociology* (1955; reprint, Garden City, NY: Doubleday, 1956), 27, 38–39, 263.

30. Mark Silk, "Notes on the Judeo-Christian Tradition in America," *American Quarterly* 36, no. 1 (1984): 65–66.

31. Ibid., 69.

32. Quoted in ibid., 65.

33. Ibid., 70.

34. Revilo Oliver to Alain de Benoist, May 14, 1975, at http://www.revilo-oliver.com /papers/De%20Benoist,%20Alain/19750514_to_DeBenoist.jpg.

35. Wilmot Robertson, *The Dispossessed Majority* (1966; reprint, Cape Canaveral, FL: Howard Allen Enterprises, 1972), xxi. This work was originally published in 1966 and presents many of the statements from Oliver about the peril of civilization due to the supposed unreason of racial integration and liberalization.

36. Revilo P. Oliver, "Superstitious Materialism," *National Review*, Mar. 15, 1958, 258–59. This article was also significant enough that Oliver chose to include it in *America's Decline*, 122–24.

37. Ibid., 258, 259.

38. Ibid.

39. Revilo P. Oliver, "Christianity and the Survival of the West," in *Against the Grain*, 5.

40. Ibid., 6, 12, 27.

41. Ibid., 6, 17.

42. Ibid., 51, 58, 60, 67.

43. Ibid., 69.

44. Revilo P. Oliver, "Postscript," in *Against the Grain*, 71–72. This essay was also published as a small book by Sterling Enterprises in 1973.

45. Ibid., 72.

46. Ibid., 73.

47. Ibid., 27–28.

48. Francis Parker Yockey, *The Enemy of Europe* (York, SC: Liberty Bell, 1981), reprinted in Francis Parker Yockey and Revilo P. Oliver, *The Enemy of Europe / The Enemy of Our Enemies* (York, SC: Liberty Bell, 2003), 1–147. It is important to our initial awareness of the interconnections between these leading figures to note that the reprint collected both Yockey's manuscript and Oliver's essays but was also dedicated to Louis T. Byers, the founder of the Francis Parker Yockey Society, who died in October 1981.

49. Revilo Oliver, "The Enemy of Our Enemies," in Yockey and Oliver, *The Enemy of Europe / The Enemy of Our Enemies*, 29.

50. Ibid.

51. Ibid., 38.

52. Ibid., 29. See also Lawrence R. Brown, *The Might of the West* (New York: Obelensky, 1963).

53. Oliver, "The Enemy of Our Enemies," 29, 31, 33.

54. Revilo Oliver, "The Jews Love Christianity," in *Against the Grain*, 109, 113.

55. Ibid., 113, 111, 118.

56. Ibid., 120, 135.

57. "Major" Donald V. Clerkin, "Appendix A: A White Christian Defends His Faith—Major D. V. Clerkin Responds to 'The Jews Love Christianity,'" in Oliver, *Against the Grain*, 214.

58. Revilo P. Oliver, "Religion and Race," in *Against the Grain*, 175.

59. Ibid., 203.

60. Revilo P. Olivier, "The Old Actor and the Jews," in *Against the Grain*, 139, 141.

61. Revilo P. Oliver, *The Origins of Christianity* (Uckfield, UK: Historical Review Press, 2001), 15.

62. Ibid., 65.

63. Ibid., 68.

64. Ibid., 151–52, 157.

65. Sam D. Dickson, introduction to Oliver, *America's Decline*, v.

66. Swain, *The New White Nationalism*.

67. Greg Johnson, "Remembering Revilo P. Oliver: July 7, 1908–August 20, 1984," *Counter-Currents*, July 7, 2011, at http://www.counter-currents.com/2011/07/remembering -revilo-oliver/.

68. Kevin A. Strom, "About," Kevin Alfred Strom website, n.d., at http://www.kevin alfredstrom.com/about/, accessed Feb. 12, 2014.

69. Kevin A. Strom, introduction to Oliver, *Origins of Christianity*, 11.

2. William Pierce and the Cosmotheist Critique of Christianity

1. Southern Poverty Law Center, "William Pierce," Intelligence Files, n.d., at http:// www.splcenter.org/get-informed/intelligence-files/profiles/william-pierce, accessed Feb. 22, 2014.

2. See, for example, H. Leroy, "Hunter d'Andrew MacDonald," Jeune Nation, Oct. 16, 2013, at http://jeune-nation.com/2013/10/andrew-macdonald-hunter-par-h-leroy/.

3. For further discussion of Pierce's transatlantic connections, see Nick Ryan, *Into a World of Hate: A Journey among the Extreme Right* (New York: Routledge, 2004), 346–47. See also William Pierce, "The National Alliance in Europe: Commentary by Dr. William Pierce, 1998," *The Legacy of Dr. William Pierce* (blog), posted Mar. 27, 2012, at http:// williamlutherpierce.blogspot.com/2012/03/national-alliance-in-europe.html, where Pierce discusses the favorable reception of National Alliance abroad.

4. Greg Johnson, "Remembering William Luther Pierce: September 11, 1933–July 23, 2002," *Counter-Currents*, Sept. 11, 2013, at http://www.counter-currents.com/2013/09 /remembering-william-luther-pierce/.

5. Jacob Young, dir., *Dr. No?* VHS (Morgantown, WV: WNPB, 1991).

6. Griffin, *Fame of a Dead Man's Deeds*, 27.

7. Ibid., 27, 34–35.

8. Carol Mason, *Reading Appalachia from Left to Right: Conservatives and the Kanawha County Textbook Controversy* (New York: Columbia Univ. Press, 2009), 77; Barkun, *Religion and the Racist Right*, 226; Griffin, *Fame of a Dead Man's Deeds*, 37.

9. Griffin, *Fame of a Dead Man's Deeds*, 83.

10. Brad Whitsel, "Aryan Visions of the Future in the West Virginia Mountains," *Terrorism and Political Violence* 7, no. 4 (1995): 119.

11. Quoted in Griffin, *Fame of a Dead Man's Deeds*, 85.

12. Whitsel, "Aryan Visions," 120; Griffin, *Fame of a Dead Man's Deeds*, 87.

13. Fredrick J. Simonelli, *American Fuehrer: George Lincoln Rockwell and the American Nazi Party* (Urbana: Univ. of Illinois Press, 1999), 54.

14. George Lincoln Rockwell, *This Time the World*, 7th ed. (York, SC: Liberty Bell, 2004), 413–14.

15. Simonelli, *American Fuehrer*, 131.

16. Ibid., 137, 138.

17. Ibid., 131.

18. Griffin, *Fame of a Dead Man's Deeds*, 103.

19. Ibid., 104.

20. Nicholas Goodrick-Clarke, *Hitler's Priestess: Savitri Devi, the Hindu–Aryan Myth, and Neo-Nazism* (New York: New York Univ. Press, 1998), 4, 6.

21. Quoted in ibid., 6.

22. Griffin, *Fame of a Dead Man's Deeds*, 104.

23. Goodrick-Clarke, *Hitler's Priestess*, 206.

24. Frank Mintz, *The Liberty Lobby and the American Right: Race, Conspiracy, and Culture* (New York: Praeger, 1985), 129.

25. Durham, *White Rage*, 27.

26. Michael, *Willis Carto*, 2.

27. Griffin, *Fame of a Dead Man's Deeds*, 119.

28. Barkun, *Religion and the Racist Right*, 226.

29. Leonard Zeskind, *Blood and Politics: The History of the White Nationalist Movement from the Margins to the Mainstream* (New York: Farrar, Straus and Giroux, 2009), 20.

30. Durham, *White Rage*, 27.

31. Ibid., 27; Griffin, *Fame of a Dead Man's Deeds*, 119.

32. William Pierce, "Why Conservatives Can't Win," in *The Best of* ATTACK! *and National Vanguard Tabloid*, ed. Kevin Alfred Strom (Arlington, VA: National Vanguard Books, 1984), 6.

33. Durham, *White Rage*, 27, 28.

34. Martin Durham, "From Imperium to Internet: The National Alliance and the American Extreme Right," *Patterns of Prejudice* 36, no. 3 (2002): 54.

35. William Pierce, "Our Cause," *National Vanguard*, 1976 (specific date unknown), posted Sept. 11, 2010, at http://nationalvanguard.org/2010/09/our-cause/.

36. Ibid.

37. William Pierce, "America Is a Changing Country," talk given in 2002 (specific date unknown), video posted in the Dr. William L. Pierce Archive, Nov. 13, 2012, at https://www.youtube.com/watch?v=X5ko1OYYDr8.

38. Griffin, *Fame of a Dead Man's Deeds*, 130.

39. Ibid.

40. Ibid., 28; Barkun, *Religion and the Racist Right*, 226.

41. Griffin, *Fame of a Dead Man's Deeds*, 121.

42. Ibid., 120.

43. Ibid., 122. See also William Gayley Simpson, *Which Way Western Man* (Cooperstown, NY: Yeoman Press, 1978).

44. Griffin, *Fame of a Dead Man's Deeds*, 122.

45. The *National Vanguard* former website, natvan.com, now redirects to nationalvanguard.org.

46. Durham, *White Rage*, 31.

47. William Pierce, "Death and Black Metal by William Pierce," Stormfront, posted by Proud Saxon, Oct. 13, 2011, at http://www.stormfront.org/forum/t838248-2/. For more discussion on the topic of music in American white nationalism and more details concerning Resistance Records, see Nancy Love, *Trendy Fascism: White Power Music and the Future of Democracy* (Albany: State Univ. of New York Press, 2016).

48. Adam Cohen, "All You Need Is Hate," *Time*, special issue, Feb. 10, 2010, at http://content.time.com/time/magazine/article/0,9171,1960595,00.html.

49. Griffin, *Fame of a Dead Man's Deeds*, 184.

50. Ibid.

51. Kevin Alfred Strom, "Dr. William Pierce: Preparing the Way, Part 2," *National Vanguard*, Sept. 19, 2015, at http://www.kevinalfredstrom.com/2015/09/dr-william-pierce-preparing-the-way-part-2/.

52. Durham, *White Rage*, 75.

53. Quoted in Griffin, *Fame of a Dead Man's Deeds*, 183.

54. Pierce, "Our Cause."

55. William Pierce, "A Program for Our Survival," in *Extremism in America: A Reader*, ed. Lyman Tower Sargent (New York: New York Univ. Press, 1995), 179, 181.

56. William Pierce, *Cosmotheism Trilogy* [*The Path* (1977), *On Living Things* (1979), and *On Society* (1984)], n.d., at https://archive.org/details/CosmotheismTrilogyByWilliamLutherPierce, accessed Oct. 22, 2015, 2.

57. Ibid., 3.

58. Ibid., 3, 4.

59. Ibid., 6–7.

60. William Pierce, "Cosmotheism—Wave of the Future," 1977 (specific date unknown), *The Legacy of Dr. William Pierce* (blog), posted July 30, 2013, at http://williamlutherpierce.blogspot.com/2013/07/cosmotheism-wave-of-future.html. All quotations from this talk are from this online publication of it.

61. Ibid.

62. Pierce, *Cosmotheism Trilogy*, 14.

63. Ibid.

64. Ibid., 16.

65. *The John Franklin Letters* (New York: Bookmailer, 1959).

66. For more discussion of *The Turner Diaries*, especially in the context of the survivalist milieu, see Richard G. Mitchell Jr., *Dancing at Armageddon: Survivalism and Chaos*

in Modern Times, new ed. (Chicago: Univ. of Chicago Press, 2004). Also see Brad Whitsel, "*The Turner Diaries* and Cosmotheism: William Pierce's Theology," *Novo Religio: The Journal of Alternative and Emergent Religions* 1, no. 2 (1998): 183–97.

67. William Pierce [as Andrew MacDonald], *The Turner Diaries: A Novel* (Fort Lee, NJ: Barricade Books, 1978), 195.

68. Ibid., 64.

69. Ibid., 203.

70. Ibid., 202.

71. William Pierce [as Andrew MacDonald], *Hunter* (Arlington, VA: National Vanguard Books, 1989), 9–10.

72. Ibid., 101.

73. Ibid., 16.

74. Ibid., 44.

75. Ibid., 104–5.

76. Ibid., 257–58.

77. William Pierce, *The Saga of White Will*, New World Order Comix no. 1 (Hillsboro, WV: National Vanguard Books, 1993), 6.

78. Ibid., 7–8, 22.

79. Ibid., 22, capitalization in the original.

80. Ibid., 37.

81. Ibid., inside front cover page.

82. Ibid., inside back cover page.

83. Griffin, *Fame of a Dead Man's Deeds*, 186–87.

84. Ibid., 187.

85. Whitsel, "Aryan Visions," 122.

86. Pierce, *Cosmotheism Trilogy*, 7.

87. William Pierce, "On Christianity," *National Vanguard*, 1982 (specific date unknown), posted Oct. 26, 2010, at http://nationalvanguard.org/2010/10/on-christianity. All quotations from this article come from its reprint at this website.

88. Mark Potok, "Ten Years after Founder's Death, Key Neo-Nazi Movement 'A Joke,'" Southern Poverty Law Center, July 23, 2012, at http://www.splcenter.org/get-informed/news/shipwreck-ten-years-after-the-death-of-its-founder-the-once-dominant-national-alli.

89. Martin Durham, "Upward Path: Palingenesis, Political Religion, and the National Alliance," *Totalitarian Movements and Political Religions* 5, no. 3 (2004): 465.

90. Ibid., 467.

3. Anti-Christianity in Ben Klassen's "Racial Holy War"

1. For example, see Hannah Arendt, *The Origins of Totalitarianism* (New York: Houghton Mifflin Harcourt, 1968), and Aimé Césaire, *Discourses on Colonialism*, trans. Joan Pinkham (1972; reprint, New York: Monthly Review Press, 2000).

2. Quoted in Martin Gilbert, *Churchill and the Jews: A Lifelong Friendship* (New York: Holt, 2007), 120.

3. Charles Long, *Significations: Signs, Symbols, and Images in the Interpretation of Religion* (Aurora, CO: Davis Group, 1995), 115.

4. Henry F. Osborn, "The Second International Congress of Eugenics: Address of Welcome," *Science* 54, no. 1397 (1921): 312–13.

5. Quoted in Steven G. Koven and Frank Gotzke, *American Immigration Policy: Confronting the Nation's Challenges* (New York: Springer, 2010), 11.

6. Quoted in Paul Lombardo, *Three Generations, No Imbeciles: Eugenics, the Supreme Court, and Buck v. Bell* (Baltimore: John Hopkins Univ. Press, 2008), 285.

7. Nancy Ordover, *American Eugenics: Race, Queer Anatomy, and the Science of Nationalism* (Minneapolis: Univ. of Minnesota Press, 2003), 3.

8. David Theo Goldberg, *Racist Culture: Philosophy and the Politics of Meaning* (Oxford: Blackwell, 1993), 3.

9. Durham, *White Rage*, 75.

10. Michael, *Theology of Hate*, viii.

11. Ben Klassen, *Nature's Eternal Religion* (Lighthouse Point, FL: Church of the Creator, 1973), 351.

12. Michael, *Theology of Hate*, 1; Ben Klassen, *Against the Evil Tide: An Autobiography* (Otto, NC: Church of the Creator, 1991), 4.

13. Klassen, *Against the Evil Tide*, 4.

14. Ibid., 96.

15. George Michael, "RAHOWA! A History of the Church of the Creator," *Terror and Political Violence* 18 (2006): 562.

16. Klassen, *Against the Evil Tide*, 152–53.

17. Ibid., 209–15; Michael, *Theology of Hate*, 5.

18. Klassen, *Against the Evil Tide*, 234.

19. Ibid., 294–95.

20. State of Florida, *Journal of the House of Representatives*, Extraordinary Session, Jan. 9, 1967, through Jan. 28, 1967, 3–4, at http://ufdc.ufl.edu/UF00027772/00054/1j.

21. Klassen, *Against the Evil Tide*, 339.

22. Ibid., 369.

23. Michael, *Theology of Hate*, 7–8.

24. Ibid., 8–9. Klassen is often lauded on white nationalist websites as having described the JBS and its anti-Communist activities as a "smoke screen for Jews." See, for example, an article on Jew Watch titled "Real Nazis, or More Zionist Hoaxes," at http://www.jewwatch.com/jew-hatehoaxes-american-nazis.html.

25. Michael, *Theology of Hate*, 9.

26. Klassen, *Against the Evil Tide*, 338.

27. Ibid., 387, 394.

28. Ibid., 394–95, 396.

29. Ibid., 398, emphasis in original.

30. Ibid., 410, 411.

31. Ben Klassen, RAHOWA! This Planet Is All Ours (Otto, NC: Church of the Creator, 1987); A Revolution of Values through Religion (Otto, NC: Church of the Creator, 1991); and On the Brink of Bloody Racial War (Niceville, FL: Church of the Creator, 1993).

32. Ibid., 498.

33. Durham, White Rage, 141.

34. Quoted in Michael, Theology of Hate, 94.

35. Ibid., 99–100.

36. Steven Atkins, Encyclopedia of Right Wing Extremism in American History (Santa Barbra, CA: ABC-CLIO, 2011), 169.

37. Michael, Theology of Hate, 120.

38. Ibid., 120–21.

39. Michael, "RAHOWA!" 573.

40. Southern Poverty Law Center, "Church of the Creator: A History," Intelligence Report, no. 95 (Summer 1999), at http://www.splcenter.org/intel/intelreport/article.jsp?sid =219.

41. Michael, Theology of Hate, 123, 124, 120.

42. "Midwest Shooting Spree Ends with Apparent Suicide of Suspect," CNN, July 5, 1999, at http://www.cnn.com/US/9907/05/illinois.shootings.02/.

43. Michael A. Fletcher, "Behind the Hate: A Racist 'Church,'" Washington Post, July 6, 1999, at http://www.washingtonpost.com/wp-srv/national/daily/july99/church6.htm.

44. Michael, Theology of Hate, 159–60.

45. Robert Salladay, Lynda Gledhill, and Kelly St. John, "Sacramento Rampage—5 Shot Dead. Slayer Kills Himself during Gun Battle with Police," Sept. 10, 2001, at http://www.sfgate.com/news/article/Sacramento-rampage-5-shot-dead-Slayer-kills-2881164.php.

46. Michael, Theology of Hate, 173, 174, 175, 177, 182, 184.

47. Ibid., 183.

48. Ibid., 161.

49. Klassen, Nature's Eternal Religion, 7.

50. Ibid.

51. Ibid., 21. See also Grant, Passing of the Great Race.

52. Klassen, Nature's Eternal Religion, 142–43.

53. Ibid., 132.

54. Ibid., 144.

55. Ibid., 355.

56. Ibid., 357.

57. Ibid., 331.

58. Ibid., 28.

59. Ben Klassen, *The White Man's Bible* (Lighthouse Point, FL: Church of the Creator, 1981), 6, 11, bold in the original.

60. Ibid., 306.

61. Ibid., 351–53.

62. Ibid., 440.

63. Ibid., 38.

64. Ibid., 39–40.

65. Ibid., 38.

66. Ibid., bold in the original.

67. Ibid., 155.

68. Ibid., 164.

69. See Alexandra Minna Stern, *Eugenic Nation: Faults and Frontiers of Better Breeding in Modern America* (Berkeley and Los Angeles: Univ. of California Press, 2005), and Lombardo, *Three Generations, No Imbeciles.*

70. Klassen, *White Man's Bible*, 158–62.

71. Ibid., 160–63.

72. Ben Klassen, *Salubrious Living* (Otto, NC: Church of the Creator, 1982), 8.

73. Ibid.

74. Arnold DeVries, "The Fountain of Youth," in Klassen, *Salubrious Living*, 237.

75. Klassen, *Salubrious Living*, 241.

76. Ibid., 243.

77. Ben Klassen, "Recognize Your Enemies! RAHOWA! *Racial Loyalty* Issue No. 36, June 1986," in *RAHOWA: This Planet Is All Ours*, 15.

78. Ibid., 17.

79. Ibid., 26–27.

80. Ibid., 30.

81. Ibid.

82. Ibid., 28.

83. Ibid., 31.

84. Ibid., 30.

85. Ibid., 16.

86. Ibid., 15.

87. Klassen, *Nature's Eternal Religion*, 343, 352.

88. Klassen, *White Man's Bible*, 191.

89. Klassen, *Nature's Eternal Religion*, 402.

90. Ibid., 313.

4. "Authentic" Whiteness and Protectionism in Racialist Odinism

1. Gardell, *Gods of the Blood*, 342–43.

2. Michael Omi and Howard Winant, *Racial Formation in the United States: From the 1960s to the 1990s*, 2nd ed. (New York: Routledge, 1994), 120.

3. Matthew Frye Jacobson, *Roots Too: The White Ethnic Revival in Post–Civil Rights America* (Cambridge, MA: Harvard Univ. Press, 2006), 4, 9.

4. Bjorn, "Why We Are Odinists," *Odinist*, no. 13 (Sept. 1974): 10.

5. "Declaration 127," Huginn's Heathen Hoff, n.d., at http://www.declaration127 .com/, accessed Oct. 7, 2016.

6. Stevie Miller, "There Is No Folkish and Universalist Debate in Heathenry," *Grundsau Burrow*, Sept. 6, 2016, at https://grundsauburrow.wordpress.com/2016/09/06/there-is-no -folkish-and-universalist-debate-in-heathenry/.

7. For further reading on the complexity of Heathenry, see James R. Lewis and Murphy Pizza, eds., *Handbook of Contemporary Paganism* (Leiden, Netherlands: Koninklijke NV Brill, 2009), in particular the essay by Jenny Blain and Robert J. Wallis, "Heathenry," 413–32.

8. Garman Lord, *The Way of the Heathen: A Handbook of Greater Theodism* (Watertown, NY: Theod, 2000), 1.

9. David Lane, "Wotanism (Odinism)," in *Victory or Valhalla: The Final Compilation of Writings*, edited by Java and Sissy (Butte, MT: THORINK, 2008), 195.

10. Orestes A. Brownson, "A Letter to Protestants," in *The Works of Orestes A. Brownson: Controversy*, comp. Henry F. Brownson (Detroit: Thorndike Nourse, 1883), 256–57.

11. See Ronald Hutton, *Triumph of the Moon: A History of Modern Pagan Witchcraft* (New York: Oxford Univ. Press, 1999).

12. Margot Adler, *Drawing Down the Moon: Witches, Druids, Goddess-Worshipers, and Other Pagans in America*, rev. and updated ed. (New York: Penguin Books, 2006), 285.

13. Jeffrey Kaplan, "The Reconstruction of the Ásatrú and Odinist Traditions," in *Magical Religion and Modern Witchcraft*, ed. Jeffrey R. Lewis (Albany: State Univ. of New York Press, 1996), 193–236.

14. Gardell, *Gods of the Blood*, 274, 275.

15. Adler, *Drawing Down the Moon*, 284, 285, 288, 289.

16. Gardell, *Gods of the Blood*, 17.

17. Ibid., 165.

18. Stephen McNallen, "Three Decades of Asatru Revival in America," *TYR: Myth–Culture–Tradition* 2 (2004): 205, 206.

19. Stephen McNallen, "Asatru . . . the Way of Our Ancestors . . . Calling Us Home," Asatru Folk Assembly, Nov. 24, 2014, at http://www.runestone.org/.

20. Stephen McNallen, *Asatru/Odinism—A Native European Religion*, DystopiaUK, YouTube, posted Mar. 24, 2011, http://www.youtube.com/watch?v=ngdTa4IMRuE.

21. Mark Noll, *God and Race in American Politics* (Princeton, NJ: Princeton Univ. Press, 2009), 136.

22. Ibid., 156.

23. Gardell, *Gods of the Blood*, 276.

24. Ibid., 259.

25. Quoted in ibid., 178.

26. McNallen, "Three Decades of Asatru Revival," 206.

27. "A Brief Biography of Alexander Rud Mills," Odinic Rite Australia, n.d., at http://www.reocities.com/osred/Rud_Mills_Brief_Biography.htm, accessed Dec. 20, 2014.

28. Michael Moynihan, "Odinism," in *The Encyclopedia of Religion and Nature*, ed. Bron Taylor (London: Continuum, 2006), 1219.

29. Gardell, *Gods of the Blood*, 167.

30. Ibid.

31. Alexander Rud Mills, *The Call of Our Ancient Nordic Religion: Reflections on the Theological Content of the Sagas* (Melbourne, Australia: A. Rud Mills, 1957), 26.

32. Else Christensen, *An Introduction to Odinism* (Chrystal River, FL: Gjallerhorn Book Service, 1980), 14.

33. Quoted in ibid., 6.

34. Ibid., 15.

35. Amos Morris-Reich, "Race, Ideas, and Ideals: A Comparison of Franz Boas and Hans F. K. Günther," *History of European Ideas* 32, no. 3 (2006): 314.

36. Quoted in "Chapter One: Nazi Race-Science," Archives for the Institute for the Study of Academic Racism, n.d., at http://www.ferris.edu/HTMLS/othersrv/isar/archives2/billig/chapter1.htm, accessed Dec. 22, 2013.

37. Christensen, *Introduction to Odinism*, 3, 7.

38. Moynihan, "Odinism," 1219.

39. Gardell, *Gods of the Blood*, 166.

40. Ibid., 171.

41. Ibid., 168; Kaplan and Weinberg, *Emergence of the Euro-American Right*, 106.

42. Christensen, *Introduction to Odinism*, 1.

43. Ibid., 2–3.

44. Ibid., 3.

45. Ibid., 4.

46. Ben Klassen to Else Christensen, Mar. 26, 1986, in Ben Klassen, "Odinism," in *A Revolution of Values through Religion* (Otto, NC: Church of the Creator, 1991), 103, 109.

47. Else Christensen to Ben Klassen, May 8, 1986, in Klassen, "Odinism," 109.

48. Ibid.

49. Christensen, *Introduction to Odinism*, 14, 1.

50. Abby L. Ferber, *White Man Falling: Race, Gender, and White Supremacy* (Lanham, MD: Rowman and Littlefield, 1999), 5–6. See also Abbey L. Ferber, ed., *Home-Grown Hate: Gender and Organized Racism* (New York: Routledge, 2004).

51. Ron McVan, *Creed of Iron: Wotansvolk Wisdom* (Saint Marie, ID: Fourteen Words Press, 1997), 17.

52. David Lane, "Wotansvolk," in *Victory or Valhalla*, 208.

53. David Lane, "Open Letter to a Dead Race," in *Victory or Valhalla*, 327.

54. Gardell, *Gods of the Blood*, 191.

55. George Michael, "David Lane and the 14 Words," *Totalitarian Movements and Political Religions* 10, no. 1 (2009): 43.

56. A fan video that compiles scenes from *Brotherhood of Murder* and an iconic photograph of Matthews confronting antiracist activists can be found at http://www.youtube.com/watch?v=3cHadlUoFbI. For more on Saga, see her website at http://www.thisissaga.com/. Saga also composed a tribute song for David Lane, "Goodbye David Lane," to the tune of "Candle in the Wind" by Elton John. Saga's performance of the song can be viewed at http://www.youtube.com/watch?v=A9TmfSwntOg.

57. "Inside the Hate Conspiracy," *Turning Point*, ABC, Oct. 5, 1995; Martin Bell, dir., *Brotherhood of Murder* (Los Angeles: DEJ Productions, 1999).

58. Mark S. Hamm, *Terrorism as Crime: From Oklahoma City to al-Qaeda and Beyond* (New York: New York Univ. Press, 2007), 144.

59. Durham, *White Rage*, 101–2.

60. Daniel Levitas, *The Terrorist Next Door: The Militia Movement and the Radical Right* (New York: Thomas Dunne Press, 2002), 106.

61. Barkun, *Religion and the Racist Right*, 230, 231.

62. Ibid., 228.

63. Magnus Söderman and Henrick Holappa, eds., *Unbroken Warrior: The Richard Scutari Letters* (Stockholm: Nationellt Motstånd Förlag, 2011).

64. David Lane, "88 Precepts," in *Victory or Valhalla*, 174, 175.

65. Ibid., 181.

66. David Lane, "Valhalla—Fact or Fiction," in *Victory or Valhalla*, 191.

67. Ibid.

68. Quoted in Durham, *White Rage*, 73.

69. David Lane, "Open Letter to All Christians," in *Victory or Valhalla*, 217, full capitals in the original.

70. Ibid.

71. Ferber, *White Man Falling*, 12, 13.

72. Ibid., 131.

73. David Lane, "White Genocide Manifesto," in *Victory or Valhalla*, 321.

74. Quoted in Davis R. Davies and Judy Smith, "Jimmy Ward and the *Jackson Daily News*," in *The Press and Race: Mississippi Journalists Confront the Movement*, ed. Davis R. Davies (Jackson: Univ. Press of Mississippi, 2001), 94.

75. Lane, "White Genocide Manifesto," 321.

76. Ibid.

77. Ibid.

78. Arjun Appadurai, *Fear of Small Numbers: An Essay on the Geography of Anger* (Durham, NC: Duke Univ. Press, 2006), 7–9.

79. Lane, "White Genocide Manifesto," 323.

80. Gardell, *Gods of the Blood*, 343.

81. Bergson, *Two Sources*, 15.

82. Ferber, *White Man Falling*, 131.

83. Goodrick-Clarke, *Black Sun*, 2.

84. Ibid., 3.

5. Esoteric Racialism and Christianity

1. Quoted in "Pope Calls for Religions to Oppose Racism Together," *New York Times*, Aug. 19, 2005, at http://www.nytimes.com/2005/08/19/world/europe/19iht-web.0819pope.html?_r=0.

2. US House of Representatives, Un-American Activities Committee, *Preliminary Report on Neo-fascist and Hate Groups* (Washington, DC: US Government Printing Office, 1954).

3. Antoine Faivre and Christine Rhone, *Western Esotericism: A Concise History* (Albany: New York Univ. Press, 2010), 1.

4. Ibid., 2–6.

5. Ibid., 21. See also Nicholas Goodrick-Clarke, *The Occult Roots of Nazism: The Ariosophists of Austria and Germany, 1890–1935* (New York: New York Univ. Press, 1992).

6. Kennet Granholm, "The Left-Hand Path and Post-Satanism: The Temple of Set and the Evolution of Satanism," in *The Devil's Party: Satanism in Modernity*, ed. Peter Faxneld and Jesper Aa. Petersen (New York: Oxford Univ. Press, 2013), 212–13. See also Jesper Aagaard Petersen, "The Carnival of Dr. LaVey: Articulations of Transgression in Modern Satanism," in *The Devil's Party*, ed. Faxneld and Petersen, 167–88.

7. Nicholas Goodrick-Clarke, *The Western Esoteric Traditions: A Historical Introduction* (New York: Oxford Univ. Press, 2008), 13.

8. Arthur M. Schlesinger Jr., *The Age of Roosevelt: The Politics of Upheaval* (Boston: Houghton Mifflin, 1960), 69.

9. Leo Ribuffo, *The old Christian Right: The Protestant Far Right from the Great Depression to the Cold War* (Philadelphia: Temple Univ. Press, 1983), 73.

10. Ibid., 3.

11. For more biographical details, see Ribuffo's chapter on Pelley in *The Old Christian Right*, and Scott Beekman's biography of Pelley, *William Dudley Pelley: A Life in Right-Wing Extremism and the Occult* (Syracuse, NY: Syracuse Univ. Press, 2005).

12. Ribuffo, *Old Christian Right*, 50; Beekman, *William Dudley Pelley*, 54.

13. William Dudley Pelley, "My Seven Minutes in Eternity—The Amazing Experience That Made Me Over," *American Magazine*, Mar. 1928, reprinted as *Seven Minutes in Eternity, with Their Aftermath* (New York: Robert Collier, 1929), 13.

14. Pelley, *Seven Minutes in Eternity*, 15.

15. Beekman, *William Dudley Pelly*, 75.

16. Ribuffo, *Old Christian Right*, 53.

17. Beekman writes more in depth than I can in the space of this section both on Pelley's previous efforts to organize and the changes that came from his reorganization of the League for the Liberation into the Silver Shirt Legion of America as well as on Pelley's school, Galahad College, and the role it served in his new endeavor (see Beekman, *William Dudley Pelly*, esp. 81).

18. William Dudley Pelley, *No More Hunger* (1933; reprint, Nobsville, IN: Aquila Press, 1961), 172.

19. Quoted in Suzanne G. Ledeboer, "The Man Who Would Be Hitler: William Dudley Pelley and the Silver Shirt Legion," *California History* 65, no. 2 (1986): 132.

20. Pelley, *Seven Minutes in Eternity*, 16.

21. Betty Dobratz, *White Power, White Pride: The White Separatist Movement in the United States* (New York: Twayne, 1997), 57.

22. Kaplan and Weinberg, *Emergence of a Euro-American Right*, 107.

23. Goodrick-Clarke, *Black Sun*, 72–73. The sedition trial was officially titled *United States v. McWilliams, et al.*, US District Court, Southern District of West Virginia, Cr. 73086, Feb. 28, 1944. The description of it as the "Sedition Trial" came from the media coverage of it and from a book written by one of the attorneys for the defense, Maximillian St. George, and one of the infamous defendants, Lawrence Dennis: *A Trial on Trial: The Great Sedition Trial of 1944* (1946; reprint, Newport Beach, CA: Institute for Historical Review, 1984).

24. Gary Alan Fine and Terence McDonnell, "Erasing the Brown Scare: Referential Afterlife and the Power of Memory Templates," *Social Problems* 54, no. 2 (2007): 170.

25. Goodrick-Clarke, *Black Sun*, 75.

26. Ibid., 74.

27. Ibid. Hitler's last "political testament" in German as well as facsimiles of this letter can be viewed at http://www.ns-archiv.de/personen/hitler/testament/politisches-testament .php and http://www.ns-archiv.de/personen/hitler/testament/faksimile/polit-02.php.

28. Goodrick-Clarke, *Black Sun*, 81.

29. *The Secret Doctrine: The Synthesis of Science, Religion, and Philosophy* was originally published in 1888. It followed *Isis Unveiled*, published in 1877. These two works

represent the major works by Helena Blavatsky as she sought to articulate what she stated to be the esoteric truth of all life and doctrine transmitted to her by instruction from ancient adepts and masters of this tradition. Other texts written by other people came to influence theosophy today, of course, but Blavatsky's works are the most recognized and are cited by Madole and others in the NRP. See Helena Blavatsky, *The Secret Doctrine: The Classic Work, Abridged and Annotated*, abridged and annotated by Michael Gomes (New York: TarcherPerigee, 2009), and *Isis Unveiled: Secrets of the Ancient Wisdom Tradition, Madame Blavatsky's First Work*, abridged by Michael Gomes (Wheaton, IL: Philosophical Publishing House, 1997).

30. James Madole, "The Leadership Principle: A Heritage of Aryan Man," *National Renaissance Bulletin* 21, nos. 1–2 (1970): 4–5.

31. Ibid., 5, 6.

32. Ibid., 6.

33. Ibid., 7.

34. Ibid., 9.

35. James Madole, "'Nature's Eternal Religion'—the New *Mein Kampf* of the NRP," *National Renaissance Bulletin* 24, nos. 1–2 (1973): 4, 8.

36. James Madole, "A Stern Rebuke to the Critics of the National Renaissance Party," *National Renaissance Bulletin* 22, nos. 9–10 (1971): 6–7, 8.

37. Robert Bayer, "The Aryan Concept of Race, Religion, and History (Part IV)," *National Renaissance Bulletin* 23, nos. 7–8 (1972): 7.

38. Ibid.

39. James Madole, "'The New Atlantis': A Blueprint for an Aryan 'Garden of Eden' in North America!" *National Renaissance Bulletin* 24, nos. 5–6 (1973): 4, 5.

40. Ibid., 8.

41. James Madole, "'The New Atlantis': A Blueprint for an Aryan 'Garden of Eden' in North America! (Part V)," *National Renaissance Bulletin* 26, nos. 1–2 (1975): 5.

42. Jeffery Kaplan, "The Postwar Paths of Occult National Socialism: From Rockwell and Madole to Manson," in *The Cultic Milieu: Oppositional Subcultures in an Age of Globalization*, ed. Jeffrey Kaplan and Helén Loöw (Walnut Creek, CA: Altamira Press, 2002), 237.

43. Simonelli, *American Fuehrer*, 24–26, 117.

44. Ibid., 25.

45. Rockwell, *This Time the World*, 154, 254, 157.

46. Ibid., 81.

47. Ibid., 82.

48. Goodrick-Clarke, *Hitler's Priestess*, 6.

49. Ibid., 25, 43, 91.

50. Savitri Devi, *Defiance* (Calcutta: n.p., 1951), 26–27, 505, available at the Savitri Devi Archive, http://www.savitridevi.org/PDF/defiance.pdf, accessed Feb. 29, 2012.

51. Ibid., 517.

52. The phrase "el ultimo avatāra" comes from Miguel Serrano's most important book, *Adolph Hitler, el ultimo avatāra* (Santiago, Chile: Ediciones la Nueva Edad, 1987). Serrano is discussed in more detail in Goodrick-Clarke, *Black Sun*, chap. 9.

53. Madole's suggestion concerning *The Satanic Bible* and *Satanic Rituals* appeared primarily in the *National Renaissance Bulletin* in 1973, but he did not consistently mention them.

54. Blanche Barton, *The Secret Life of a Satanist: The Authorized Biography of Anton LaVey* (Los Angeles: Feral House Books, 1992), 214.

55. Gavin Baddeley, *Lucifer Rising: Sin, Devil Worship, and Rock 'n' Roll* (London: Plexus, 1999), 76.

56. Peter H. Gilmore, "The Fascism Question," in *The Satanic Scriptures* (Baltimore: Scapegoat, 2007), 82–91.

57. For more about these contacts, see Goodrick-Clark, *Black Sun*, 83, 214–16.

58. Ibid., 83, 215.

59. Ibid., 83.

60. Anton LaVey, interview in Baddeley, *Lucifer Rising*, 66.

61. This interview, originally aired on public-access television in California in 1988, is still available in full at YouTube: see "Tom Metzger Interviews Nicholas Schreck," YouTube, uploaded by Styxhexenhammer666, Dec. 30, 2010, at http://www.youtube.com/watch?v=eS47cjbZkGM, accessed Mar. 22, 2014; all quotes from the discussion between Schreck and Metzger come from this version of the interview.

62. Petersen, "The Carnival of Dr. LaVey," 177.

63. Ibid., 178.

64. Étienne Balibar, "Is There a 'Neo-racism'?" in *Race, Nation, Class: Ambiguous Identities*, trans. Chris Turner (New York: Verso, 1991), 22, emphasis in the original.

6. The North American New Right and Contemporary White Nationalism's Latest Religious Adaptations

1. Johnson, "Toward a North American New Right," 1.

2. Greg Johnson, "New Right vs. Old Right," *Counter-Currents*, May 11, 2012, at http://www.counter-currents.com/2012/05/new-right-vs-old-right/; all quotations from this essay come from this online publication.

3. Tamir Bar-On, *Where Have All the Fascists Gone?* (Hampshire, UK: Ashgate, 2007), 7.

4. There is certainly more written on the ENR than I can discuss in this section. For more, see Bar-On, *Where Have All the Fascists Gone?*; Anne-Marie Duranton-Crabol, *Visages de la Nouvelle Droite: Le G.R.E.C.E. et son histoire* (Paris: Presses de la Fondation nationale des sciences politiques, 1988); and Pierre-Andre Taguieff, *Sur la Nouvelle Droite: Jalons d'une analyse critique* (Paris: Descartes & Cie, 1994). GRECE is still operational,

though it has undergone transformations in its history. One can still visit the organization's website at http://grece-fr.com/.

5. GRECE, "Manifeste du GRECE," n.d., at http://grece-fr.com/?page_id=64, accessed Mar. 16, 2004, my translation.

6. Pierre Vial, *Pour une renaissance culturelle: Le G.R.E.C.E. prend la parole* (Paris: Editions Copernic, 1979).

7. Bar-On, *Where Have All the Fascists Gone?* 169.

8. René Rénard's preface to Duranton-Crabol's book *Visages de la Nouvelle Droite* states the common conclusion that the FNR's animosity toward Christianity and its "exaltation of ancient paganism" have set it quite apart from other right-wing movements in France (11).

9. James Shields, *The Extreme Right in France: From Pétain to Le Pen* (New York: Routledge, 2007), 144.

10. Tomislav Sunic, *Against Democracy and Equality: The European New Right*, 3rd ed. (London: Arktos Media, 2011), 29.

11. Ibid., 30.

12. Michael O'Meara, *New Culture, New Right: Anti-liberalism in Postmodern Europe* (Bloomington, IN: 1st Books, 2004), 43.

13. Bar-On, *Where Have All the Fascists Gone?* 23, 57.

14. Ibid., 60.

15. Ibid., 34.

16. Ibid., 98.

17. Balibar, "Is There a 'Neo-racism'?" 26.

18. Taguieff, "Origines et métamorphoses de la Nouvelle Droite," 7.

19. Alberto Spektorowski, "The New Right: Ethno-regionalism, Ethno-pluralism, and the Emergence of a Neo-fascist 'Third-Way,'" *Journal of Political Ideologies* 8, no. 1 (2003): 111–30.

20. Balibar, "Is There a Neo-racism?" 22, 26, emphasis in original.

21. Benoist, *On Being a Pagan*, 3.

22. Stephen Edred Flowers, preface to Alain de Benoist, *On Being a Pagan*, trans. Jon Graham, ed. Greg Johnson (Atlanta: ULTRA, 2004), ii–iii.

23. Ibid., 4, 195, 196, 199.

24. Ibid., 201, emphasis in original.

25. Ibid., 14, 15.

26. Alain de Benoist, *The Problem of Democracy*, trans. Sergio Knipe (1985; reprint, London: Arktos Media, 2011), 29, 98.

27. Guillaume Faye, *Archeofuturism: European Visions of the Post-catastrophic Age* (1998; reprint, London: Arktos Media, 2010), 14, 20, 21.

28. Ibid., 88–89.

29. Ibid., 35.

30. Pierre Krebs, *Fighting for the Essence: Western Ethnosuicide or European Renaissance?* trans. Alexander Jacob (London: Arktos Media, 2012), 19, 29.

31. Flowers, preface to Benoist, *On Being a Pagan*; Stephen Edred Flowers, preface to Alain de Benoist and Charles Champetier, *Manifesto for a European Renaissance*, trans. Martin Bendelow and Francis Greene, ed. Stephen Edred Flowers (Smithville, TX: Runa-Raven Press, 2010), not paginated.

32. Collin Cleary, *Summoning the Gods: Essays on Paganism in a God-Forsaken World*, ed. Greg Johnson (San Francisco: Counter-Currents, 2011).

33. Short bios of Buckley and Moynihan can be found at http://www.radicaltradition alist.com/tyr.htm.

34. Joshua Buckley, Colin Cleary, and Michael Moynihan, "Editorial Preface," *TYR: Myth–Culture–Tradition* 1 (2002): 9.

35. Stephen Edred Flowers, "The Idea of Integral Culture: A Model for a Revolt against the Modern World," *TYR: Myth–Culture–Tradition* 1 (2002): 13, 19, 20.

36. See the Identity Europa website at https://www.identityevropa.com/identity/.

37. Flowers, "The Idea of Integral Culture," 18.

38. Buckley, Cleary, and Moynihan, "Editorial Preface," 10.

39. Joshua Buckley and Michael Moynihan, "Editorial Preface," *TYR: Myth–Culture–Tradition* 2 (2004): 7–10.

40. This biographical information is found on Sunic's website at http://www.tom sunic.com/?page_id=13. Alain de Benoist credits Sunic with having written the first English-language book on the ENR; see Alain de Benoist, "The New Right Forty Years Later," in Sunic, *Against Democracy and Equality*, 15. In Sunic's own preface to the third edition, he also states that this book grew out of his doctoral thesis presented in 1988 (*Against Democracy and Equality*, 11), which pushes this original contribution back two more years.

41. Sunic, *Against Democracy and Equality*, 43.

42. Ibid., 47.

43. Ibid., 54–55.

44. Ibid., 55.

45. Ibid., 155.

46. NPI's homepage can be found at http://www.npiamerica.org/.

47. NPI's self-description is given on its website at http://www.npiamerica.org/about/.

48. The American Freedom Party gives its "mission statement" for 2015 on its website at http://american3rdposition.com/?page_id=195.

49. The list of American Freedom Party officers as of 2015 can be found at http://american3rdposition.com/?cat=1019.

50. Kevin MacDonald, *A People That Shall Dwell Alone: Judaism as a Group Evolutionary Strategy, with Diaspora Peoples* (Lincoln, NE: Writers Club Press, 2002).

51. Sander Gilman, "Review: *A People That Shall Dwell Alone: Judaism as a Group Evolutionary Strategy* by Kevin MacDonald," *Jewish Quarterly Review*, New Series, 86, nos. 1–2 (1995): 200.

52. Tomislav Sunic, presentation at NPI conference, Sept. 10, 2011, *Voice of Reason*, at http://reasonradionetwork.com/index.php?s=NPI+conference+2011.

53. Tomislav Sunic, foreword to Krebs, *Fighting for the Essence*, 12, 13.

54. Tomislav Sunic, *Homo Americanus: Child of the Postmodern Age* (N.p.: Book-Surge, 2007), xii, 24, 93, 100, 107.

55. Ibid., 114.

56. Biographical information on some figures in the New Right, such as Michael O'Meara, is often difficult to obtain. A reason for this may be that they, like Greg Johnson, purposefully hide the full details of their identity and background to prevent the collection of this information by those they regard as enemies. Johnson admits to this strategy in an interview with Tom Sunic on the latter's radio show. See Tomislav Sunic, "The Sunic Journal: Dr. Greg Johnson on the New Right," *Voice of Reason*, Aug. 9, 2011, audio only, at http://reasonradionetwork.com/20110809/the-sunic-journal-dr-greg-johnson -on-the-new-right. A researcher must rely on their self-descriptions and how they are known within the community. The background on O'Meara given here comes from the description of him on the Counter-Currents website at http://www.counter-currents.com /author/momeara/.

57. The *Occidental Quarterly* is both a print journal and a website at http://www .toqonline.com/. According to the "About" page, "THE OCCIDENTAL QUARTERLY: WESTERN PERSPECTIVES ON MAN, CULTURE, AND POLITICS is published by The Charles Martel Society four times yearly, in the Spring, Summer, Fall, and Winter." Michael O'Meara is on the print advisory board, and Kevin MacDonald sits as the journal's editor.

58. O'Meara, *New Culture, New Right*, 216, 217, 97. See also James C. Russell, *The Germanization of Early Medieval Christianity: A Socio-historical Approach to Religious Transformation* (Oxford: Oxford Univ. Press, 1994).

59. O'Meara, *New Culture, New Right*, 97, 216–17.

60. Michael O'Meara, "Against White Reformists," Vanguard News Network, 2007, reprinted in *Counter-Currents*, July 17, 2012, at http://www.counter-currents.com/2012/07 /against-white-reformists/.

61. This date is arrived at by statements in Greg Johnson, "Frequently Asked Questions, Part 1," *Counter-Currents*, June 5, 2012, at http://www.counter-currents.com/2012/06 /frequently-asked-questions-part-1/.

62. Sunic, "The Sunic Journal: Dr. Greg Johnson on the New Right."

63. Johnson, "New Right vs. Old Right." Counter-Currents recently released a book collecting this essay and many others authored by Johnson and using this same title, with a foreword by Kevin MacDonald. See Greg Johnson, *New Right versus Old Right* (San Francisco: Counter-Currents, 2013).

64. Johnson, "New Right vs. Old Right."

65. Ibid.

66. Johnson, "Frequently Asked Questions."

67. Greg Johnson, "The Christian Question in White Nationalism," *Occidental Observer*, May 14, 2010, at http://www.theoccidentalobserver.net/authors/Johnson-Christianity .html; all quotations from the article come from this online publication of it.

68. Edmund Connelly, "Harold Covington's Northwest Quartet," *Occidental Observer*, Mar. 30, 2011, at http://www.theoccidentalobserver.net/2011/03/harold-covingtons -northwest-quartet/. The fifth book in the series, *Freedom's Sons*, was published later in 2011. The homepage for Covington's Northwest Front series can be found at http://north westfront.org/.

69. Johnson, "Toward a North American New Right," 1, 2, 8.

70. folkabovedogma, forum entry, Stormfront, posted July 11, 2013, at https://www .stormfront.org/forum/t979461/.

71. Some American, forum entry, Stormfront, posted July 11, 2013, at https://www .stormfront.org/forum/t979461/.

72. WhiteNationalist, forum entry, Stormfront, posted July 11, 2013, at https://www .stormfront.org/forum/t979461/.

73. Grey Fang, forum entry, Stormfront, posted July 12, 2013, at https://www.storm front.org/forum/t979461-3/.

Conclusion

1. Jacques Chevalier, *Entretiens avec Bergson* (Paris: Librarie Plon, 1959), 15.

2. Uriel Tal, "Political Faith of Nazism prior to the Holocaust," in *Religion, Politics, and Ideology in the Third Reich: Selected Essays*, edited by Saul Friedländer (New York: Routledge, 2004), 16–54; Doris Bergen, *The Twisted Cross: The German Christian Movement in the Third Reich*, 2nd ed. (Chapel Hill: Univ. of North Carolina Press, 1996); Susannah Heschel, *The Aryan Jesus: Christian Theologians and the Bible in Nazi Germany* (Princeton, NJ: Princeton Univ. Press, 2008).

3. Tal, "Political Faith of Nazism," 33–34.

4. Bergson, *Two Sources*, 266.

5. Anthony Parel, "Values of Closed Society," *International Political Science Review* 3, no. 2 (1982): 234.

6. "Why We Hate," *The Insurgent*, n.d., at http://www.resist.com/JOOMJournal /WHY%20WE%20HATE.html, accessed Mar. 16, 2014.

7. Bergson, *Two Sources*, 286.

8. Ben Adler, "White Christian Nationalism at CPAC," *The Nation*, Feb. 10, 2012, at http://www.thenation.com/blog/166176/white-christian-nationalism-cpac#.

9. This story is discussed most concisely in Benjamin Hart and Jack Merkinson, "*National Review* Fires John Derbyshire, Writer Who Penned Racist Screed," *Huffington*

Post, Feb. 7, 2012, at http://www.huffingtonpost.com/2012/04/07/national-review-fires -john-derbyshire_n_1410273.html.

10. On his own webpage, Derbyshire has been candid about his relationship with V-Dare; see his comments at http://www.johnderbyshire.com/, where a fund has been set up in his name.

11. Peter Brimelow, "Why V-Dare? / Why the White Doe?" V-Dare, n.d., at http:// www.vdare.com/about, accessed Mar. 5, 2014.

12. Peter Brimelow, *Alien Nation: Common Sense about America's Immigration Disaster* (New York: Harper Perennial, 1996), xix.

13. Lauren Fox, "White Nationalist at CPAC Does Not Fit In," *U.S. News & World Report*, Mar. 7, 2014, at http://www.usnews.com/news/blogs/washington-whispers/2014/03/07 /white-nationalist-at-cpac-doesnt-fit-in.

14. Roberta Costa and Ed O'Keefe, "House Majority Whip Scalise Confirms He Spoke to White Supremacists in 2002," *Washington Post*, Dec. 12, 2014, at https://www.washington post.com/politics/house-majority-whip-scalise-confirms-he-spoke-to-white-nationalists -in-2002/2014/12/29/7f80dc14-8fa3-11e4-a900-9960214d4cd7_story.html?utm_term=.41a 74f7ed2eb.

15. Barkun, *Religion and the Racist Right*, xiii.

Epilogue

1. National Policy Institute (NPI), "NPI Events," n.d., at http://npievents.com/, accessed Nov. 29, 2016.

2. Sarah Posner, "How Donald Trump's New Campaign Chief Created an Online Haven for White Nationalists," *Mother Jones*, Aug. 22, 2016, at http://www.motherjones .com/politics/2016/08/stephen-bannon-donald-trump-alt-right-breitbart-news.

3. Eric Bradner, "Alt-Right Leader: 'Hail Trump! Hail Our People! Hail Victory!'" CNN, Nov. 22, 2016, at http://www.cnn.com/2016/11/21/politics/alt-right-gathering-donald-trump/.

4. RAMZPAUL, Twitter post, Nov. 23, 2016, at https://twitter.com/ramzpaul/status /801531616816496640.

5. Greg Johnson, "Obituary for a Brand?" *Counter-Currents*, Nov. 29, 2016, at https:// www.counter-currents.com/2016/11/the-alt-right-obituary-for-a-brand/.

6. Paul Gottfried, "The Decline and Rise of the Alternative Right," *Taki's Magazine*, Dec. 8, 2008, at http://takimag.com/article/the_decline_and_rise_of_the_alternative _right/print#axzz4RuMRmodP; all quotations from Gottfried's talk come from this publication of it.

7. "Theme: The Egalitarian Temptation," H. L. Mencken Club conference, Nov. 21–23, 2008, Linthicum, MD., at http://hlmenckenclub.org/2008-conference/, accessed Nov. 30, 2016.

8. Paul Gottfried, "A Call to the Alternative Right," *Taki's Magazine*, Nov. 10, 2009, at http://takimag.com/article/a_call_to_the_alternative_right/print#axzz4RuMRmodP.

9. Allum Bokhari and Milo Yiannopoulos, "An Establishment Conservative's Guide to the Alt-Right," *Breitbart*, Mar. 29, 2016, at http://www.breitbart.com/tech/2016/03/29/an-establishment-conservatives-guide-to-the-alt-right/.

10. Andrew Anglin, *"Breitbart's Alt-Right Analysis Is the Product of a Degenerate Homosexual and an Ethnic Mongrel,"* *Daily Stormer*, Mar. 31, 2016, at http://www.daily stormer.com/breitbarts-alt-right-analysis-is-the-product-of-a-degenerate-homosexual-and -an-ethnic-mongrel/.

11. Greg Johnson, "The Alt-Right Means White Nationalism . . . or It Means Nothing at All," *Counter-Currents*, Aug. 30, 2016, at http://www.counter-currents.com/2016/08/the-alt-right-means-white-nationalism/.

12. John Daniszewski, "Writing about the 'Alt-Right,'" Associated Press, Nov. 28, 2016, at https://blog.ap.org/behind-the-news/writing-about-the-alt-right.

13. Eleanor Beardsley, "Trump's Election Gives Hope to Europe's Far Right," National Public Radio, Nov. 9, 2016, at http://www.npr.org/sections/parallels/2016/11/09/501398066/trumps-election-gives-hope-to-europes-far-right.

14. Peters, "Among Donald Trump's Biggest U.S. Fans."

15. Gregory A. Smith and Jessica Martínez, "How the Faithful Voted: A Preliminary 2016 Analysis," Pew Research Center, Nov. 9, 2016, at http://www.pewresearch.org/fact-tank/2016/11/09/how-the-faithful-voted-a-preliminary-2016-analysis/.

16. Daniel Cox, "White Christians Side with Trump," PRRI, Nov. 9, 2016, at http://www.prri.org/spotlight/religion-vote-presidential-election-2004-2016/.

17. Betsey Cooper, Daniel Cox, Rachel Lienesch, and Robert P. Jones, "Nearly One in Five Female Clinton Voters Say Husband or Partner Didn't Vote, PRRI/Atlantic Survey," PRRI, Dec. 1, 2016, at http://www.prri.org/research/prri-atlantic-december-2016-post -election-survey/.

18. Betsey Cooper, Daniel Cox, Rachel Lienesch, and Robert P. Jones, "The Divide over America's Future: 1950 or 2050?" PRRI, Oct. 25, 2016, http://www.prri.org/research/divide-americas-future-1950-2050/.

19. Robert P. Jones, *The End of White Christian America* (New York: Simon & Schuster, 2016), 230–31.

20. Jennifer Rubin, "'End of White Christian America' Author: Evangelicals Are in a Fix," *Washington Post*, Nov. 17, 2016, https://www.washingtonpost.com/blogs/right-turn/wp/2016/11/17/end-of-white-christian-america-author-evangelicals-are-in-a-fix/?utm_term =.d29bf16bc3cd.

21. Nathan Damingo, "#PROJECTSIEGE," Identity Europa, Oct. 2, 2016, at https://www.identityevropa.com/action-report/2016/9/27/projectsiege.

22. Thomas Frank, *What's The Matter with Kansas? How Conservatives Won the Heart of America* (New York: Holt, 2004), 5.

Bibliography

Adler, Ben. "White Christian Nationalism at CPAC." *The Nation*, Feb. 10, 2012. At http://www.thenation.com/blog/166176/white-christian-nationalism-cpac#.

Adler, Margot. *Drawing Down the Moon: Witches, Druids, Goddess-Worshipers, and Other Pagans in America*. Rev. and updated ed. New York: Penguin Books, 2006.

Aho, James A. *This Thing of Darkness: A Sociology of the Enemy*. Seattle: Univ. of Washington Press, 1994.

Anderson, Benedict. *Imagined Communities: Reflections on the Origin and Spread of Nationalism*. Rev. ed. New York: Verso, 1991.

Anglin, Andrew. "Breitbart's Alt-Right Analysis Is the Product of a Degenerate Homosexual and an Ethnic Mongrel." *Daily Stormer*, Mar. 31, 2016. At http://www.dailystormer.com/breitbarts-alt-right-analysis-is-the-product-of-a-degenerate-homosexual-and-an-ethnic-mongrel/.

Appadurai, Arjun. *Fear of Small Numbers: An Essay on the Geography of Anger*. Durham, NC: Duke Univ. Press, 2006.

Arendt, Hannah. *The Origins of Totalitarianism*. New York: Houghton Mifflin Harcourt, 1968.

Atkins, Steven E. *Encyclopedia of Right Wing Extremism in American History*. Santa Barbra, CA: ABC-CLIO, 2011.

Baddeley, Gavin. *Lucifer Rising: Sin, Devil Worship, and Rock 'n' Roll*. London: Plexus, 1999.

Baker, Kelly. *Gospel according to the Klan: The KKK's Appeal to Protestant America, 1915–1930*. Lawrence: Univ. Press of Kansas, 2011.

Balibar, Etienne. "Is There a 'Neo-racism'?" In *Race, Nation, Class: Ambiguous Identities*, translated by Chris Turner, 17–28. New York: Verso, 1991.

Barkun, Michael. *Religion and the Racist Right: The Origins of the Christian Identity Movement*. Rev. ed. Chapel Hill: Univ. of North Carolina Press, 1997.

Bar-On, Tamir. *Where Have All the Fascists Gone?* Hampshire, UK: Ashgate, 2007.

Barton, Blanche. *The Secret Life of a Satanist: The Authorized Biography of Anton LaVey*. Los Angeles: Feral House Books, 1992.

Bayer, Robert. "The Aryan Concept of Race, Religion, and History (Part IV)." *National Renaissance Bulletin* 23, nos. 7–8 (1972): 5–9.

Beardsley, Eleanor. "Trump's Election Gives Hope to Europe's Far Right." National Public Radio, Nov. 9, 2016. At http://www.npr.org/sections/parallels/2016/11/09/501398066/trumps-election-gives-hope-to-europes-far-right.

Beekman, Scott. *William Dudley Pelley: A Life in Right-Wing Extremism and the Occult*. Syracuse, NY: Syracuse Univ. Press, 2005.

Bell, Martin, dir. *Brotherhood of Murder*. Los Angeles: DEJ Productions, 1999.

Benoist, Alain de. "The New Right Forty Years Later." In Tomislav Sunic, *Against Democracy and Equality: The European New Right*, 3rd ed., 15–29. London: Arktos Media, 2011.

———. *On Being a Pagan*. Translated by Jon Graham. Edited by Greg Johnson. Atlanta: ULTRA, 2004.

———. *The Problem of Democracy*. Translated by Sergio Knipe. 1985. Reprint. London: Arktos Media, 2011.

Benoist, Alain de, and Charles Champetier. *Manifesto for a European Renaissance*. Translated by Martin Bendelow and Francis Greene. Edited by Stephen Edred Flowers. Smithville, TX: Runa-Raven Press, 2010.

Bergson, Henri. *The Two Sources of Morality and Religion*. Translated by Ashley Audra and Cloudesley Brereton, with W. Horsfall Carter. Garden City, NY: Doubleday Anchor Books, 1935. Published originally in French in 1932.

Bergen, Doris. *The Twisted Cross: The German Christian Movement in the Third Reich*. 2nd ed. Chapel Hill: Univ. of North Carolina Press, 1996.

Bjorn. "Why We Are Odinists." *Odinist*, no. 13 (Sept. 1974): 2–12.

Blavatsky, Helena. *Isis Unveiled: Secrets of the Ancient Wisdom Tradition, Madame Blavatsky's First Work*. Abridged by Michael Gomes. Wheaton, IL: Philosophical Publishing House, 1997.

———. *The Secret Doctrine: The Classic Work, Abridged and Annotated*. Abridged and annotated by Michael Gomes. New York: TarcherPerigee, 2009.

Bogus, Carl T. *William F. Buckley Jr. and the Rise of the American Conservative Movement*. New York: Bloomsbury, 2011.

Bokhari, Allum, and Milo Yiannopoulos. "An Establishment Conservative's Guide to the Alt-Right." *Breitbart*, Mar. 29, 2016. At http://www.breitbart.com/tech/2016/03/29/an-establishment-conservatives-guide-to-the-alt-right/.

Bradner, Eric. "Alt-Right Leader: 'Hail Trump! Hail Our People! Hail Victory!'" CNN, Nov. 22, 2016. At http://www.cnn.com/2016/11/21/politics/alt-right -gathering-donald-trump/.

"A Brief Biography of Alexander Rud Mills." Odinic Rite Australia, n.d. At http:// www.reocities.com/osred/Rud_Mills_Brief_Biography.htm. Accessed Dec. 20, 2014.

Brimelow, Peter. *Alien Nation: Common Sense about America's Immigration Disaster.* New York: Harper Perennial, 1996.

————. "Why V-Dare?/Why the White Doe?" V-Dare, n.d. At http://www.vdare .com/about. Accessed Mar. 8, 2014.

Brown, Lawrence R. *The Might of the West.* New York: Obelensky, 1963.

Brownson, Orestes A. "A Letter to Protestants." In *The Works of Orestes A. Brownson: Controversy,* compiled by Henry F. Brownson, 241–330. Detroit: Thorndike Nourse, 1883.

Broyels, John Allen. *The John Birch Society: Anatomy of a Protest.* Boston: Beacon Press, 1964.

Buckley, Joshua, Collin Cleary, and Michael Moynihan. "Editorial Preface." *TYR: Myth–Culture–Tradition* 1 (2002): 7–10.

Buckley, Joshua, and Michael Moynihan. "Editorial Preface." *TYR: Myth–Culture–Tradition* 2 (2004): 7–10.

Césaire, Aimé. *Discourses on Colonialism.* Translated by Joan Pinkham. 1972. Reprint. New York: Monthly Review Press, 2000.

"Chapter One: Nazi Race-Science." Archives for the Institute for the Study of Academic Racism, n.d. At http://www.ferris.edu/HTMLS/othersrv/isar/archives2 /billig/chapter1.htm. Accessed Dec. 22, 2013.

Chevalier, Jacques. *Entretiens avec Bergson.* Paris: Librarie Plon, 1959.

Christensen, Else. *An Introduction to Odinism.* Chrystal River, FL: Gjallerhorn Book Service, 1980.

Cleary, Collin. *Summoning the Gods: Essays on Paganism in a God-Forsaken World.* Edited by Greg Johnson. San Francisco: Counter-Currents, 2011.

Clerkin, "Major" Donald V. "Appendix A: A White Christian Defends His Faith—Major D. V. Clerkin Responds to 'The Jews Love Christianity.'" In Revilo P. Oliver, *Against the Grain: The Writings of Professor Revilo Pendleton Oliver,* 213–18. York, SC: Liberty Bell, 1995.

Cohen, Adam. "All You Need Is Hate." *Time,* special issue, Feb. 5, 2010. At http:// content.time.com/time/magazine/article/0,9171,1960595,00.html.

Connelly, Edmund. "Harold Covington's Northwest Quartet." *Occidental Observer*, Mar. 30, 2011. At http://www.theoccidentalobserver.net/2011/03/harold-covingtons-northwest-quartet/.

Cooper, Betsey, Daniel Cox, Rachel Lienesch, and Robert P. Jones. "The Divide over America's Future: 1950 or 2050?" Public Religion Research Institute (PRRI), Oct. 25, 2016. At http://www.prri.org/research/divide-americas-future-1950-2050/.

———. "Nearly One in Five Female Clinton Voters Say Husband or Partner Didn't Vote, PRRI/*Atlantic Post* Survey." Public Religion Research Institute (PRRI), Dec. 1, 2016. At http://www.prri.org/research/prri-atlantic-december-2016-post-election-survey/.

Costa, Roberta, and Ed O'Keefe. "House Majority Whip Scalise Confirms He Spoke to White Supremacists in 2002." *Washington Post*, Dec. 12, 2014. At https://www.washingtonpost.com/politics/house-majority-whip-scalise-confirms-he-spoke-to-white-nationalists-in-2002/2014/12/29/7f80dc14-8fa3-11e4-a900-9960214d4cd7_story.html?utm_term=.41a74f7ed2eb.

Cox, Daniel. "White Christians Side with Trump." Public Religion Research Institute (PRRI), Nov. 9, 2016. At http://www.prri.org/spotlight/religion-vote-presidential-election-2004-2016/.

Damingo, Nathan. "#PROJECTSIEGE." Identity Europa, Oct. 2, 2016. At https://www.identityevropa.com/action-report/2016/9/27/projectsiege.

Daniszewski, John. "Writing about the 'Alt-Right.'" Associated Press, Nov. 28, 2016. At https://blog.ap.org/behind-the-news/writing-about-the-alt-right.

Davies, Davis R., and Judy Smith. "Jimmy Ward and the *Jackson Daily News*." In *The Press and Race: Mississippi Journalists Confront the Movement*, edited by Davis R. Davies, 85–110. Jackson: Univ. Press of Mississippi, 2001.

"Declaration 127." Huginn's Heathen Hoff, n.d. At http://www.declairation127.com. Accessed Oct. 7, 2016.

Deleuze, Gilles. *Bergsonism*. Translated by Hugh Tomlinson and Barbara Habberjam. 1966. Reprint. Brooklyn, NY: Zone Books, 1990.

Deleuze, Gilles, and Félix Guattari. *Anti-Oedipus: Capitalism and Schizophrenia*. Translated by Robert Hurley. 1972. New ed. New York: Penguin Classics, 2009.

———. *Thousand Plateaus: Capitalism and Schizophrenia*. Translated by Brian Massumi. 1980. Reprint. New York: Continuum, 2002.

Devi, Savitri. *Defiance*. Calcutta: n.p., 1951. Available at the Savitri Devi Archive, http://www.savitridevi.org/PDF/defiance.pdf. Downloaded Feb. 29, 2012.

DeVries, Arnold. "The Fountain of Youth." In Ben Klassen, *Salubrious Living*, 11–238. Otto, NC: Church of the Creator, 1982.

Dickson, Sam D. Introduction to Revilo P. Oliver, *America's Decline: Education of a Conservative*, v–xi. London: Londinium Press, 1981.

Dobratz, Betty. "The Role of Religion in the Collective Identity of the White Racialist Movement." *Journal for the Scientific Study of Religion* 40, no. 2 (2001): 287–301.

———. *White Power, White Pride: The White Separatist Movement in the United States*. New York: Twayne, 1997.

Duranton-Crabol, Anne-Marie. *Visages de la Nouvelle Droit: Le G.R.E.C.E. et son histoire*. Paris: Presses de la Fondation nationale des sciences politiques, 1988.

Durham, Martin. "From Imperium to Internet: The National Alliance and the American Extreme Right." *Patterns of Prejudice* 36, no. 3 (2002): 50–61.

———. "The Upward Path: Palingenesis, Political Religion, and the National Alliance." *Totalitarian Movements and Political Religions* 5, no. 3 (2004): 454–68. doi:10.1080/1469076042000312212.

———. *White Rage: The Extreme Right and American Politics*. New York: Routledge, 2007.

Faivre, Antoine, and Christine Rhone. *Western Esotericism: A Concise History*. Albany: New York Univ. Press, 2010.

Faye, Guillaume. *Archeofuturism: European Visions of the Post-catastrophic Age*. Translated by Sergio Knipe. Edited by John B. Morgan. 1998. Reprint. London: Arktos Media, 2010.

Ferber, Abbey L., ed. *Home-Grown Hate: Gender and Organized Racism*. New York: Routledge, 2004.

———. *White Man Falling: Race, Gender, and White Supremacy*. Lanham, MD: Rowman and Littlefield, 1999.

Fine, Gary Allen, and Terence McDonnell. "Erasing the Brown Scare: Referential Afterlife and the Power of Memory Templates." *Social Problems* 54, no. 2 (2007): 170–87.

Fletcher, Michael A. "Behind the Hate: A Racist 'Church.'" *Washington Post*, July 6, 1999. At http://www.washingtonpost.com/wp-srv/national/daily/july99/church6.htm.

Flowers, Stephen Edred. Editor's preface to Alain de Benoist and Charles Champetier, *Manifesto for a European Renaissance*, translated by Martin Bendelow and Francis Greene, edited by Stephen Edred Flowers, unpaginated. Smithville, TX: Runa-Raven Press, 2010.

———. "The Idea of Integral Culture: A Model for a Revolt against the Modern World." *TYR: Myth–Culture–Tradition* 1 (2002): 11–22.

———. Preface to Alain de Benoist, *On Being a Pagan*, translated by Jon Graham, edited by Greg Johnson, i–iii. Atlanta: Ultra, 2004.

Fox, Lauren. "White Nationalist at CPAC Does Not Fit In." *U.S. News & World Report*, Mar. 7, 2014. At http://www.usnews.com/news/blogs/washington-whispers/2014/03/07/white-nationalist-at-cpac-doesnt-fit-in.

Frank, Thomas. *What's The Matter with Kansas? How Conservatives Won the Heart of America*. New York: Holt, 2004.

Gardell, Matthias. *Gods of the Blood: The Pagan Revival and White Separatism*. Durham, NC: Duke Univ. Press, 2003.

Gilbert, Martin. *Churchill and the Jews: A Lifelong Friendship*. New York: Holt, 2007.

Gilman, Sander. "Review: *A People That Shall Dwell Alone: Judaism as a Group Evolutionary Strategy* by Kevin MacDonald." *Jewish Quarterly Review*, New Series, 86, nos. 1–2 (1995): 198–201.

Gilmore, Peter H. "The Fascism Question." In *The Satanic Scriptures*, 82–91. Baltimore: Scapegoat, 2007.

Goldberg, David Theo. *Racist Culture: Philosophy and the Politics of Meaning*. Oxford: Blackwell, 1993.

Goodrick-Clarke, Nicholas. *Black Sun: Aryan Cults, Esoteric Nazism, and the Politics of Identity*. New York: New York Univ. Press, 2003.

———. *Hitler's Priestess: Savitri Devi, the Hindu–Aryan Myth, and Neo-Nazism*. New York: New York Univ. Press, 1998.

———. *The Occult Roots of Nazism: The Ariosophists of Austria and Germany, 1890–1935*. New York: New York Univ. Press, 1992.

———. *The Western Esoteric Traditions: A Historical Introduction*. New York: Oxford Univ. Press, 2008.

Gottfried, Paul. "A Call to the Alternative Right." *Taki's Magazine*, Nov. 10, 2009. At http://takimag.com/article/a_call_to_the_alternative_right/print#axzz4RuMRmodP.

———. "The Decline and Rise of the Alternative Right." *Taki's Magazine*, Dec. 8, 2008. At http://takimag.com/article/the_decline_and_rise_of_the_alternative_right/print#axzz4RuMRmodP.

Granholm, Kennet. "The Left-Hand Path and Post-Satanism: The Temple of Set and the Evolution of Satanism." In *The Devil's Party: Satanism in Modernity*, edited by Peter Faxneld and Jesper Aa. Petersen, 209–28. New York: Oxford Univ. Press, 2013.

Grant, Madison. *The Passing of the Great Race, or The Racial Basis of European History*. 1916. Reprint. New York: Scribner's, 1936.

Griffin, Robert S. *The Fame of a Dead Man's Deeds: An Up-close Portrait of White Nationalist William Pierce*. Bloomington, IN: 1st Books, 2001.

Groupement de Recherche et d'Études pour la Civilisation Européenne (GRECE). "Manifeste du GRECE." n.d. At http://grece-fr.com/?page_id=64. Accessed Mar. 16, 2014.

Hamm, Mark S. *Terrorism as Crime: From Oklahoma City to al-Qaeda and Beyond*. New York: New York Univ. Press, 2007.

Hart, Benjamin, and Jack Merkinson. "*National Review* Fires John Derbyshire, Writer Who Penned Racist Screed." *Huffington Post*, Feb. 7, 2012. At http://www.huffingtonpost.com/2012/04/07/national-review-fires-john-derbyshire_n_1410273.html.

Herberg, Will. *Protestant, Catholic, Jew: An Essay on American Religious Sociology*. 1955. Reprint. Garden City, NY: Doubleday, 1956.

Heschel, Susannah. *The Aryan Jesus: Christian Theologians and the Bible in Nazi Germany*. Princeton, NJ: Princeton Univ. Press, 2008.

Hutton, Ronald. *Triumph of the Moon: A History of Modern Pagan Witchcraft*. New York: Oxford Univ. Press, 1999.

Jacobson, Matthew Frye. *Roots Too: White Ethnic Revival in Post–Civil Rights America*. Cambridge, MA: Harvard Univ. Press, 2006.

The John Franklin Letters. New York: Bookmailer, 1959.

Johnson, Greg. "The Alt-Right Means White Nationalism . . . or It Means Nothing at All." *Counter-Currents*, Aug. 30, 2016. At http://www.counter-currents.com/2016/08/the-alt-right-means-white-nationalism/.

———. "The Christian Question in White Nationalism." *Occidental Observer*, May 14, 2010. At http://www.theoccidentalobserver.net/authors/Johnson-Christianity.html.

———. "Frequently Asked Questions, Part 1." *Counter-Currents*, June 5, 2012. At http://www.counter-currents.com/2012/06/frequently-asked-questions-part-1/.

———. "New Right vs. Old Right." *Counter-Currents*, May 11, 2012. At http://www.counter-currents.com/2012/05/new-right-vs-old-right/. Reprinted in Greg Johnson, *New Right versus Old Right*, 1–9. San Francisco: Counter-Currents, 2013.

———. "Obituary for a Brand?" *Counter-Currents*, Nov. 29, 2016. At https://www
.counter-currents.com/2016/11/the-alt-right-obituary-for-a-brand/.

———. "Remembering Revilo Oliver: July 7, 1908–August 20, 1984." *Counter-Currents*, July 7, 2011. At http://www.counter-currents.com/2011/07/remembering-revilo-oliver/.

———. "Remembering William Luther Pierce: September 11, 1933–July 23, 2002." *Counter-Currents*, Sept. 11, 2013. At http://www.counter-currents.com/2013/09/remembering-william-luther-pierce/.

———. "Toward a North American New Right." *North American New Right* 1 (2012): 1–9.

Jones, Robert P. *The End of White Christian America*. New York: Simon & Schuster, 2016.

Kaplan, Jeffrey. "The Postwar Paths of Occult National Socialism: From Rockwell and Madole to Manson." In *The Cultic Milieu: Oppositional Subcultures in an Age of Globalization*, edited by Jeffrey Kaplan and Helén Lööw, 225–65. Walnut Creek, CA: Altamira Press, 2002.

———. "The Reconstruction of the Ásatrú and Odinist Traditions." In *Magical Religion and Modern Witchcraft*, edited by Jeffrey R. Lewis, 193–236. Albany: State Univ. of New York Press, 1996.

Kaplan, Jeffrey, and Leonard Weinberg. *The Emergence of a Euro-American Right*. New Brunswick, NJ: Rutgers Univ. Press, 1998.

Klassen, Ben. *Against the Evil Tide: An Autobiography*. Otto, NC: Church of the Creator, 1991.

———. *Nature's Eternal Religion*. Lighthouse Point, FL: Church of the Creator, 1973.

———. "Odinism." In *A Revolution of Values through Religion*, 1002–116. Otto, NC: Church of the Creator, 1991.

———. *On the Brink of Bloody Racial War*. Niceville, FL: Church of the Creator, 1993.

———. *RAHOWA! This Planet Is All Ours*. Otto, NC: Church of the Creator, 1987.

———. "Recognize Your Enemies! RAHOWA! *Racial Loyalty* Issue No. 36, June 1986." In *RAHOWA! This Planet Is All Ours*, 15–33. Otto, NC: Church of the Creator, 1987.

———. *Salubrious Living*. Otto, NC: Church of the Creator, 1982.

———. *The White Man's Bible*. Lighthouse Point, FL: Church of the Creator, 1981.

Koven, Steven G., and Frank Gotzke. *American Immigration Policy: Confronting the Nation's Challenges*. New York: Springer, 2010.

Krebs, Pierre. *Fighting for the Essence: Western Ethnosuicide or European Renaissance?* Translated by Alexander Jacob. London: Arktos Media, 2012.

Lane, David. *Victory or Valhalla: The Final Compilation of Writings.* Edited by Java and Sissy. Butte, MT: THORINK, 2008.

Ledeboer, Suzanne G. "The Man Who Would Be Hitler: William Dudley Pelley and the Silver Shirt Legion." *California History* 65, no. 2 (1986): 126–36.

Lefebvre, Alexandre, and Melanie White. "Introduction: Bergson, Politics, and Religion." In *Bergson, Politics, and Religion,* edited by Alexandre Lefebvre and Melanie White, 1–21. Durham, NC: Duke Univ. Press, 2012.

Leroy, H. "Hunter d'Andrew MacDonald." Jeune Nation, Oct. 16, 2013. At http://www.jeune-nation.com/culture/andrew-macdonald-hunter-par-h-leroy.html.

Levitas, Daniel. *The Terrorist Next Door: The Militia Movement and the Radical Right.* New York: Thomas Dunne Press, 2002.

Lewis, James R., and Murphy Pizza, eds. *Handbook of Contemporary Paganism.* Leiden, Netherlands: Koninklijke NV Brill, 2009.

Lincoln, Bruce. *Discourse and the Construction of Society: Comparative Studies of Myth, Ritual, and Classification.* New York: Oxford Univ. Press, 1989.

Lipset, Seymour Martin, and Earl Raab. *The Politics of Unreason: Right Wing Extremism in America from 1790–1977.* 2nd ed. Chicago: Univ. of Chicago Press, 1978.

Lombardo, Paul. *Three Generations, No Imbeciles: Eugenics, the Supreme Court, and Buck v. Bell.* Baltimore: John Hopkins Univ. Press, 2008.

Long, Charles. *Significations: Signs, Symbols, and Images in the Interpretation of Religion.* Aurora, CO: Davis Group, 1995.

Lord, Garman. *The Way of the Heathen: A Handbook of Greater Theodism.* Watertown, NY: Theod, 2000.

Love, Nancy. *Trendy Fascism: White Power Music and the Future of Democracy.* Albany: State Univ. of New York Press, 2016.

MacDonald, Kevin. *A People That Shall Dwell Alone: Judaism as a Group Evolutionary Strategy, with Diaspora Peoples.* Lincoln, NE: Writers Club Press, 2002.

Madole, James. "The Leadership Principle: A Heritage of Aryan Man." *National Renaissance Bulletin* 21, nos. 1–2 (1970): 4–9.

———. "'Nature's Eternal Religion'—the New *Mein Kampf* of the NRP." *National Renaissance Bulletin* 24, nos. 1–2 (1973): 4–8.

———. "'The New Atlantis': A Blueprint for an Aryan 'Garden of Eden' in North America!" *National Renaissance Bulletin* 24, nos. 5–6 (1973): 3–8.

———. "'The New Atlantis': A Blueprint for an Aryan 'Garden of Eden' in North America! (Part V)." *National Renaissance Bulletin* 26, nos. 1–2 (1975): 5–9.

———. "A Stern Rebuke to the Critics of the National Renaissance Party." *National Renaissance Bulletin* 22, nos. 9–10 (1971): 6–8.

Mason, Carol. *Reading Appalachia from Left to Right: Conservatives and the Kanawha County Textbook Controversy.* New York: Columbia Univ. Press, 2009.

McNallen, Stephen. *Asatru/Odinism—A Native European Religion.* DystopiaUK, Mar. 24, 2011. At http://www.youtube.com/watch?v=ngdTa4IMRuE.

———. "Asatru . . . the Way of Our Ancestors . . . Calling Us Home." Asatru Folk Assembly, Nov. 24, 2014. At http://www.runestone.org/.

———. "Three Decades of Asatru Revival in America." *TYR: Myth–Culture–Tradition* 2 (2004): 203–20.

McVan, Ron. *Creed of Iron: Wotansvolk Wisdom.* Saint Marie, ID: Fourteen Words Press, 1997.

Michael, George. "David Lane and the 14 Words." *Totalitarian Movements and Political Religions* 10, no. 1 (2009): 43–61.

———. "RAHOWA! A History of the Church of the Creator." *Terror and Political Violence* 18 (2006): 561–83.

———. *Theology of Hate: A History of the World Church of the Creator.* Gainesville: Univ. of Florida Press, 2009.

———. *Willis Carto and the American Far Right.* Gainesville: Univ. of Florida Press, 2008.

"Midwest Shooting Spree Ends with Apparent Suicide of Suspect." CNN, July 5, 1999. At http://cnn.com./US/9907/05/illinois.shootings.02/.

Miller, Stevie. "There Is No Folkish and Universalist Debate in Heathenry." *Grundsau Burrow*, Sept. 6, 2016. At http://grundsauburrow.wordpress.com/2016/09/06/there-is-no-folkish-and-universalist-debate-in-heathenry/.

Mills, Alexander Rud. *The Call of Our Ancient Nordic Religion: Reflections on the Theological Content of the Sagas.* Melbourne, Australia: A. Rud Mills, 1957.

Mintz, Frank. *The Liberty Lobby and the American Right: Race, Conspiracy, and Culture.* New York: Praeger, 1985.

Mitchell, Richard G., Jr. *Dancing at Armageddon: Survivalism and Chaos in Modern Times.* New ed. Chicago: Univ. of Chicago Press, 2004.

Morris-Reich, Amos. "Race, Ideas, and Ideals: A Comparison of Franz Boas and Hans F. K. Günther." *History of European Ideas* 32, no. 3 (2006): 313–32.

Moynihan, Michael. "Odinism." In *The Encyclopedia of Religion and Nature*, edited by Bron Taylor, 1218–20. London: Continuum, 2006.

Noll, Mark. *God and Race in American Politics*. Princeton, NJ: Princeton Univ. Press, 2009.

Oliver, Revilo P. *After Fifty Years*. Advance offprint. Washington, DC: National Youth Alliance, 1970.

———. *Against the Grain: The Writings of Professor Revilo Pendleton Oliver*. York, SC: Liberty Bell, 1995.

———. *America's Decline: The Education of a Conservative*. London: Londinium Press, 1981.

———. "The Enemy of Our Enemies: A Critique of Francis Parker Yockey's *The Enemy of Europe*." In Francis Parker Yockey and Revilo P. Oliver, *The Enemy of Europe / The Enemy of Our Enemies*, 1–147. York, SC: Liberty Bell, 2003.

———. *The Jewish Strategy*. Earlysville, VA: Kevin Alfred Strom, 2002.

———. *The Origins of Christianity*. Uckfield, UK: Historical Review Press, 2001.

———. "Superstitious Materialism." *National Review*, Mar. 15, 1958, 258–59.

———. "The Testimony of Professor Revilo Pendelton Oliver before the Warren Commission." Sept. 9, 1964. At http://www.revilo-oliver.com/rpo/Warren_Commission_Testimony.html.

O'Meara, Michael. "Against White Reformists." Vanguard News Network, 2007. Reprinted in *Counter-Currents*, July 17, 2012. At http://www.counter-currents.com/2012/07/against-white-reformists/.

———. *New Culture, New Right: Anti-liberalism in Postmodern Europe*. Bloomington, IN: 1st Books, 2004.

———. *Toward the White Republic, and Other Essays*. Edited by Greg Johnson. San Francisco: Counter-Currents, 2010.

Omi, Michael, and Howard Winant. *Racial Formation in the United States: From the 1960s to the 1990s*. 2nd ed. New York: Routledge, 1994.

Ordover, Nancy. *American Eugenics: Race, Queer Anatomy, and the Science of Nationalism*. Minneapolis: Univ. of Minnesota Press, 2003.

Osborn, Henry F. "The Second International Congress of Eugenics: Address of Welcome." *Science* 54, no. 1397 (1921): 311–13.

Parel, Anthony. "Values of Closed Society." *International Political Science Review* 3, no. 2 (1982): 230–37.

Pelley, William Dudley. "My Seven Minutes in Eternity—The Amazing Experience That Made Me Over." *American Magazine*, Mar. 1928.

———. *No More Hunger.* 1933. Reprint. Nobsville, IN: Aquila Press, 1961.

———. *Seven Minutes in Eternity, with Their Aftermath.* New York: Robert Collier, 1929.

Peters, Jeremy W. "Among Donald Trump's Biggest U.S. Fans: Hindu Nationalists." *New York Times,* Oct. 15, 2016. At http://www.nytimes.com/2016/10/15/us/politics/indian-americans-trump.html?_r=0.

Petersen, Jesper Aagaard. "The Carnival of Dr. LaVey: Articulations of Transgression in Modern Satanism." In *The Devil's Party: Satanism in Modernity,* edited by Peter Faxneld and Jesper Aa. Petersen, 167–88. New York: Oxford Univ. Press, 2013.

Pierce, William. "America Is a Changing Country." Talk given in 2002 (specific date unknown). Video posted in the Dr. William L. Pierce Archive, Nov. 13, 2012. At https://www.youtube.com/watch?v=X5ko1OYYDr8.

———. *Cosmotheism Trilogy* [*The Path* (1977), *On Living Things* (1979), and *On Society* (1984)]. N.d. At https://archive.org/details/CosmotheismTrilogyBy WilliamLutherPierce. Accessed Oct. 22, 2015.

———. "Cosmotheism—Wave of the Future." 1977 (specific date unknown). *The Legacy of Dr. William Pierce* (blog), posted July 30, 2013. At http://william lutherpierce.blogspot.com/2013/07/cosmotheism-wave-of-future.html.

———. "Death and Black Metal by William Pierce." Stormfront, posted by Proud Saxon, Oct. 13, 2011. At http://www.stormfront.org/forum/t838248-2/.

——— [as Andrew MacDonald]. *Hunter.* Arlington, VA: National Vanguard Books, 1989.

———. "The National Alliance in Europe: Commentary by Dr. William Pierce, 1998." *The Legacy of Dr. William Pierce* (blog), posted Mar. 27, 2012. At http:// williamlutherpierce.blogspot.com/2012/03/national-alliance-in-europe.html.

———. "On Christianity." *National Vanguard,* 1982 (specific date unknown). Posted Oct. 26, 2010 at http://nationalvanguard.org/2010/10/on-christianity. Accessed May 22, 2012.

———. "Our Cause." *National Vanguard,* 1976 (specific date unknown), posted Sept. 11, 2010. At http://nationalvanguard.org/2010/09/our-cause/.

———. "A Program for Our Survival." In *Extremism in America: A Reader,* edited by Lyman Tower Sargent, 176–82. New York: New York Univ. Press, 1995.

———. *The Saga of White Will.* New World Order Comix no. 1. Hillsboro, WV: National Vanguard Books, 1993.

——— [as Andrew MacDonald]. *The Turner Diaries: A Novel.* Fort Lee, NJ: Barricade Books, 1978.

———. "Why Conservatives Can't Win." In *The Best of* ATTACK! *and* National Vanguard *Tabloid*, edited by Kevin Alfred Strom, 6. Arlington, VA: National Vanguard Books, 1984.

"Pope Calls for Religions to Oppose Racism Together." *New York Times*, Aug. 19, 2005. At http://www.nytimes.com/2005/08/19/world/europe/19iht-web.0819 pope.html?_r=0.

Posner, Sarah. "How Donald Trump's New Campaign Chief Created an Online Haven for White Nationalists." *Mother Jones*, Aug. 22, 2016. At http://www .motherjones.com/politics/2016/08/stephen-bannon-donald-trump-alt-right -breitbart-news.

Potok, Mark. "Ten Years after Founder's Death, Key Neo-Nazi Movement 'A Joke.'" Southern Poverty Law Center, July 23, 2012. At http://www.splcenter .org/get-informed/news/shipwreck-ten-years-after-the-death-of-its-founder-the -once-dominant-national-alli.

Rénard, René. Preface to Anne-Marie Duranton-Crabol, *Visages de la nouvelle droite: Le G.R.E.C.E. et son histoire*, 9–12. Paris: Presses de la Fondation nationale des sciences et politiques, 1988.

Ribuffo, Leo P. *The Old Christian Right: The Protestant Far Right from the Great Depression to the Cold War*. Philadelphia: Temple Univ. Press, 1983.

Robertson, Wilmot. *The Dispossessed Majority*. 1966. Reprint. Cape Canaveral, FL: Howard Allen Enterprises, 1972.

Rockwell, George Lincoln. *This Time the World*. 7th ed. York, SC: Liberty Bell, 2004.

Rubin, Jennifer. "'End of White Christian America' Author: Evangelicals Are in a Fix." *Washington Post*, Nov. 17, 2016. At https://www.washingtonpost .com/blogs/right-turn/wp/2016/11/17/end-of-white-christian-america-author -evangelicals-are-in-a-fix/?utm_term=.d29bf16bc3cd.

Russell, James C. *The Germanization of Early Medieval Christianity: A Socio-historical Approach to Religious Transformation*. Oxford: Oxford Univ. Press, 1994.

Ryan, Nick. *Into a World of Hate: A Journey among the Extreme Right*. New York: Routledge, 2004.

Salladay, Robert, Lynda Gledhill, and Kelly St. John. "Sacramento Rampage—5 Shot Dead. Slayer Kills Himself during Gun Battle with Police." *SFGate*, Sept. 10, 2001. At http://www.sfgate.com/news/article/Sacramento-rampage -5-shot-dead-Slayer-kills-2881164.php.

Schlesinger, Arthur M., Jr. *The Age of Roosevelt: The Politics of Upheaval*. Boston: Houghton Mifflin, 1960.

Serrano, Miguel. *Adolph Hitler, el ultimo avatāra*. Santiago, Chile: Ediciones la Nueva Edad, 1987.

Shields, James. *The Extreme Right in France: From Pétain to Le Pen*. New York: Routledge, 2007.

Silk, Mark. "Notes on the Judeo-Christian Tradition in America." *American Quarterly* 36, no. 1 (1984): 65–85.

Simi, Pete, and Robert Futrell. *American Swastika: Inside the White Power Movement's Hidden Spaces of Hate*. Lanham, MD: Rowman and Littlefield, 2010.

Simonelli, Fredrick J. *American Fuehrer: George Lincoln Rockwell and the American Nazi Party*. Urbana: Univ. of Illinois Press, 1999.

Simpson, William Gayley. *Which Way Western Man*. Cooperstown, NY: Yeoman Press, 1978.

Smith, Gregory A., and Jessica Martínez. "How the Faithful Voted: A Preliminary 2016 Analysis." Pew Research Center, Nov. 9, 2016. At http://www.pew research.org/fact-tank/2016/11/09/how-the-faithful-voted-a-preliminary-2016 -analysis/.

Söderman, Magnus, and Henrick Holappa, eds. *Unbroken Warrior: The Richard Scutari Letters*. Stockholm: Nationellt Motstånd Förlag, 2011.

Soulez, Philippe. "Bergson as Philosopher of War and Theorist of the Political." Translated by Melissa McMahon. In *Bergson, Politics, and Religion*, edited by Alexandre Lefebvre and Melanie White, 99–125. Durham, NC: Duke Univ. Press, 2012.

Southern Poverty Law Center. "Church of the Creator: A History." *Intelligence Report*, no. 95 (Summer 1999). At http://www.splcenter.org/intel/intelreport /article.jsp?sid=219.

————. "William Pierce." Intelligence Files, n.d. At http://www.splcenter.org/get -informed/intelligence-files/profiles/william-pierce. Accessed Feb. 22, 2014.

Spektorowski, Alberto. "The New Right: Ethno-regionalism, Ethno-pluralism, and the Emergence of a Neo-fascist 'Third-Way.'" *Journal of Political Ideologies* 8, no. 1 (2003): 111–30.

Spiro, Jonathan. *Defending the Master Race: Conservation, Eugenics, and the Legacy of Madison Grant*. Burlington: Univ. of Vermont Press, 2008.

Stern, Alexandra Minna. *Eugenic Nation: Faults and Frontiers of Better Breeding in Modern America*. Berkeley and Los Angeles: Univ. of California Press, 2005.

St. George, Maximilian, and Lawrence Dennis. *A Trial on Trial: The Great Sedition Trial of 1944*. 1946. Reprint. Newport Beach, CA: Institute for Historical Review, 1984.

Stoddard, Lothrop. *The Rising Tide of Colour against White-World Supremacy*. New York: Scribner's, 1920.

Stone, Barbara S. "The John Birch Society: A Profile." *Journal of Politics* 36, no. 1 (1974): 184–97.

Strom, Kevin A. "About." Kevin Alfred Strom website, n.d. At http://www.kevin alfredstrom.com/about/. Accessed Feb. 12, 2014.

———. "Dr. William Pierce: Preparing the Way, Part 2." *National Vanguard*, Sept. 19, 2015. At http://nationalvanguard.org/2015/09/dr-william-pierce-preparing -the-way-part-2/.

———. Introduction to Revilo P. Oliver, *The Origins of Christianity*, 9–12. Uck-field, UK: Historical Review Press, 2001.

Sunic, Tomislav. *Against Democracy and Equality: The European New Right*. 3rd ed. London: Arktos Media, 2011.

———. Foreword to Pierre Krebs, *Fighting for the Essence: Western Ethnosuicide or European Renaissance?* translated by Alexander Jacob, 11–15. London: Arktos Media, 2012.

———. *Homo Americanus: Child of the Postmodern Age*. N.p.: Booksurge, 2007.

———. "The Sunic Journal: Dr. Greg Johnson on the New Right." *Voice of Reason*, Aug. 9, 2011, audio only. At http://reasonradionetwork.com/20110809 /the-sunic-journal-dr-greg-johnson-on-the-new-right.

Swain, Carol. *The New White Nationalism in America: Its Challenge to Integration*. New York: Cambridge Univ. Press, 2002.

Taguieff, Pierre-André. "Origines et métamorphoses de la Nouvelle Droite." *Vingtième Siècle: Revue d'histoire*, no. 40 (Oct.–Dec. 1993): 3–22.

———. *Sur la Nouvelle Droite: Jalons d'une analyse critique*. Paris: Descartes & Cie, 1994.

Tal, Uriel. "Political Faith of Nazism prior to the Holocaust." In *Religion, Politics, and Ideology in the Third Reich: Selected Essays*, edited by Saul Friedländer, 16–54. New York: Routledge, 2004.

"Tom Metzger Interviews Nicholas Schreck." YouTube, video, uploaded by Styx-hexenhammer666, Dec. 30, 2010. At http://www.youtube.com/watch?v=eS47 cjbZkGM. Accessed Mar. 22, 2014.

US House of Representatives, Un-American Activities Committee. *Preliminary Report on Neo-fascist and Hate Groups*. Washington, DC: US Government Printing Office, 1954.

Vial, Pierre. *Pour une renaissance culturelle: Le G.R.E.C.E. prend la parole*. Paris: Editions Copernic, 1979.

Welch, Robert. *The Blue Book of the John Birch Society.* 8th printing. Belmont, MA: John Birch Society, 1961.

———. *The Neutralizers.* Belmont, MA: John Birch Society, 1963.

Whitsel, Brad. "Aryan Visions of the Future in the West Virginia Mountains." *Terrorism and Political Violence* 7, no. 4 (1995): 117–39.

———. "*The Turner Diaries* and Cosmotheism: William Pierce's Theology." *Novo Religio: The Journal of Alternative and Emergent Religions* 1, no. 2 (1998): 183–97.

"Why We Hate." *The Insurgent,* n.d. At http://www.resist.com/JOOMJournal /WHY%20WE%20HATE.html. Accessed Mar. 16, 2014.

Yockey, Francis Parker. *The Enemy of Europe.* York, SC: Liberty Bell, 1981.

———. *Imperium: The Philosophy of History and Politics.* 1948. Reprint. Costa Mesa, CA: Noontide Press, 1991.

Yockey, Francis Parker, and Revilo P. Oliver. *The Enemy of Europe / The Enemy of Our Enemies.* York, SC: Liberty Bell, 2003.

Young, Jacob, dir. *Dr. No?* VHS. Morgantown, WV: WNPB, 1991.

Zeskind, Leonard. *Blood and Politics: The History of the White Nationalist Movement from the Margins to the Mainstream.* New York: Farrar, Straus and Giroux, 2009.

Index

Damon T. Berry is assistant professor of religion at St. Lawrence University in Canton, New York. He has published in the *Journal of Hate Studies* and the *Security Journal* and has two essays in edited volumes forthcoming.